THE rahui

Legal pluralism in Polynesian traditional management of resources and territories

THE rahui

Legal pluralism in Polynesian traditional management of resources and territories

EDITED BY
TAMATOA BAMBRIDGE

PACIFIC SERIES

Published by ANU Press
The Australian National University
Acton ACT 2601, Australia
Email: anupress@anu.edu.au
This title is also available online at press.anu.edu.au

National Library of Australia Cataloguing-in-Publication entry

Title: The Rahui : legal pluralism in Polynesian traditional management of resources and territories / edited by Tamatoa Bambridge.

ISBN: 9781925022797 (paperback) 9781925022919 (ebook)

Subjects: Legal polycentricity--Polynesia.
Polynesia--History.

Other Creators/Contributors:
Bambridge, Tamatoa, editor.

Dewey Number: 340.5

All rights reserved. No part of this publication may be reproduced, stored in a retrieval system or transmitted in any form or by any means, electronic, mechanical, photocopying or otherwise, without the prior permission of the publisher.

Cover design and layout by ANU Press
Cover art by Raina Chaussoy

This edition © 2016 ANU Press

Contents

Foreword ix

Introduction: The *rahui*: A tool for environmental protection
or for political assertion? 1
Tamatoa Bambridge

Part I – *Tapu* and *rahui*: Traditions and pluralistic organisation of society

1. Political power and *rahui* in ancient Polynesian society 15
   Bernard Rigo
2. Ancient magic and religious trends of the *rāhui* on the atoll
   of Anaa, Tuamotu 25
   Frédéric Torrente
3. *Tapu* and *kahui* in the Marquesas 43
   Pierre Ottino-Garanger, Marie-Noëlle Ottino-Garanger,
   Bernard Rigo and Edgar Tetahiotupa
4. *I uta i tai* — a preliminary account of *ra'ui* on Mangaia,
   Cook Islands 79
   Rod Dixon
5. Technical exploitation and 'ritual' management of resources
   in Napuka and Tepoto (Tuamotu Archipelago). 105
   Eric Conte
6. The law of *rahui* in the Society Islands 119
   Tamatoa Bambridge

Part II – *Rahui* today as state-custom pluralism

7. Protection of natural resources through a sacred prohibition:
   The *rahui* on Rapa iti. 139
   Christian Ghasarian
8. From traditional to modern management in Fakarava 155
   Lorin Thorax

9. European contact and systems of governance
    on Tongareva 165
    Charlotte N. L. Chambers

10. Traditional marine resources and their use in contemporary
    Hawai'i 177
    Alan M. Friedlander, Janna M. Shackeroff and John N. Kittinger

11. Providing for *rāhui* in the law of Aotearoa New Zealand 195
    Jacinta Ruru and Nicola Wheen

12. Uncanny rights and the ambiguity of state authority
    in the Gambier Islands 211
    Alexander Mawyer

Conclusion: What are the lessons to be learned from the *rahui*
and legal pluralism? The political and environmental efficacy
of legal pluralism. 227
Tamatoa Bambridge

Postscript: What are the consequences of *rahui*? 231
Jean Guiart

References 243

This book is dedicated to Ron Crocombe and his family

Foreword

The indigenous societies of Eastern Polynesia have long held a central place in anthropological and archaeological theory on the political transformation of fragmented and antagonistic chiefdoms into unified, centralised states. Eastern Polynesia is generally understood to include the islands encompassed by contemporary French Polynesia, Cook Islands, Hawai'i, Aotearoa New Zealand, and Rapanui. These small, relatively discrete islands or archipelagos are populated by peoples of common ancestry and have been viewed as ideal social laboratories for fieldwork to study social and political evolution in a comparative perspective. Prominent Pacific scholars in these disciplines used their Eastern Polynesian research to make influential interventions into wider theoretical debates within their fields — most notably in the past generation, Marshall Sahlins on culture contact and adaptation in the 1980s and 1990s, and transitions from simple to complex social and political organisation from the 1950s onwards; Douglas Oliver on constructions of cultural realities from the 1950s until the 1980s; and Patrick Kirch on ecological circumvention as a factor in the evolution of chiefly power from the early 1980s onwards. Underlying these debates have been the longer term, fundamental issues about the relative influence of ecological and cultural factors in human activities, and the interactions between these two sets of variables. To what extent do our environmental habitats channel our thinking and actions, and to what extent are our uses of potential natural resources influenced by our cultural views of ourselves as members of human communities with broadly shared and learned values and perceptions of our physical world?

Another important body of scholarship on Eastern Polynesian societies, which emerged parallel to these streams from the 1980s, has received less recognition globally, but may influence the future of the region in far more telling ways. In this era, over a century of Aotearoa

New Zealand Maori protest at land alienation and breaches of faith by the Crown finally led to the formation of the Waitangi Tribunal to investigate injustices against Maori to assist the Crown's attempts to address grievances. A great deal of research on indigenous histories and ways of viewing land, sea and social relations was conducted to make the case for compensation and restitution before the work of the tribunal, combined with a renaissance in Maori assertions of cultural identity, and this produced a profound cultural and academic revolution. In Hawai'i, another body of long-stifled but long-remembered indigenous knowledge and practice gained increasing official recognition in state education institutions in this period, with a parallel and interacting cultural renaissance to that of Maori. Hawai'ian representation on state decision-making bodies on resource allocation and use still remains far from satisfactory. Cook Islanders are the only Eastern Polynesians with the dominant say in use of their lands, seas and economy, while indigenous French Polynesians still struggle to have a voice in political, economic and environmental decision-making bodies; although momentum for meaningful change and just representation is gathering. Across Eastern Polynesia, indigenous scholars and community leaders are emphasising that political power was always more concensus based than most academics claim, and that the exercise of this community-based, consensual power required a strong basis of environmental guardianship.

This message of the interrelationship between environmental guardianship and consent-based political power across Eastern Polynesian indigenous societies pervades the chapters of this book in ways that are compelling, credible and intellectually revolutionary. Indeed, this collection may well turn out to be one of the most important works on Eastern Polynesia to emerge in a generation in that it addresses four major divisions and shortcomings in scholarship on the region. First, all contributors have spent a great deal of time working with specific indigenous communities and the result is a collection of rich and never-before-published studies of local environmental management techniques in which politics and ecological management merge. This is particularly true for the material relating to the Marquesas, Tuamotu, and Austral islands. Second, this material reveals the continuous and ongoing importance of local *rahui* as central components of locally based institutions for resource management and social relations throughout the colonial era down to the present day, and their central importance in cultural revivals and reassertions of community *mana*. In so doing, this volume questions many of the ideas about the efficacy of centralised institutions at the core of much political centralisation theory on pre-European state formation and community and state discourse in contemporary Pacific nations. Third, this is a reassertion of the importance of comparative studies in that the sum is greater than the individual parts combined. The combination of common themes and specific solutions and configurations works well and the differences reveal much about the underlying assumptions and practices. Lastly, this collection represents a long-overdue and welcome combining of francophone and anglophone Pacific scholarship in an accessible format. Most Pacific scholars are aware of and influenced by top French scholars of the Pacific who write in English, such as Maurice Godelier and Serge Tcherkézoff. Here, readers gain English-language access to a host of French scholars working on francophone Pacific communities about which little has been written in English. The result is stimulating and vitally important.

Eastern Polynesians mastered environments that were initially less well endowed than those they sailed from, but yet flourished in the majority of cases. Locally controlled *rahui* have been at the heart of environmental management and concensus-based social relations for generations across Eastern Polynesia. The current revival and reassertion of *rahui* across the region have lessons for all of humanity in this era of rising environmental degradation and looming climate-induced displacement.

Paul D'Arcy
Department of Pacific and Asian History
The Australian National University
6 June 2015

INTRODUCTION
The *rahui*: A tool for environmental protection or for political assertion?

Tamatoa Bambridge

This collection deals with an ancient institution in Eastern Polynesia called the *rahui*, a form of restricting access to resources and/or territories. Strictly speaking, even though several new meanings have been added throughout history,[1] the definition of *rahui* has essentially been the same since the mid-nineteenth century. The Polynesian Lexicon (Pollex) proposes the protoform *raafui* for East Polynesia and gives the restrictive definition 'prohibit'. According to the Pollex, *rahui* is variously defined as 'prohibit' (Easter Island), 'prohibition or restriction laid on hogs, fruit … by the chief', 'to lay on such a *rahui*' (Tahiti), or as 'a restriction' (Manihiki–Rakahanga). These definitions are applicable to the whole geographical area of Eastern Polynesia.[2]

Most authors agree that concepts like *mana*, *tapu* and others can only be fully understood when viewed in combination as interrelated and mutually influential concepts that are central to Polynesian perceptions

---

1   Maxwell, K.H. & Penetito, W., 2007. 'How the use of rāhui for protecting taonga has evolved over time'. *MAI Review* 2: 1; www.review.mai.ac.nz.
2   Dieffenbach, E., 1843. 'Dictionary, PART III: Grammar and Dictionary', in *Travels in New Zealand with Contributions to the Geography, Geology, Botany, and Natural History of that Country*, Vol. II. London, England: John Murray, Albemarle Street; Davies, J., 1851. *A Tahitian and English Dictionary with Introductory Remarks on the Polynesian Language and a Short Grammar of the Tahitian Dialect*. Tahiti, printed at the London Missionary Society's Press.

of their social, political, spiritual and natural worlds.³ In one sense, *tapu* is the state of a person, thing, place or period where *mana* (power from divine influence) is present. Another meaning of *tapu* is 'forbidden to certain categories of persons in specific contexts'.⁴

In the literature, *tapu* (a sacred prohibition) and *rahui* are considered fundamental institutions in Polynesia and are often defined as synonymous. From this perspective, in relation with *tapu*, *rahui* appears as a form of *tapu* applied to a class of resources or to a territory. A *rahui* allows for *mana* to be present among resources or on a territory. Nevertheless, through the case studies that are presented in this book, the difference between *tapu* and *rahui* may not only be a matter of degree ('*rahui* as a form of *tapu*'). There is also a difference in nature. As a matter of fact, the prohibition reflects a power or an authority and these concepts also need to be related to the enactment of sociopolitical groups.⁵ *Tapu* and *rahui* appear as two types of prohibition, reflecting two types of political and religious power. As Ottino-Garanger, Ottino-Garanger, Rigo and Tetahiotupa indicate:

> In Polynesia, as in many cultures, power was both political and religious. Yet, it is important to distinguish between what is in the nature of *tapu*, which has to be obeyed by all components of society … and what is the result of decisions made by those in whom sacred power is vested and who subject others to provisional prohibitions that, to their minds, seem to be required by a political, weather-related or environmental situation. In times of food shortage, drought, in anticipation of sumptuary ceremonies, for prestige reasons or in order to save resources, Marquesan *haka'iki* (*ariki*, Society Islands) or *tau'a* (sacred, specialist priest) are empowered to impose *kahui* (*rahui*, Society Islands) ⁶

In the first case, the prohibition is governed by the sacred nature of the object, whereas, in the second case, the prohibition is controlled by strategies related to political and sacred power.

---

3   Firth, R., 1940. 'The analysis of mana: an empirical approach'. *Journal of the Polynesian Society* 49: 483–510; Keesing, R.M., 1984. 'Rethinking mana'. *Journal of Anthropological Research* 40(1): 137–56; Shore, B., 1989. 'Mana and Tapu: a new synthesis'. In Alan Howard and Rob Borofsky (eds), *Developments in Polynesian Ethnology*. Honolulu: University of Hawai'i Press, pp. 137–74.
4   Bambridge, T. & Vernaudon, J., 2012. 'Espace, histoire et territoire en Polynésie: une appropriation foncière de l'espace terrestre et marin'. In E. Le Roy (ed.), *La Terre et l'homme*. Paris: Editions Khartala, pp. 33–53.
5   Firth, 1940.
6   See Chapter 3, this volume.

In the Polynesian context, *tapu* or *rahui* have less to do with a mystical abstract power than with the manifestation of efficiency in such domains as success, health, food and fertility.

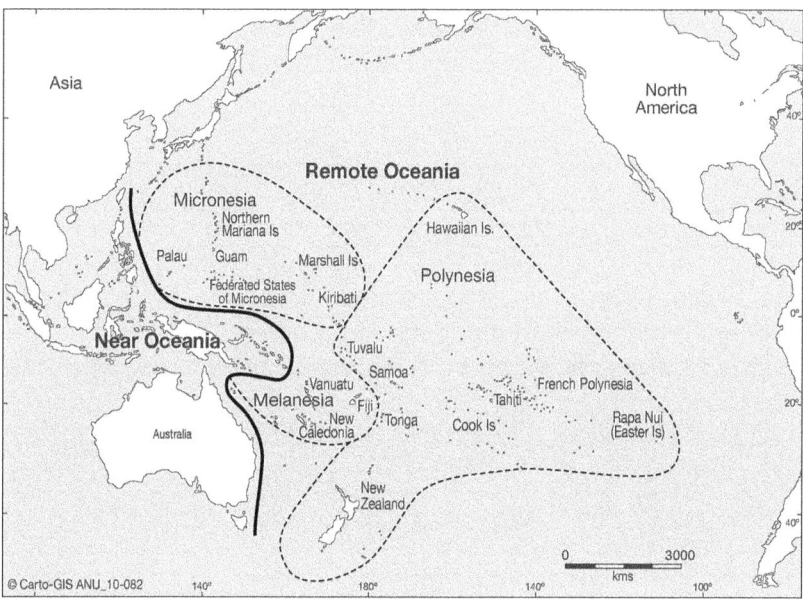

Figure 1: Map of Eastern Polynesia in Oceania
Source: © The Australian National University Carto-GIS ANU_10-082

Based on fieldwork in the Marquesas, Tuamotu and Society islands archipelagos, the first essays in this volume from — Rigo; Torrente; Ottino-Garanger et al.; and Bambridge — revisit concepts such as *tapu* and *rahui* from nineteenth-century sources. The chapters from Ottino-Garanger et al. and Torrente are especially based on primary sources from insiders (Tuamotu) or first settlers or explorers (Marquesas) who, in the case of the Marquesas, were mainly Catholic. These chapters offer a reconstruction of the *rahui* institution from sources that have not previously been been used or revealed.

While *tapu* has been extensively discussed in the scientific literature on Oceanian anthropology, the *rahui* is absent from secondary modern literature. This situation is problematic because individual actors, societies and states in the Pacific are readapting such concepts to their current needs, such as environment regulation or cultural legitimacy.

Many contemporary Polynesian states and local communities have re-established the *rahui*, mainly to facilitate more sustainable management of their resources and environment. In addition to covering this aspect of *rahui*, most of the chapters in this collection ask another fundamental question: What of the political dimension of the *rahui*? Indeed, the *rahui* was traditionally linked to the *tapu*, which was a form of political assertion when imposing restrictions on specific resources.[7] The political implication of the *rahui* are still relevant today as modern states — and indigenous communities in Eastern Polynesia conceptualise *rahui* from a political perspective rather than from an environmental one.

Taking the political orientation into account, this book assembles a comprehensive collection of current works on the *rahui* from the perspective of legal pluralism. Most authors more or less agree with the definition of legal pluralism that is suggested by Griffith, which is 'the coexistence within a social group of legal orders that do not belong to a single "system"'.[8] This definition, when linked to the study of the *rahui*, has two advantages. First, it allows us to analyse to what extent pre-European Polynesian society was dominated by a context of legal pluralisms in keeping with the diffusion of power and authority within the social structure.[9] Second, it allows us to pursue the study of legal pluralism in Polynesian society in a situation where the notion of legal centralism based on state authority has prevailed from the nineteenth century until today.[10] Furthermore, this descriptive definition of legal pluralism encourages the elaboration of a legal anthropological theory that is neither normative nor ideologically linked to the exclusive definition of law that is usually given by the state.[11] With this shared perspective, the following chapters also tackle various theories

---

7   Best, E., 1904. 'Notes on the custom of Rahui, its application and manipulation, as also its supposed powers, its rites, invocations and superstitions'. *Journal of the Polynesian Society* 13(2): 83–88; Oliver, D., 1974. *Ancient Tahitian Society*. Honolulu: The University Press of Hawai'i.
8   Griffith, J., 1986. 'What is legal pluralism?' *Journal of Legal Pluralism* 24: 8.
9   Firth, R., 1965. *Essays on Social Organization and Values*. Monograph on social anthropology no. 28. University of London, London School of Economics: The Athlone Press.
10 Bambridge, T., 2009. *La terre dans l'archipel des îles Australes. Étude du pluralisme juridique et culturel en matière foncière*. Institut de Recherche pour le Développement (IRD) et Aux Vents des îles; Bambridge, T., 2007. 'Généalogie des droits autochtones en Nouvelle-Zélande (Aotearoa) et à Tahiti (1840–2005)'. *Droits et Sociétés* 22(1).
11 von Benda-Beckmann, F., 2002. 'Who's afraid of legal pluralism?' *Journal of Legal Pluralism* 47: 37–83; von Benda-Beckmann, F. & K., 2006. 'The dynamics of change and continuity in plural legal orders'. *Journal of Legal Pluralism* 53–54: 1–44.

and methodologies while stressing the mutual relevance of diverse historical, cultural and political dimensions. This study, therefore, aims to contribute to the renewal of debate on the core problems and analytical methods of legal pluralism.

While studying the *rahui* in the realm of environmental management, the following chapters demonstrate that the political dimension remains important to both states and the local communities. This volume underlines the new assertion of identity that has flowed from the cultural dimension of the *rahui*. Today, *rahui* have become a means for indigenous communities to be recognised on a political level. Some indigenous communities choose to restore the *rahui* in order to preserve political control of their territory or, in some cases, to get it back.[12] On a political level, Chambers examines the *rahui* in Tongareva through the changes in power structure that led to unification. After the 1889 annexation by the British, a council of elders — called *hau* — was created. This was replaced by the council of the island in 1901 and was put under the authority of the central government of the Cook Islands in 1957.

For the state, better control of the *rahui* represents a way of asserting its legitimacy and its sovereignty in the face of this reassertion by indigenous communities (see essays by Thorax; Ruru and Wheen; Friedlander, Shakeroff and Kittinger; Mawyer; and Chambers).

While there is broad general agreement over the meaning of the *rahui*, the historical context varies considerably between localities. The states in the Pacific region are subjected to a 'double bind'[13] at the local and international levels. On the one hand, local communities have realised the importance of environmental legitimacy as a way of strenghtening their political voice. On the other hand, states must take into consideration several international pressures. As early as 1975, the International Union for the Conservation of Nature and Natural Resources (IUCN) adopted a resolution that sought to conciliate the rights of indigenous peoples and the principles of environmental preservation. In 1996, the World Wildlife Fund for Nature (WWF) approved a declaration of principles that supported the United Nations

---

12   See Chapters 7 and 8 in this volume; Mawyer, A., 2006. '"TV Talk" and Processes of Media Receptivity in the Production of Identities in the Gambier Islands, French Polynesia'. PhD thesis. The University of Chicago.
13   Elias, N., 1993. *Engagement et distanciation*. Paris: Fayard, pp. 69–169.

Declaration on the Rights of Indigenous Peoples. In 1999, the World Commission on Protected Areas (WCPA) — one of the six commissions of the IUCN — advocated the joint management of protected areas. In these circumstances, the notion of legal pluralism — linked to the tradition of the *rahui* — has been relevant to academic research as well as to local, national and regional institutions. Legal pluralism also gained new meanings. Before European influences in Polynesia, legal pluralism was associated with the fact that sociopolitical groups had multiple ways of organising authority over *rahui*, and multiple ways to implement sanctions about infringing *rahui* regulations. Today, legal pluralism has moved from within communities to between communities and is more concerned with state–custom interactions at local, national and international levels. New actors, such as non-government organisations (NGOs), also have the capacity to influence internal regulations as well as providing new models for regulating society–resources–culture interactions.

The authors in this book discuss *rahui* in light of the main contemporary and scientific issues related to legal pluralism in Eastern Polynesia. They cover a number of environmental and societal contexts within the Pacific from which many more lessons can be learned. The following chapters are the result of intensive fieldwork beginning in the early 2000s in Aotearoa New Zealand, the Cook Islands, Hawai'i, and in the Gambier, Tuamotu and Society islands in French Polynesia.

The authors examine two main issues related to the *rahui*: traditions and social changes and the establishment of legal pluralism within the social changes.

Traditions and pluralistic organisation of society

In the first chapter of this book, Rigo argues that, in order to define a society as pluralistic according to Griffith's terms,[14] one must first analyse its social organisation. Society is pluralistic if organised as such conceptually and practically. Rigo puts the *rahui* in the category of Polynesian political concepts related to the notion of sacredness

---

14   Griffith, 1986.

and shows the nature of this categorisation. To Rigo, the *rahui* is a sacred institution, not because of the Western dichotomy between the profane and the sacred,[15] but because the whole society revolves around sacredness, specific rites or ceremonies, in which group organisation and leadership networks allow and require upward and downward movements of sacredness. Ancestral characters exist only because living beings affiliated with them make them exist, hence — as the author indicates — the fact that tutelary family gods are sometimes invoked to implement a *rahui* on a specific territory. In this context, ongoing political changes and reorganisation occur that can alter these ancestral affiliations, since society — organised in networks — depends on the chiefs' decisions to create or recreate networks, as new opportunities arise and circumstances dictate.

Torrente offers an ethnographic analysis of the *rahui* in the atoll of Anaa (Tuamotu), based on the vernacular manuscript of Paea-a-Avehe. Torrente emphasises the fact that, if a society is plural from the perspective of its social organisation, the core of its pluralism has to be found in the religious and ceremonial aspects that govern social life. For example, discussing the *tiorega* ritual (the lifting of the *rahui*), he describes the plurality of authorities and powers that receive special aknowledgment through rituals:

> Paea talks about a special walled enclosure he calls *marae tiore haga katiga; marae* for the offering of first fruits, of which he has left a drawing. He adds that when a coconut tree gave its first ripe nuts (*teke*) they were to be carried to this *marae* and could not be eaten before the rite of the lifting of the prohibition had taken place, otherwise the nuts would be found bad (*kiro*) or would fall down before being ripe, or would be found dry. The *ariki*, the *tahuga* and the principal warrior (*kaito*) were to receive these first fruits before they could be eaten by the common people. The same ritual was practised for the first catches of fish during their period of abundance.[16]

---

15 Rigo, Bernard, 2004. *Altérité polynésienne ou les métamorphoses de l'espace-temps.* Paris: CNRS Editions.
16 See Chapter 2, this volume.

For their part, Ottino-Garanger et al. describe extensively the different occasions where a *rahui* may apply in the Marquesan archipaelago. Comparing *tapu* and *rahui*, their conclusion about the pluralistic organisation of Marquesan society has profound consequences for the anthropology of law in the Pacific. As a matter of fact,

> *tapu*'s efficiency is predicated on the punishment for transgression. The punishment may be automatic as soon as there is contact with a material that is hazardous in itself: madness, leprosy or blindness, for example. This idea is so deeply rooted that every plague is construed as punishment for a fault. Disease or drought don't necessarily originate in a transgression and it is important to identify its author ... When a *kahui* is involved, the transgression is perceived first as a challenge to the power of the *ariki/haka'iki* or the *tau'a*. Punishment first falls within their competence; it reflects flouted authority and, in the final analysis, the *ariki/haka'iki* or the *tau'a* is seen only as the privileged tool. It is not that the transgression of a perennial *tapu* cannot be punished inasmuch as the whole community is in danger; rather, punitive watchfulness involves first and foremost temporary prohibitions.[17]

Focusing on social organisation, my chapter[18] utilises Tahitian historical sources to demonstrate that all leaders, and not exclusively the *ari'i* (chiefs) — the highest status in the hierarchy — had the power to establish a *rahui*. The study of the relationships between the types of territories and the *rahui*, and between family groups and different territories, proves that the *rahui* is fundamentally a political institution that allows the conveyor to affirm control on resources in a specific territory. This plural reality has also been described for the Maori (Aotearoa New Zealand) by Wilson.[19]

In many of the territories studied in this book, Polynesian encounters with Europeans significantly transformed the authority and the pluralism that characterised these societies. Indeed, major historical events have altered and have redefined the tradition of the *rahui*. The first major event corresponds to the evangelising process in the Polynesian islands, which led to profound changes in belief systems and the main institutions. Other influential events include drastic

---

17 See Chapter 3, this volume.
18 Chapter 6.
19 Wilson, 1874, quoted in Frédéric Torrente, 2012. *Buveurs de mers, Mangeurs de terres, Histoire des guerriers de Anaa, archipel des Tuamotu*. Pape'ete: Te Pito o te Fenua.

demographic decline and the beginning of international trade. In a more general perspective, the colonisation process — whether it be British or French — affected the political organisation and traditions of indigenous societies.

Among the numerous social changes, Conte's work on the Tuamotu Archipelago reveals how new fishing practices in Tepoto and Napuka modified the practices related to the *rahui*. These new techniques, combined with traditional beliefs, transformed the economy into one revolving solely around economic predation. Traditionally, the end of the *rahui* in the Tuamotu Islands represented the prelude to turtle fishing. According to post-European local beliefs, the turtles were sent to the living by their ancestors, and refusing to catch them was an affront to the ancestors and jeopardised the access to these resources for future periods. Thus, traditional practices become an alibi to justify the commercial activities carried out by the fishermen. The capitalist system implemented by missionaries in the nineteenth century thus diverted the tradition of the *rahui* from its initial principles.

On a political level, Dixon examines the evolution of the *rahui* in Mangaia through the changes in power structures that led to unification. Based on archeological evidence, this work explores the change in *rahui* organisation through the analysis of political changes and how the land is managed today.

Social changes and ambivalent pluralism

Pluralism is historically and geographically dissimilar and often contradictory. Two types of ambivalence within the social sphere can be detected. First, on a historical level, colonial ideology in Polynesia has become a state ideology in various forms. The independent state constantly attempts to maintain a monopoly on the definition and elaboration of environmental norms[4] in the Pacific. The emerging legal pluralism thus appears as a minimalist one that denies traditional pluralism in Polynesian societies while conceding some autonomy to local communities regarding decision-making and general management. Second, the issues tackled in this book reveal that the *rahui*, while linked to environmental matters, seems above all to represent a political contest between local traditional authorities and the state government, and also between specific individuals. These two ambivalences — the *rahui* as a political stake and the modern state as the bearer of a disputed centralising ideology — are discussed by means of three theoretical avenues: that of the viewpoints of all categories of individuals (Mawyer); that of institutions (Ruru and Wheen, Thorax, Friedlander, Shackeroff and Kittinger); and that of social organisation (Dixon, Ghasarian, Chambers).

Mawyer's work describes the Gambier archipelago through several historical periods: the renunciation of political power and territorial control by local people in favour of the Catholic community during the first years of the annexation process; the French Government's takeover of territories and the assertion of its sovereignty in marine areas; and the transfer of power over lagoons from the colonial government to the autonomous government of French Polynesia. These different historical configurations blurred identity and social roles among local people. It was unclear who had the right to impose a ban in the lagoon. One may observe that historical research on the jurisdiction of the *rahui* in the lagoon refutes the viewpoints of local actors who do not recognise the power of the Ministère de la Perle in Tahiti, and the government more broadly, to make decisions on public activities in the lagoon.

Mawyer questions the status of historical pluralism in Mangareva from an individual point of view. As far as the implementation of the *rahui* in the lagoon is concerned, he shows the ambivalent — sometimes disturbing — relationships between the individual and the centralised state authority in French Polynesia. As with the situation in Rapa described by Ghasarian, Dixon shows that, in Mangaia, the *rahui* still exists and is under the authority of the council of the island even though this institution was officially abrogated in 1915 (and in 1945 in Rapa).

The emerging legal pluralism, then, appears as a minimalist one which denies the traditional pluralism in Polynesian societies while conceding some autonomy to local communities regarding decision-making and general management. Second, the issues tackled in the essays reveal that the *rahui*, while linked to environmental matters, represents, above all, a political stake between local traditional authorities and the state government, and also among individuals. These two ambivalences — the *rahui* as a political stake and the modern state as the bearer of a disputed centralising ideology — are discussed along three theoretical analyses: that of the viewpoints of all categories of individuals (Mawyer, Chambers); that of the institutions (Ruru and Wheen); and that of social organisation (Chambers, Ghasarian, Thorax).

This duality of laws — official and unofficial, according to Chiba's terms[20] — does not encourage harmonious collaboration between state law and traditional law, but rather confusion and questioning among the people about the real control of the *rahui* today. In Rapa, the identification process is not undermined by confusion or doubt, for the people willingly ignore state regulations and can do so because of the island's relative geographical isolation from the major administrative centres.[21]

Ruru and Wheen emphasise the ambiguities that are found in reinterpretations of the *rahui* in the environmental legislation of the government of Aotearoa New Zealand. At times, the *rahui* is conceded to Maori communities, at other times the Ministry of Fisheries has the monopoly of it, as decreed by the 1996 *Fisheries Act*. With little emphasis on the changes that occurred within institutions, Ruru and Wheen analyse the use of the term *rahui* in the modern legal framework of Aotearoa New Zealand. They demonstrate that, under the aegis of a state institution, its traditional meaning is marginalised.

Friedlander, Shackeroff and Kittinger discuss efforts by the US federal government to incorporate traditional knowledge into marine management. They note, however, that these moves may be less motivated by a desire to set up a new pluralism in state management than to meet a sovereign ambition: to re-establish the federal authority on the north islands of Hawai'i. Friedlander, Shackeroff and Kittinger discuss how traditional ecological knowledge (TEK) is integrated into contemporary Hawai'ian marine resource management, giving rise to challenges deriving from power and politics, postcolonial legacies and epistemological differences.

---

20   Chiba, M., 1998. 'Droit non-occidental'. In W. Capeller and T. Kitamura, *Une introduction aux cultures juridiques non occidentales. Autour de Masaji Chiba*. Académie Européenne de Théorie du Droit de Bruxelles. Editions Bruylant, pp. 37–44.
21   See also Bambridge, T. & Ghasarian, C., 2002. 'Droit coutumier et législation française à Rapa: les enjeux d'une traduction'. *Droit et cultures*, Traduction et droits 44: 153–81.

Ghasarian describes how the *rahui* functions on a daily basis, and agrees with Friedlander, Shackeroff and Kittinger's conclusions that the *rahui* is respected because customary authorities have maintained the control of their terrestrial and marine territories. The convergence between the control of customary property and that of the *rahui* is all the more relevant on Rapa and in Tongareva as the *rahui* still exists there today — whereas it was officially repealed at the beginning of the century in Aotearoa New Zealand and Hawai'i. The legal pluralisms that emerged from colonial settlements greatly differ from the cooperative type described by Morse.[22] The preservation of a traditional institution implies some bypassing, if not some deliberate ignorance of the official laws.

In all the following cases, the preservation of contemporary legal pluralism occurs with the prevalence of a postcolonial ideology that is, by its nature, totalitarian, if we adhere to Weber's definition of the state as 'the centralisation of the legitimate domination'.[23] The dominant modern state has not been weakened in French Polynesia, the Cook Islands, Hawai'i or in Aotearoa New Zealand. The state has never ceased to exercise its prerogatives against the collective rights of indigenous peoples, with the *rahui* being the principal subject of debate.

---

22   Morse, B.W., 1988. *Indigenous Law and the State*. Foris Publications.
23   Weber, M., 2010. *Economie et Société*. Paris: Editions Flammarion.

PART I

Tapu and *rahui*: Traditions and pluralistic organisation of society

1

Political power and *rahui* in ancient Polynesian society

Bernard Rigo

Introduction

In keeping with Gell's[1] theoretical assumptions about the equivalence between ideas and object, this chapter argues that the notion of *rahui* cannot be thought of independently of the cultural logic in which it is inscribed.

In Oceania, before the sudden appearance of Westerners, the idea of power, particularly political power, was not distinguished from the idea of the sacred. The power of the Polynesian chief (*ari'i, ali'i, ariki, 'eiki*), came from *mana*; that is, it was founded on the ancestrality of the bond with a particular land (*fenua*). The practice of *rahui* was and is an effect of these structural representations of Oceanian societies, in that it is the expression of a power for which the modality is the sacred, and the stakes of which are primarily political.

In making the connection with the past, it is therefore important to take time to examine the traditional concept of *rahui*, to recall its lexical meaning as well as to locate it in a societal and representational

---

1   Gell, A., 1993. *Wrapping in Images: Tattooing in Polynesia*. Oxford: Clarendon Press; Gell, A., 1998. *Art and Agency*. Oxford: Clarendon Press.

economy. *Rahui* is a term, with some subtle phonetic nuances, that is found in all Polynesian islands; for example, in Samoa, Hawai'i, the Marquesas, Tahiti, the Tuamotu and the Mangareva islands.[2] It refers to the prohibition or restriction applied to the consumption of a resource: fruits, animals (notably the pig, in Samoa) or any product of a particular land. Literally, it is the imposition of a *tapu* brought into effect by the sacred incantation (*rahu*) of an *ari'i* or a *tahu'a* (an expert in the relations between the world of men and the invisible entities). It is this same person who also lifts the *rahui*.

It is necessary to begin with the status of those who set the *rahui* to understand its nature and its purpose, to grasp that the former is religious and that the latter is political, as far as such a distinction is relevant in Pacific societies pre-European contact.

Nature and modality of political power

The Polynesian *ari'i* are sacred, not as delegated representatives of a divine entity but as affiliated to the divine,[3] by way of genealogical networks. Vertical continuity with the gods implies a hierarchy, and that hierarchy is merely the social expression of the primacy of genealogy from which the sacred power and temporal authority of *tahu'a* and *ari'i* originate. This 'ideology of consanguinity'[4] — 'ideology of the blood'[5] — structures Polynesian society. Ancestrality is nothing other than the assertion that anteriority confers value: gods and ancestors initiate the relationship, and the principle of primogeniture defines, at least theoretically, the class of *ari'i nui*, leaders of the highest rank.

---

2 Tregear, E., 1891. *The Maori–Polynesian Comparative Dictionary*. Christchurch, Wellington and Dunedin: Whitcomb and Tombs Ltd, pp. 386–87.
3 de Bovis, E., 1978. *Etat de la société tahitienne à l'arrivée des européens*. Publication no. 4. Tahiti: Société des Études Océaniennes, p. 51; Ellis, W., 1972. *A la recherche de la Polynésie d'autrefois*. Paris: Publication de la Société des océanistes, p. 91; Ellis, W., 1829. *Polynesian Researches, During a Residence of Nearly Six Years in the South Sea Islands*, Vols 1 & 2. Fisher, Son & Jackson.
4 Oliver, D., 1974. *Ancient Tahitian Society*. 3 vols. Honolulu: The University Press of Hawai'i, p. 636.
5 Testart, A., 1986. *Essai sur les fondements de la division du travail chez les chasseurs-cueilleurs*. Paris: EHESS.

1. POLITICAL POWER AND *RAHUI* IN ANCIENT POLYNESIAN SOCIETY

The prestige of different social classes is proportional to their degree of genealogical proximity in relation to the elder lineage. This geneaological distribution, which confers functions — first born / *ari'i* / political power; younger / *tahu'a* / religious power — and distinguishes social groups (*ari'i, ra'atira, manahune*), at the same time constructs a clan network that includes the tutelary deities. There is no dividing line between the divine and that which is not divine, as with the distinction between feminine and masculine: the chiefs are equally as sacred as gods, and they are sacred in fact and not symbolically. The extensive ethnographic literature of the early European observers described the effects in Tahiti of this divine power; for instance the customs of *amo* and *pi'i*, which were not the least spectacular. The person of the chief was so sacred that everything that touched him became *tapu*, including the ground he trod on,[6] or syllables contained in his name.[7] That a chief had to move on the backs of men as soon he left his sacred territory, and the entire community had to reform its vocabulary, under threat of having eyes gouged out, demonstrates the rather exorbitant powers linked to the *ari'i*.

It must be stressed that this power was not ceremonial or symbolic, but a practical reality. As one must not meet the eye of a god, commoners must bow before the *ari'i*, or risk losing their lives for not doing so.[8] *Ari'i* were perceived as gods and lived as such,[9] which placed them at the top of the social hierarchy but did not cut them off from the community; quite to the contrary. The leader was not the concentration of *mana* or the divine, but rather diffused it through his network of social and political associations. This means that every man was more or less sacred according to his genealogical distance from the leader. Under this logic of the clan based on blood, the head of the chief was not exclusively sacred, just more sacred. And it is in this sense, at least theoretically, that the *mana* of each individual, just like the *mana* of the community, is directly dependent on that of the chief.[10] A genealogical system has a network-based logic, and there is no network without this idea of a permanent circulation

---

6   Ellis, 1972, pp. 533–36.
7   *Bulletin de la Société d'Études Océaniennes* (*BSEO*) March–June 1994, 261–62: 14–34.
8   Sahlins, M., 1989. *Des îles dans l'histoire*. Paris: Gallimard/Le Seuil, p. 76 (1985. *Islands of History*. The University of Chicago, pp. 35, 143).
9   Oliver, 1974, pp. 1047–48.
10 See Handy, E.S.C., 1930. *History and Culture in the Society Islands*. Bulletin no. 79. Honolulu: Bernice P. Bishop Museum, p. 46.

which assumes continuity of circulation: from top to bottom, from the tutelary gods to the *manahune*, something must circulate — *mana*, *mauri* (sacred, prestige)[11] — like a sap that comes up from the roots (*tumu*) and irrigates the slenderest twigs.

Staying with the social aspect, the chief was the one who, through his alliances, his wars, his successes and his failures, gave both form and subsistence methods to the community. He was at once a warrior chief and also a religious leader; through him passes the tutelary god's *mana* (Ta'aroa, Tane, Oro, whichever). Thanks to this *mana*, abundance and fertility were provided for all men. In the domain of the chiefdom, the *ari'i* activated both natural and human resources. Different anthropologists have understood that the majesty of the chief is linked to his power to stimulate and redistribute wealth. The prestige belonged to he who could create an abundant circulation system within his network. The various ceremonies and rituals were ways of boosting the network to enable circulation of goods; sacrifices were accompanied by feasts: each time was an opportunity to circulate goods and people, to share and spend, under the aegis of *ari'i* and his *atua* (deity in the old system of belief). Morrison was not mistaken when he noted, 'The first fruits of all kinds are offered to the god, then the chief and lord of the place before being consumed and it is the same for fish …'.[12] Everything is an opportunity for a ceremony: 'If a man has a new net to use for fishing or a new canoe to launch, he organises a celebration on the *marae* (lithic platform where the old worships were held) for the priests …'.[13]

This is because it took the help of the gods and their representatives for the net to be filled up and for the *va'a* (dugout, canoe) to be efficient in the waves. When one considers the considerable number of sacred sites in Polynesia, it seems that social space is covered by a dense network of places of worship: *marae tupuna* (dedicated to the ancestries), specialist *marae* (fishermen, boatmen, healers), *marae ra'atira* (minor local chiefs), *ari'i marae*, *marae mata'eina'a va'a* (members of a chiefdom), inter-island *marae*, not to mention the ocean itself (considered to be the first *marae*).[14] Every aspect of social life was

---

11   Conte, E., 2000. *L'archéologie en Polynésie Française*. Tahiti: Au vent des îles, p. 233.
12   Morrison, J., 1981. 'Journal'. Paris: Société des Études Océaniennes, p. 151.
13   Morrison, J., 1981, p. 151.
14   Henry, T., 1988 (1968). *Tahiti aux temps anciens*. Paris: Publication de la Société des océanistes no. 1, p. 365.

affected by a sacred circulation, whose steady rhythm accompanies all of the important moments of everyday life and marks all levels of the hierarchy, and all aspects of human activity.

It was precisely for this reason that chiefs, as chiefs, could die, that is to say, they could be deposed.[15] The same applied to gods: 'Gods can and do die, when there are no priestly mediums to keep them alive'.[16] The superior, whatever form it took, depended on the inferior because an ascending circulation must necessarily happen and legitimise the chief or god by converging towards him. It is in this sense that the imperative of redistribution imposed at all levels of the hierarchy must be understood. Only the one who has received can give. The great chief or the great god was certainly a being that redistributed a great deal, but he was only great because he had received — or taken — a great deal. It is not surprising that if the Polynesians have always preferred to give rather than to receive,[17] it is not in the hope of receiving a significant gift in return, nor is it just to implement, in the medium term, a desire for power, it is first and foremost the perfect and immediate expression of a hierarchical valorisation: the power to give is *the* power. It is immediately experienced in terms of prestige. Sociopolitical circulation involves receiving goods (dependence) in order to give (*mana*), and providing — notably for prestige — in order to receive — especially loyalty. In this respect, the hierarchy of the gods was not determined by the intrinsic ontological qualities of a particular deity but rather their unequal power for (re)distribution.

Since the gods were part of a network, and sought to grow by increasing their network, they needed chiefs and active 'priests'. Thus, it can be understood that the great chief, even if he received more material goods than he redistributed, first distributed prestige to his network. The bad chief was one who did not redistribute enough material goods; he held back or failed in his political or military undertakings.

---

15 Adams, H., 1964. *Mémoires d'Ari'i Tamai*. Paris: Publication de la Société des Océanistes no. 12, Musée de l'Homme, p. 7; Hanson, A., 1973. *Rapa*. Paris: Publication de la Société des Océanistes no. 33, p. 18; Morrison, 1981, p. 138.

16 Te Rangi Hiroa (Sir Peter Buck), 1987. *The Coming of the Maori*. Wellington: Maori Purposes Fund Board; Whicoulls Limited, p. 473.

17 See Morrison, J., 1981, p. 174; and Crook, W.P., quoted by Oliver, 1974, p. 848: 'none of them know what it is to possess property in our sense of the word. If a native possesses many articles of property, he must distribute and cannot withhold; all his friends have a kind of positive claim, and to refuse to give would be shocking. He would be a *taata hamani ino*, literally a man that works evil.'

Of each, it can be said that 'he does not descend very well from the gods',[18] or that his god lacks power. In both cases, 'it causes shame' (*e mea haama*) because it is the whole community that is deprived of *mana*.

Rahui as sacred modality of a political power

Polynesian gods, ancestors and leaders, did not take their place in a cosmos like the Greek pantheon of deities. The word *fenua* is not an equivalent of the word 'nature' (adapted in Tahitian as *natura*). It refers first of all to the particular land to which one is connected, because it is also the land of one's ancestors. In this sense, it does not refer to the whole world, but a space to which a human network is attached, or more precisely with which something is exchanged: the power exercised on Earth (*mana ari'i*) is also a power exercised by the Earth (*mana fenua*).[19] If we wish to understand the concept of *rahui* and respect the originality of cultural logic, we cannot project contemporary representations and concerns onto a past where they are separated from their cultural and circumstantial context.[20]

Traditional cosmogonies, sacred myths and chants are framed around the themes of procreation, parthenogenesis and sexuality. It is against this background that warrior exploits and heroic deeds of a few gods, demigods or heroes provide a counterbalance to the erotic and cosmic movements. If natural events and biological functions are everywhere in these stories, 'nature', as a holistic and encompassing entity, is nowhere. In other words, the genealogical and energetic constitution of networks, particularly in the form of connecting by procreation, is the trademark of the main Polynesian texts.[21] But nature plays no role here: missing from the lexicon, it is also missing from the representations. Nature is not enchanted, because there is no nature:

---

18   Morrison, 1981, p. 171.
19   Sahlins, 1989, p. 76.
20   See Rigo, B., 2005, 'L'espace et le temps, expression culturelle privilégiée'. In Rigo, B., *L'espace-temps*. Bulletin du LARSH no. 2. Papeete: Au vent des îles.
21   Beckwith, M., 1972, *The Kumulipo*. Honolulu: University of Hawai'i Press; Henry, T., 1988, p. 343–68; Krämer, A., 1994. *The Samoa Islands*. Aotearoa: Polynesian Press; Métraux, A., 1941. *L'île de Pâques*. Paris: Gallimard, p. 108.

visible and invisible forces, female strength and male powers, gods and men are entangled in a game whose unstable forces create the precarious rules. Before contact with the West, the Polynesians did not live in nature, they lived in relationship with entities more or less loaded with sacredness in their network. The notion of *rahui* must then be linked to the economy of a human network defined by a sacred circulation, the extension of which marks the limits of a *fenua*: that particular sacred, ancestral land to which one is affiliated. The *rahui* is an act set by a sacred authority: power and sacredness are inseparable in Oceanian societies.[22] The nature of this sacredness must be remembered; it does not reside in a being or an intangible substance, transcending god or cosmic order, but in the power of circulation.[23]

The Polynesian leader, his guardian gods and his ancestors have a precarious status defined by their effective capacity to bring wealth, and their ability to redistribute it to their community of descendants and affiliates. In this, the leader is dependent on the members of his network. If the leader fails, the goods will no longer come back to him, the circulation will continue without him. It will travel elsewhere and he will literally be bypassed, losing *mana*; that is, to be socially eliminated. It is clear that this double movement constructs, on the one hand, the network in its maximum extension — from the earth and its products to the invisible entities, to whom the leader is genealogically the closest — and, on the other hand, the network in its hierarchical structure — upstream, the direction of the convergence of wealth indicates the axis of power and, downstream, redistribution, subject to formal and strategic preoccupations, designates the place and function of each member of the community.

The notion of *rahui* must, therefore, be associated with the economy of a human network defined by a sacred circulation, whose extension marks the limits of a *fenua*. The *rahui* is an act set by an authority. The prerogative of the *rahui* should, therefore, be understood in two ways: first, it is the implementation of the sacred power of the person who sets it; second, it is part of a logic which seeks to strengthen the entire network in terms of both its extension as well as in its hierarchy.

---

22 Rigo, B., 2007. 'Le pouvoir politique et le sacré en Polynésie'. In M. Chatti, N. Clinchamps and S. Vigier (eds), *Pouvoir(s) et politique(s) en Océanie*. Paris: L'Harmattan, pp. 197–22.
23 Babadzan, A., 1993. *Les dépouilles des dieux*. Paris: Editions de la Maison des Sciences de L'Homme, pp. 114–18.

It could be thought that segmentation and increasing hierarchy in certain Oceanian societies has diverted, for the benefit of a more centralised power, what was perhaps originally the implementation of social cohesion in order to manage resources. If the *tapu* is structural, the *rahui* is occasional: it adapts to the occasional demands of the natural world or of political power. All the events that affect the network — the death of an important person, alliances, the birth of a chief's son, and so on — are opportunities for important ceremonies. In these great moments of the community's life, the strength of the network is asserted by making its sacred modality into spectacle: the movement of goods. The *rahui* does not obey an ecological logic, but the sacred economy of a network society. Hence, substantiated facts all over Oceania can be easily understood: the sumptuous feast, as a demonstration of power,[24] is a constituent part of any exchange custom. If we cannot speak of potlatch for Oceanian societies, we can talk about agonistic logics: whether it is a question of traditional offerings on sacred *marae*, or gifts of contemporary parishioners in the Evangelical church during the *me* (collection which takes place each year in May in the Evangelical church and which results in special ceremonies) in French Polynesia, or the generosity of the Wallisians towards their Catholic parish on the occasion of communions, it is always human networks that are reaffirmed and which appear in their plurality.

We understand that the traditional ban provisionally set on products of land or sea is a necessity, less an ecological concern to maintain a resource than a religious and political calculation; one must provide oneself with the means to make available, when the time comes, the necessary abundance for the representation of the reality and the vitality of the network. This representation is in fact a necessary demonstration both for the members of the community itself and for all the others. Somehow, the *rahui* boosts the circulation and renders human networks competitive. One also grasps the dynamic ambiguity contained in the universal game of any political power involving sacredness: the *rahui* emanates from the recognised authority of a person; when used efficiently, it reinforces this authority considerably. Fortunately, Oceanian societies were, and still are, sufficiently fluid to

---

24 Douaire-Marsaudon, F., 1998. *Les premiers fruits*. Paris: CNRS Editions/Editions de la Maison des Sciences de L'Homme, p. 123.

deter chiefs from the excessive use of this power.[25] In these societies, displays of wealth or status that are not grounded in reality are not forgiven. Abusive *rahui* that demand too many sacrifices of the population will result in the diversion of all circulation away from imprudent *ari'i*.

Conclusion

For Polynesia in particular, and Oceania in general, there was not an encompassing nature to share, but competing networks in which all things — human or non-human — were linked. Not a common house (*oikos*, which could set up an ecologic preoccupation) but — to use a more Oceanian metaphor — rather a banyan among other banyans, each one multiplying the number of roots in land and air, both invisible and visible, in order to grow higher than the others by absorbing, for its own benefit, as much water or light as possible.[26]

The essential driving force behind Oceanian societies was the need to establish their status as primary and constituent in relationship to other societies. Thus, they are defined as network societies. The relationship is not status but an action whose renewal defines social space and hierarchies. The action in this case is put into circulation. The abundance of the circulation is the strength and extension of the human network.[27] Just as strength is not a potential assertion but an exercise actually demonstrated, the staging of circulation assumes a sacred economy of conservation for the purpose of sumptuous expenditure. The forbidden, just like a dam used to raise the level of the water, which will be released spectacularly, works to strengthen the sacred circulation and, hence, also to strengthen a religious and political social structure. This is not to say that the *rahui* had no ecological effects — the *ari'i* or the *tahu'a* had no interest in exhausting a natural resource (especially if it is dedicated exclusively for their consumption as, for example, the turtle). Rather, the *rahui*'s primary logic was economical, political and religious all at once: the renewed

---

25   Baré, J-F., 1987. *Tahiti, Les Temps et Les Pouvoirs: Pour Une Anthropologie Historique du Tahiti Post-Européen*. Paris: Éditions de l'Orstom, pp. 75, 89.
26   Henry, T., 1988 (1968), p. 350 ; Godin, P., 2000, 'Les ancêtres, essai de définition'. In F. Angleviel (ed.), *Religion et sacré en Océanie*. Paris: L'Harmattan, pp. 25–47.
27   Rigo, B., 2004. *Altérité polynésienne ou les métamorphoses de l'espace-temps*, Paris, CNRS Editions, pp. 125–89.

need for an abundant and prestigious circulation imposed temporary restrictions which simultaneously showed and demonstrated the reality of a power and of a human network.

Thus the practice of *rahui* doubly reaffirms the hierarchy: within the network and in relation to other chiefdoms. Its logic is not that of economy but that of expense, or more precisely, it participates in an economy of expense whose aim, to be demonstrative, must be reasonably excessive.

2

Ancient magic and religious trends of the *rāhui* on the atoll of Anaa, Tuamotu

Frédéric Torrente

This paper is based on vernacular material that was obtained from one of the last of the ancient *vanaga*, masters of pre-Christian lore, Paea-a-Avehe, of Anaa[1] Island.

Introduction

Throughout the last century, in the Tuamotuan archipelago, the technical term *rāhui* has been applied to 'sectors' (*secteurs*): specified areas where the intensive monoculture of the coconut tree was established, at that time and still today, according to the principle of letting these areas lie fallow between periods of cropping. The religious reasons for this method have been forgotten. The link between Christian conversion and the development of coconut plantations has changed the Tuamotuan atoll's landscape through the introduction

---

1   Anaa is the Tahitian name of this atoll ('Ana'a). In Tuamotuan language, it should be noted 'Ganaa' or 'Ganaia'. This atoll is situated in western Tuamotu, in the Putahi or Parata linguistic area.

of new modes of land occupation and resource management. In old Polynesia, the political and the religious were intertwined, as well as man and his symbolic and ritual environment.

Political and social aspects are studied elsewhere in this book. This essay considers the religious and ritual picture of pre-European life on the islands, and shows how religious concepts influenced man in his environment.

The Tuamotuan group of islands represents the greatest concentration of atolls worldwide; they are a unique, two-dimensional universe, close to water level and lacking environmental features, such as high ground, that could provide a place of refuge. This explains the extreme mobility of the vulnerable Tuamotuan societies, and their adaptability to change, be it of human origin or environmental. The Polynesian religion was based on prohibitions organised inside systems. Man was, thus, able to know where he stood according to his rank, in a world that identified sacred things or locations that had to be set apart. Shore asserts that this separation was translated within the opposition *tapu/noa*, which is undistinguishable from the concept of *mana*.[2] This strict opposition, much less porous to outside factors than the one of *Ao/Po* (life and visible world/death and invisible world), is key to understanding how Polynesian societies function. Man was obliged to respect the rules that governed social behaviour, including moral or practical responsibilities and those things or actions that were strictly prohibited.[3]

The functions of these permanent or temporary prohibitions varied according to one's point of view. They allowed one to find his place on the continuum god/humans/ancestors/origin of life, and during religious rites that perpetuated the cosmic order. Such prohibitions protected the god's power (*mana*), and fed the dread (*rikarika*) of supernatural sanctions. The same prohibitions reinforced the divine power of a chief's legitimacy, keeper of world order and holder of the group's perennial identity, maintainer of social cohesion.

---

2   Shore, B., 1989. '*Mana* and *Tapu*: a new synthesis'. In A. Howard & R. Borofsky (eds), *Developments in Polynesian Ethnology*. Honolulu: University of Hawai'i Press, pp. 137–74.
3   Bender, A. & Beller, S., 2003, 'Polynesian *tapu* in the deontic square. A cognitive concept, its linguistic expression and cultural context'. In R. Alterman & D. Kirch (eds), *Proceedings of the Twenty Fifth Conference of the Cognitive Sciences Society*, pp. 131–38.

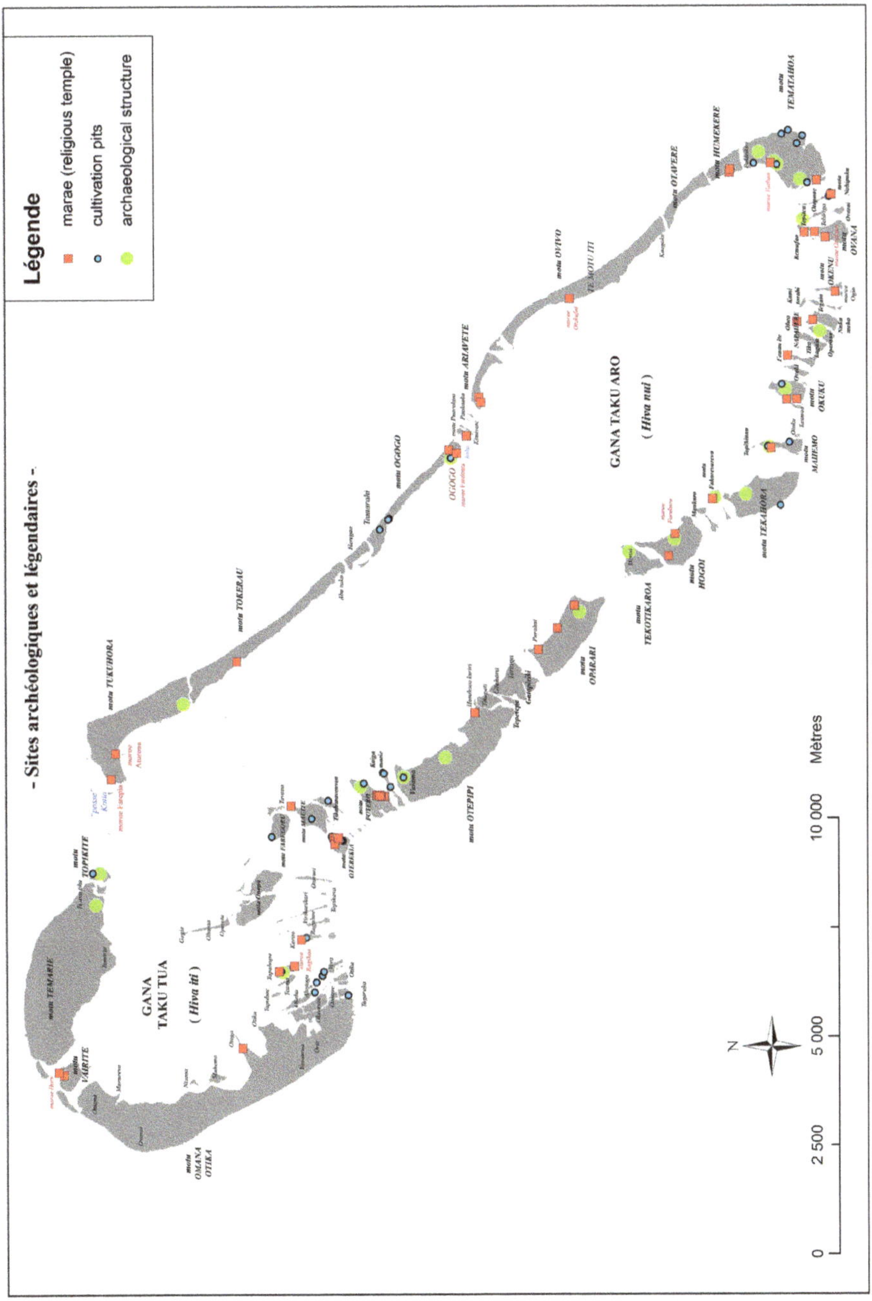

Figure 2: Map showing the locations of *marae* and archaeological structures on Anaa
Source: Frédéric Torrente

The word *rāhui* derives from the Eastern Polynesian root *raafui*, which means to prohibit (Polynesian Lexicon — Pollex). The Maori give the following definition: 'to protect by a rahui — i.e. by a mark set up to prohibit persons from taking fruit, birds etc., on certain lands, or to prevent them from trespassing on lands made *tapu*'.[4] On Mangaia: '*raui*, sacred, restricted by *tapu*, a mark of *tapu*, generally shown by the setting up of a coconut leaf plaited in a particular way'.[5] Williams notes: 'A mark denoting a sacred spot, as a burial place, a mark to indicate that shellfish, timber, flax or any other commodity in the neighbourhood is to be preserved. Made sacred, preserved'.[6]

In the Tuamotu, *rāhui* means: 'to prohibit, interdict, forbid taking, as the food of certain lands. A prohibition laid on lands or on crops. Closed, forbidden, as a land from which certain foods may not be taken'.[7] *Rāhui* is, thus, a temporary prohibition, the area of which is indicated by a physical sign, that is established on a food resource and on one's own land. The fear of supernatural sanctions derived from the invisible active power of the *rāhui* was enough for it to be respected.

To establish a *rāhui*

Any man inside greater Polynesia, notwithstanding his rank, could put a *rāhui* on his own land or on a particular type of resource,[8] which shows the importance of the *rāhui* inside the private sphere. This is still well entrenched in Maori culture.

The *rāhui* could be applied to resources obtained from the land, as well as to marine resources (portions of lagoons, portions of reefs).

In the Tuamotus, the divine chief (*ariki*) was also the master of rites on his sacred temple called *marae ariki*. Each descent line (*gāti*) had a tutelary god who was recognised as belonging to the whole atoll, as being the father of a divine succession that gave birth to a succession

---

4   Williams, H.W., 1852. *A Dictionary of the Maori Language*, London: D.C.L.
5   Tregear, E., 1891. *The Maori-Polynesian Comparative Dictionary*. Wellington, New Zealand, p. 385.
6   Williams, 1852.
7   Stimson, J.F. & Marshall, D.S., 1964. *A Dictionary of Some Tuamotuan Dialects of the Polynesian Language*. Massachusetts: Peabody Museum of Salem & The Hague: The Royal Institute of Linguistics and Anthropology, p. 427.
8   Wilson, W., 1799, *A Missionary Visit to the Southern Pacific Ocean, Performed in the Years 1796, 1797, 1798, in the Ship Duff, Commanded by Captain James Wilson*. London.

of chiefs.[9] One of the *ariki*'s prerogatives was to place temporary prohibitions linked to the important milestone ceremonies: stages of the chief's life, prestigious visitors, wars and seasonal rituals. When a chief wanted to put a *rāhui* on a food resource as a preliminary to a feast, he acted through a *tahuga* (the priest on the *marae*), who called upon the gods, taking the oath that they would be invited to the feast.

If a person of inferior rank wished to protect his plantations, he would go through a *tāura* (expert in divination and magic), who buried an object at the base of the tree made *mana* by the incantation called *karakia* (in the Tuamotus and among the Maori). A symbol would be put on the tree as a message for potential transgressors. The incantation was to the *mauri* (life-giving energy) of the tree, for it to become full of fruit and protected through the awakening (*faka ara*) of the destructive power of the *rāhui* applied against a potential thief.

Davies claims that in the Society Islands, *rahu* is the name of the incantation made to apply a prohibition, another sense of the word being 'to engender, to produce, to create, to make appear, to bring to the world, synonymous with *arahu*, to spring, as seed or young shoot. *Rahurahu* is an expression of the sacred or of the prohibition, synonymous with *tapu*, as in the phrase *ai rahurahu* (to eat prohibited food)'.[10]

The *rāhui* inside a system

The *rāhui* is first of all a physical sign indicating a prohibition. More than a simple sign, however, it is part of a system of association by which a material symbol that can be seen by everyone is a mark of the prohibition on access to an invisible but active world. The *rāhui* is positive in that it protects the physical elements that are not to be touched, and negative and destructive in its effect on the one who would violate the *rāhui*.

Among the Maori, carved posts (*pou rāhui*) indicated that a temporary prohibition was placed (*rāhuitia*) on natural resources such as land, forests, shores or rivers. A piece of material or another object belonging to the custodian would be attached to the post, which might be a simple stake, as a mark of his invisible power.

---

9   Caillot, E., 1932, *Histoire des Religions de l'Archipel des Tuamotu*. Paris: Ernest Leroux.
10   Davies, J., 1851, *A Tahitian and English Dictionary with Introductory Remarks on the Polynesian Language and a Short Grammar of the Tahitian Dialect*. Tahiti: printed at the London Missionary Society's Press.

The *pou rāhui* is inhabited by the active power of the *rāhui*. The image's threatening aspect underscored the danger of going further. The 'heart' of the *rāhui* was a hidden stone (*whatu, fatu, pofatu*) which contained the *mauri*, hidden so as not to be manipulated by an expert diviner (*tāura*) enfeebling its *mauri*. At first, the power entrusted inside the stone had to be woken up, or activated (*fakaoho*) through a *karakia* calling upon the vertical continuum between *Ao* and *Po* and, so to speak, charging this stone with *mana* and sharpening its teeth.[11]

Near the *pou rāhui* was meant to be the abyss (*waro*) the entrance to the *Po* into which the violator would fall. The *pou rāhui* wore a man's girdle (*maro*), which was a decoy, the real *maro* being hidden at some distance. The functional physical whole of the hidden *maro* and *whatu* was called the *kapu* of the *pou rāhui*. Eventually there was attached on the *pou rāhui* only a piece of the chief's clothes or a piece of material.

The planting of *pou rāhui* was linked to the ownership of the land:

> These posts were erected as indicating a taking possession of the land — a *tītiri*, or erecting the sacred mark of the rāhui.[12]

> *Titi o kura*, the setting up of the *kura*, that is painting the post supporting a house with red ochre, as *tapu* indicating the sacredness of the building.[13]

In the Society Islands, when there was a significant *rāhui* put on by the chiefs, one of the ways to ritually reactivate the existence of the cosmos and to reiterate their divine origin and their prestige was to establish on the temple a *ti'i potua ra'au* (carved posts)[14] or *potua aru* ('a tree trunk carved on its whole length with *ti'i* images, planted as a guardian of a rahui or a prohibition',[15] see Figure 3). When the chiefs had decided on a *rāhui*, these *ti'i potua ra'au* images, carved back to back, were stood on the meeting places, their bases surrounded by stones, which are reminiscent of the *whatu*. When the prohibition was lifted, the carved posts were taken out, their *mauri* having gone. There was another kind of *ti'i pū rāhui*, inside the private sphere, for provisional prohibitions

---

11   Best, E., 1904. 'Notes on the custom of *Rahui*, its application and manipulation, as also its supposed powers, its rites, invocations and superstitions'. *Journal of the Polynesian Society*, 13(2): 83–88.
12   White, T., 1892, '"The *Rahui*". Notes & Queries'. *Journal of the Polynesian Society* 1(4): 275–76.
13   White, T., 1899. 'The ceremony of *Rahui*'. *Transactions & Proceedings of the Royal Society of New Zealand 1868–1869* 32: 352–57.
14   Henry, T., 1968. *Tahiti aux temps anciens*, Paris: Publication de la société des océanistes.
15   Davies, J., 1851.

2. ANCIENT MAGIC AND RELIGIOUS TRENDS OF THE *RĀHUI* ON THE ATOLL OF ANAA

about plantations. The dimensions of the carving varies according to the rank of their owner, but anyone could carve them and practice a ritual meant to activate them, grouping them attached to stakes so as to cover all directions of the property that benefited from their protection. Stones were also put at the base of the stakes.

Figure 3: Carved post called *ti'i potua ra'au* as sign of *rāhui*
Source: Drawing by George Tobin, Mitchell Library

Making use of the coconut

The coconut palm tree has many uses in making sacred objects, including the *kaha*, *'aha* (sennit) that supports the red feathers of the god's effigy (*to'o*). It is thus logical that it would be called on as a symbolic mark of prohibition: *niu*, and its variants refers to the coconut across the Austronesian linguistic area, and the stone, which is the basis of a sacred enclosure. Images in plaited coconut palm could be used, as also in Melanesia, to indicate a prohibition. In Samoa:

> the taboo was employed chiefly for the purpose of protecting plantations and fruit trees from the thieves. Each individual was supposed to have the power of tabooing his property by means of a significant symbol, without the aid of a priest, and bring punishment to those who disregarded the taboo.[16]

Beliefs connected with taboo signs on Samoa are given by Turner:

> One of these, intended to protect a man's breadfruit trees, was a representation of a sea spike (three pointed spear), made with plaited coconut leaflets and hung from one or more trees; the idea involved was that the sea spike would run into the body of a thief, and anyone proposing to steal would be prevented by a fear, if he did so, that a sea spike would actually dart up and wound him mortally, the next time he went out to sea.[17]

In Anaa of the Tuamotus, the significative elements of the *rāhui* can be compared with those in the rest of Polynesia. At the end of the nineteenth century, the vernacular corpus of Paea-a-Avehe shows the religious importance of rites regulating fertility and the management of food resources.

Protection of plantations on Anaa

Contrary to common belief, the Tuamotuan people were as capable agriculturalists as they were sailors. The cultivating of food plants (*hamo katiga*) was done inside pits called *maite*. These pits were dug

---

16   Ella, cited in Williamson, R.R., 1937. *Religion and Social Organization in Central Polynesia*, Cambridge at the University Press. Ella later became a London Missionary Society missionary on Ouvéa, which means he was at ease with Polynesian linguistics.
17   Williamson, 1937.

with pearl shell spades[18] to sweet water level. The pits were lined with trees that produced humus through their leaves, which belonged to and was exploited by a lineage (*gāti*).

Plantations outside pits could be put under prohibitions, such as the species of *Pandanus tectorius* specifically used as a food for humans, *Pandanus tectorius var. tectorius*, or the one cultivated for the making of mats or objects that would be put under *tapu*, which is mentioned in the old songs as *fara tanu*, probably *Pandanus tectorius var. laevis*, the leaves of which are devoid of thorns.[19] Another important plant used for food was the *pia*, *Tacca leontopetaloides*, which grows around the outside face of the atoll.

Part of Paea's manuscript dwells on the techniques for making use of the coconut palm on Anaa. Although this testimony belongs to the beginning of the nineteenth century, it illustrates the minute care and knowledge that was brought to bear on the use of different parts of the coconut as regulated by a system of prohibitions. There existed a system of material and symbolic codes, as among the Maori, that made sense to the whole community.

A mark called *pūtiki* at Anaa, as described by Paea, was intended to convey a message through a plaited coconut frond (*rau gaofe*) twined around the trunk. The sole fact of being plaited all round signalled the ownership of the land. The image made of the frond embodied the *mauri* and the power of its owner. The fruit, which was the object of the restriction, was attached to the *pūtiki*, in this case a coconut at the ripe stage (*gora*). This construction was meaningful for all and indicated both ownership and prohibition.

The proto-Polynesian *pūtiki* stems from the root *fii-tiki*. The definition given by Stimson for the Tuamotu is:

> To make a circle fringe, of leaves around, upon. As around a tree as a sign of restriction; or upon the head as a protection against the sun. Marked by a girdle of leaves: a sign of formal sacred restriction, prohibition.[20]

---

18   Chazine, J-M., 1985, 'Les Fosses de Culture dans les Tuamotu. Travaux en cours et Perspectives'. *Journal de la Société des Océanistes* 61: pp. 25–62.
19   Butaud, J.F., 2010. *Guide Floristique des Atolls Soulevés de l'archipel des Tuamotu*. Papeete: Direction de l'Environnement.
20   Stimson & Marshall, 1964.

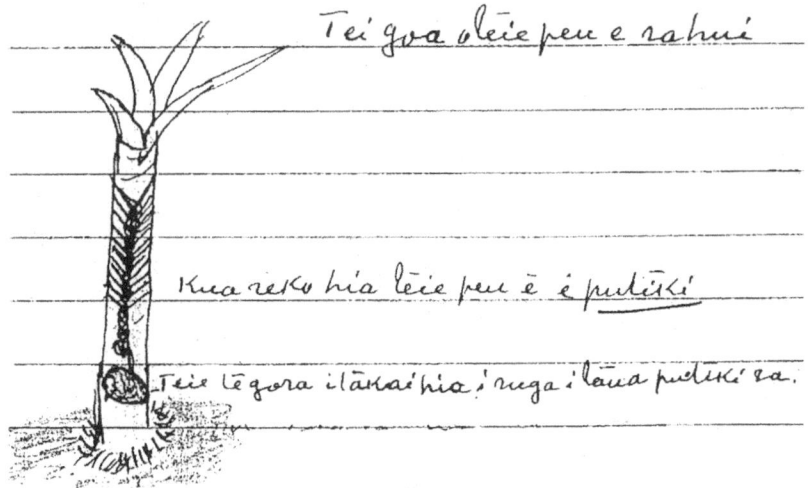

Figure 4: *Pūtiki* as sign of prohibition on the resource
Source: Drawing by Paea-a-Avehe, Stimson Mss, Torrente 2012

As Paea explains:

> *E gaohe ore, e ravehia teie peu i ruga i te hakari e te tahi atu a haga rakau, e rave katoa hia hoki ei pukohu karire haiko. Te igoa o teie peu e rāhui, kua reko hia teie peu e, e pūtiki. Teie te gora i takai hia i ruga i taua pūtiki ra.*[21] (The custom was to take green coconut fronds, which were placed round the coconut palm tree trunk, or round another tree, or at times pandanus leaves freshly cut. These coconut fronds were also used to fasten faggots of dry wood for the fire. This custom was also called *rāhui*, and more specifically *pūtiki*. A green coconut was hung under the *pūtiki*).[22]

In this symbol, two things take precedence. On one side, the fact that a coconut frond girds the trunk of the fruit tree signifies a temporary prohibition placed upon the food source, on the other side the hanging of a ripe coconut tells which category of food is being thus regulated.

The *pūrahui* is mentioned on Anaa, as a generic term designating the sacred prohibition, meaning a plantation (*pū*), put under *rāhui*, containing the concept of heart, of origin, of invisible centre: *pū*,

---

21 Paea-a-Avehe, 'Small notebooks from Paea'. In Frank Stimson Manuscripts, Microfilms, The Peabody Essex Museum of Salem, Massachusetts.
22 Torrente, F., 2012. *Buveurs de mers, Mangeurs de terres, Histoire des guerriers de Anaa, archipel des Tuamotu*, Pape'ete: Te Pito o te Fenua.

wrapped in its visible sign, *rāhui*. There exists on this atoll a piece of land called Pūrahui, on which is established a small *marae* bearing the same name.[23]

Rāhui on parts of the lagoon

The atoll of Anaa has a closed lagoon that was well known in the past for its abundance of pearl shells, *pārau* (*Pintada margaritifera*), or *te uhi taramea* (*Pinna* sp.), and its abundance of *koeha* (*Tridacna maxima*). The commercial diving campaigns that began in the second half of the nineteenth century diminished the resource, which obliged the imposition of a law forbidding the plundering of the lagoon of Anaa.[24]

The chants (*fakatara*) the function of which is to legitimate the land holdings of the ancient descent groups (*gāti*), carry the names of the lagoon areas that are rich in pearl shell (and belonging to particular chiefs), called *roto pārau*, and of the spots where the pearl shell are concentrated, called *pū pārau*. The prestigious chieftainship *gāti* Tagihia owned pearl shell as a guardian symbol (*te uhi taramea*).[25]

Ancient society gave the shell fauna of Anaa a primary religious and symbolic importance, the shells of the bivalves being understood as containing the atoll universe, as well as being host to all that is sacred (red feathers, or blood oozing from sacrifices). Pearl shell came into the making of all religious objects, or for the ornamentation of warriors, for example necklaces (*kanaenae*) and breastplates (*te uhi taramea*), including the famous Parata warriors of Anaa who were covered with shark skins and wore a sort of glove made from the jaw of the moray eel.[26]

The *tapu* on the shells was not only meant to protect a food resource but also, more widely, symbolic or sacred objects that were prestigious throughout Polynesia.

---

23 Torrente, F., 2010. *Ethnohistoire de Anaa, un atoll des Tuamotu*, Thèse de doctorat en Ethnologie, Anthropologie culturelle. Université de la Polynésie française.
24 Journal of 'Messenger de Tahiti'. Imprimerie du Gouvernement, Papeete, Aout 1878.
25 Torrente, 2012.
26 Torrente, 2012.

Certain parts of the reef were marked out by pieces of white cloth (*tapa*) on sticks so as to indicate a restriction on the fishing of *maoa* shells (*Turbo setosus*) or *pāhua*, *kohea* (*Tridacna maxima*), or wider fishing inside the area. On Anaa, numerous heaps are still known as being used to demarcate the *tauga paru*, areas of fish concentration each of which bore a specific name.

Rāhui transgression

Intentional or not, the breaking of a *tapu* or a *rāhui* is called *hara*. It is meant to bring about the gods' displeasure, or to unleash the unearthly forces on the transgressor. If the fault was known, the risk was then carried by the group as a whole and seen as a disorder threatening the social cohesion — a calamity of some sort, natural or not, being thrust upon the group. This was the reason for the person at fault to be banned from his group and land of birth.

The mechanisms of the supernatural sanction are that the destructive power of the *rāhui* penetrate (*uru*) the transgressor, deteriorates his *mauri* and brings death if nothing is done or a knowledgeable person, a *tahuga* or *tāura*, does not practice the appropriate ritual so as to reverse the destructive process. The rites were meant to restore the *mauri*, and get out of the body the destructive principle linked to the *rāhui*. Purification rituals, making use of water or of the smoke of a *tapu* fire, were practised on the *marae* also in the case of transgression (*hara*) affecting the community. Some authors claim, maybe mistakenly, that this ritual could involve human sacrifice, which is a theory proposed by the proselytising agenda of missionaries and Christian zealots.[27]

Possession of the victims by one or more destructive forces would bring about symptoms marked by shivering and uncontrolled movements called *ira*, and mostly acute pain and the swelling of the belly. As noted by Reverend Orsmond:

> The spirit of the coral, *puga*, *farero*, *kana*, lacerated the guts, the power of the stone, *fatu*, creating an intolerable weight (on the belly), the power of the wood, *rakau*, pierced the guts, bringing a strong

---

27 Henry, T., 1928. *Ancient Tahiti*. Bulletin no. 48. Honolulu: Bernice P. Bishop Museum; Pomare, T., 1971. *Mémoires de Marau Taaroa, dernière reine de Tahiti, traduits par sa fille, la princesse Takau Pomare*. Publication de la Société des Océanistes no. 27. Paris: Musée de l'Homme.

fever, palpitation and foam to the mouth. When the witnesses, choken by fright, asked the forces who they might be, they would answer and give their names, saying this word first: '*O vau ...*' (it is I).[28]

Paea explains that on Anaa the transgression of the *tapu* or *rāhui* — in this instance, it would be a *marae* located at Napahere — caused sickness, starting with an uncontrollable shaking and a swelling of the body as with a woman with child.[29] Going to a *tahuga* or *tāura*, was the only way to dominate the surnatural sickness called *pona*.[30]

Paea explains that only the purification rite performed by a *tahuga* could cure the sickness in these words: '*Kaore hoki e mehaki e ora ai tei te haga tahuga hoki te mehaki e ora ai te tagata i tupu hiai teie nei maki.*' This swelling process is known all over Polynesia and Melanesia.[31]

The *tahuga* made a miniature canoe with a sail and a paddle (*E haga rateu ki te vaka korereka te vega te hoe*) that he moved around the victim's belly while speaking to the force inside: '*Hauhari mai! Hauhari mai tateu i ruga i to tateu vaka mai ake hau tere ka vaiho atu tena tagata! Kaveke tateu!* (Come, come on our canoe and leave this man, let us go. Let us go!).'

Then he carried the canoe ceremonially unto the reef and let it run in the sea, while saying: '*Hau tere ra kauraka e noho mai kaveke tateu* (Now go! Let us not stop here, let us go!).'

It is only when the canoe went away that the sickness could take away the destructive forces of the *pona*: '*Kia tere ra taua vaka korereka nei, ei reira taua maki nei e ora ai. Ko te huru teie i te maki reko hia ra e pona.*'[32]

Elsewhere, pollution caused by the breaking of a *tapu*, or the transgression of a *rāhui*, could be attenuated by expiatory or purification rites that were meant to remove the contamination process.

---

28   Rev. Orsmond, in Henry, 1928.
29   '*E tupu hiai e taua maki kiro nei e te rikarika e goru te kopu mai te hapu te huru.*' This outworldly sickness was called *pona*: '*E reko teie no te maki rekohia ra e, e pona no Ganaia.*'
30   Paea-a-Avehe, Emory Manuscripts, folio ZG 13/ 292, Bernice Pauahi Bishop Museum Archives, Honolulu, Hawai'i, translation in Torrente, 2012.
31   Guiart, J., 2013a. *Malekula, l'explosion culturelle*. Nouméa & Pape'ete: Le Rocher-à-la-Voile; Guiart, J., 2013b. *Cultures on the Edge, Caught Between the White Man's Concept, Polynesia Opposed to Melanesia, from Efate to Epi, Central Vanuatu*. Pape'ete: Te Pito o te Fenua.
32   Paea-a-Avehe, Emory Manuscripts, in Torrente, 2012.

For that purpose, two mediums were used: the *tapu* fire (*ahi taitai*), which chased or consumed the pollution by the influence of the heat or the smoke; otherwise salt or fresh water washed the impurity.

Modes of lifting a *rāhui* or a temporary restriction

Lifting a *rāhui* was part of a complex ceremonial process at the end of which food, after having been offered to the gods, would pass from the state of *tapu* to that of *noa* (free from any restriction). This process was called *fakanoa*, which meant not only the freedom from *tapu*, but also 'to bring within one's power'.[33] The accumulated food would then be distributed on the occasion of a feast. The *rāhui* had been lifted by he who had instituted it, and the signs of the restriction were taken out with some solemnity. The action of lifting *tapu* or *rāhui* was called *hakamāma* on Anaa and *tāma* on Vahitahi; the state of freedom from *tapu* was known as *mā* or *māma*.

The offering of the first fruits from the crop or from fishing or hunting was the ritual by which the *rāhui* would be lifted on the food concerned. The first fruits were cooked on a *tapu* fire and given as an offering to the gods.

This rite demonstrates a propitiatory dimension through which the prohibition (the sacred content linked to the *tapu*) was transferred to the gods who absorbed it. As Babadzan explains, this is an inversion rite through which the ritual pollution of the offering to the gods reverses the roles, putting the gods in an inferior position to humans. Offerings and incantations thus carried a consequence that made food *noa* for the humans to eat[34] at a feast attended by the whole community.

Among the Maori, lifting the *tapu* when the building of a communal house was finished was obtained through the first-born girl of the highest rank eating a roasted kumara inside the building. First-born girls of high rank were classified as *ariki* and, as all Maori *ariki*, could be *tahunga* if they had gone through the specific training.

---

33 Smith, J., 1974. *Tapu Removal in Maori Religion*. Memoir no. 40. Wellington: The Polynesian Society.
34 Babadzan, A., 1993. *Les dépouilles des dieux*. Paris: Editions de la Maison des Sciences de L'Homme.

Lifting the restriction: The *tiorega* ritual

The *tiorega* ritual[35] was practised on Anaa so as to lift the *tapu* on food resources or on the occasion of the first captures of fish that had been placed under *rāhui*. Offerings were given first to the high-ranking people, *ariki* or *tahuga*, who acted as go-betweens so as to deliver them to the gods. The common people (*tangata rikiriki*) could eat the produce after its redistribution to all. My informant, the 75-year-old Te Neehiva-a-Horoi, still knew about this ritual, practised on a specific *marae* called *marae tiore*.

Paea talks about a special walled enclosure he calls *marae tiore haga katiga*; *marae* for the offering of first fruits, of which he has left a drawing (see Figure 5). He adds that when a coconut tree gave its first ripe nuts (*teke*) they were to be carried to this *marae* and could not be eaten before the rite of the lifting of the prohibition had taken place, otherwise the nuts would be found bad (*kiro*) or would fall down before being ripe, or would be found dry. The *ariki*, the *tahuga* and the principal warrior (*kaito*) were to receive these first fruits before they could be eaten by the common people. The same ritual was practised for the first catches of fish during their period of abundance.

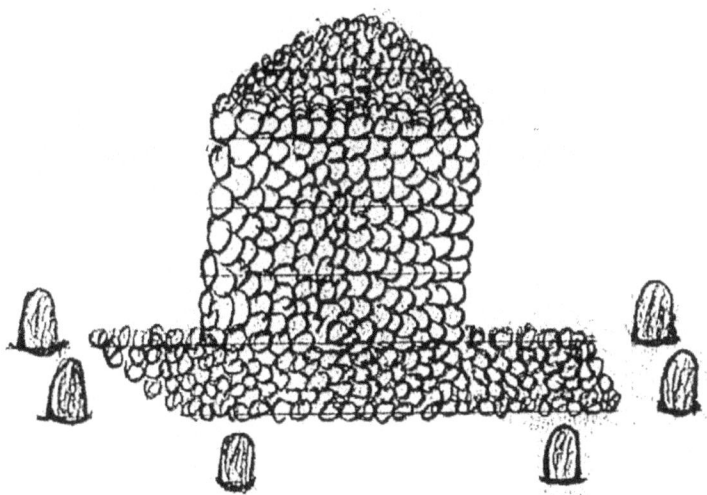

Figure 5: Temple called *Marae tiore haga katiga*
Source: Drawing by Paea-a-Avehe, Stimson Mss, Torrente 2012

---

35 The meaning of *tiorega* is 'eating of the first fruits' (Stimson & Marshall, 1964); elsewhere: *pāore* = *tiore*.

The gāvari ritual on Anaa

At the occasion of the end of community work, such as the building of a high seas canoe, the end of the *rāhui* was announced and a ritual called *gāvarihaga vaka* was introduced, which allowed the lifting of the prohibitions and the opening of the canoe for its normal use.[36] The same happened at the end of the building of a *marae* or other important community buildings.

These rites were practised on Anaa in another type of walled enclosure called *marae vaiga katiga no te haga varua o te po*, literally 'shrine for food offerings to the forces of the invisible world'. This was a small *marae* demarcated by a wall of ordinary stones, a wooden post (named *kehō*) planted exactly in the centre. The *kehō* had a horizontal platform fixed at its summit on which the food offerings meant for the gods (*atua*) or the ancestors (*tuputupūa*) were deposited. This *marae* was smaller than the ones serving as more central religious sites. On Fagatau Island, the *kehō* was a standing stone that was at times associated with a transverse stone piece on which to place offerings to the gods.[37]

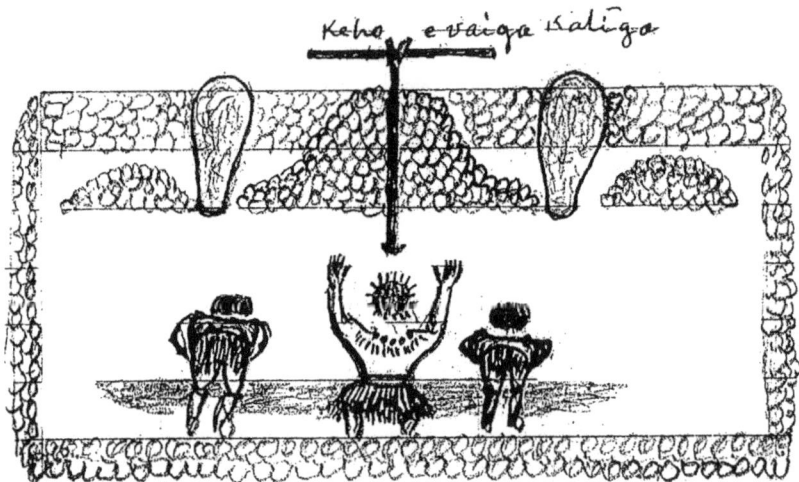

Figure 6: Temple called *Marae vaiga katiga no te haga varua o te po*
Source: Drawing by Paea-a-Avehe, Stimson Mss, Torrente 2012

---

36 Stimson & Marshall, 1964.
37 Stimson & Marshall, 1964.

Feasts were celebrated seasonally, during periods of abundance or when the first seagoing turtles (*Chelonia mydas*) came in. The first turtle to be captured was the object of complex rites.[38]

Conclusion

Thus can we say that in Polynesia, each living species (of vegetable or animal kingdom) or any inert element existed within a continuum that excluded any philosophical opposition between nature and culture. The genealogical model set out the exact place of each living species, including man.

A vertical logic drew the link between the sky as being the abode of the gods, the chiefs who controlled the human order of things, and the ancestors and the world of origins, which was deep in the earth.

Each species of creation owned a visible shape, issued from the depths (*tupu*) and a specific appearance (*huru*) visible to humans, as a kind of container, an envelope, a shell. This contained an invisible interiority made of many vital elements. First, the *vārua*, sort of an ever-unseen double living inside this body that could survive the death of its envelope. This was the living factor behind the animation of each physical body, which explains the personification of elements seen in the natural environment, such as coral.

On the other hand, each body benefited from a life-giving energy (*mauri*), which allowed the manifestation of life and the reproduction of species. A vital principle runs through all things, as the sap inside a tree (*iho* or *uho*) given to man at birth by the umbilical cord, also called *uho*, or by the roots of plants. In man, it could be carried over generations, being present in the ancestor's relics, bones and objects, and inside a chief's lineage (*iho ariki* or *uho ariki*).

But, nobody could exist without the life-giving light, shown in the person of Atea or Tane-te-vai-te-ora. That is why the pieces of the cosmos, clouds and stars, and the living objects, animals and vegetal species, are seen as the children of Atea or Tane, according

---

38   Emory, K.P., 1947. *Tuamotuan Religious Structures and Ceremonies*. Bulletin no. 191. Honululu: Bernice P. Bishop Museum.

to a genealogical model that links the ancestry (*tuputupūa*) of gods, men and animal and vegetable species, plus any understandable phenomenon that is given a mental existence.

It is not feasible here to give the details of the construction of the Polynesian cosmic order, which made of two opposing worlds: the world of light called, according to location, *Ao nei* or *Ao marama*, the world of what can be seen, of life; and the world of the *Po*, the one of the invisible, of the gods, of obscurity and of the original depths where the dead return to.[39] There is no way of studying any living species without taking into account the parallel visible and invisible worlds.

Christianisation has erased the old frontiers between *tapu* and *noa* areas. The logic of the *rāhui* has changed. Fossil forms of the old religion have been retained, nevertheless, in particular in the manipulation under *tapu* of relics (nails, hair, liquids), clothes or objects in contact with the human body, including footprints.

The signification of the word *rāhui* has also changed. It is linked today to the different concepts dealing with the protection of the environment, which was not the aim in ancient Polynesia.

Translated by Jean Guiart, July 2013.

---

39 Stimson, J.F., 1937. *Tuamotuan Legends (Island of Anaa) Part I. The Demi Gods*. Honululu: Bernice Pauahi Bishop Museum Bulletin; Salmond, A., 1978. 'Te Ao Tawhito. A semantic approach to the traditional Maori cosmos'. *Journal of the Polynesian Society* 87(1): 5–28.

3
Tapu and *kahui* in the Marquesas

Pierre Ottino-Garanger, Marie-Noëlle Ottino-Garanger, Bernard Rigo and Edgar Tetahiotupa

Nowadays in Polynesia, a path leading down to the sea or a space on a piece of land may bear a sign that says *tapu*. In such instances, however, no sacredness is implied; it means simply that it is either private property or off limits to the general public. This modern usage of an ancient Polynesian concept is not a diversion of a lost notion; the word is used because it is relevant for contemporary society.

What is posited here is the notion of prohibition, which can be found in every culture. The notion of prohibition, however, is valid only as based upon the authority that underlies its enforcement, and especially inasmuch as enforcement is possible. Now, this prerequisite is precisely the possibility that a prohibition is likely to be transgressed. What is impossible need not be prohibited, and no boundaries are set where an impassable barrier is present.

Prohibition always reflects a power or an authority. This means that there are two types of prohibition, because there are two types of danger: danger related to something that is dangerous per se, and danger related to an authority that is in a position to use dangerous powers.

In the first instance, prohibition is perennial, just like the nature of the substance involved — women's blood, dead people's skulls as well as the *fugu*'s liver (the *fugu* is a kind of globefish) are dangerous in themselves in Polynesia. This does not keep people from preparing the *fugu*'s meat, which is a delicacy, or from having children by women or setting up rituals for the dead; what matters is taking precautions to be safe from direct and clearly identified dangerous things. Everybody has to submit to these precautions, especially the *ariki/haka'iki* (chief).

In the second instance, the prohibition is determined by an authority, rather than by the nature of things. While the path is not in itself dangerous, the penalties that are likely to be meted out for trespassing on private property may be. The nature of the penalty may be provided for in the civil code or in ancestral sacredness; it is a matter of culture and societal organisation of power.

The early European observers of Pacific societies were struck by the diversity of prohibitions that ruled human behaviour and which could be accounted for by the notion of *tapu*. All things considered, it is right to preserve the specific character of this Polynesian concept, which cannot be reduced to the Western notion of 'prohibition', as the core idea in *tapu* was always shot through with sacredness.

In Polynesia, as in many cultures, power was both political and religious. Yet, it is important to distinguish between what is in the nature of *tapu*, which has to be obeyed by all components of society as the laws of nature must be obeyed by mankind, and what is the result of decisions made by those in whom sacred power is vested and who subject others to provisional prohibitions that, to their minds, seem to be required by a political, weather-related or environmental situation. In times of food shortage, drought, in anticipation of sumptuary ceremonies, for prestige reasons or in order to save resources, Marquesan *haka'iki* (*ariki*, Society Islands) or *tau'a* (sacred, specialist priest) are empowered to impose *kahui* (*rahui*, Society Islands).

It seems that all Polynesian, and even Pacific societies as a whole, are careful to make a distinction between men's space and women's space, between the space of the living and the ancestors' space. All these spaces are like ambivalent sacred powers with which it is important to come to terms. They involve boundaries and prohibitions.

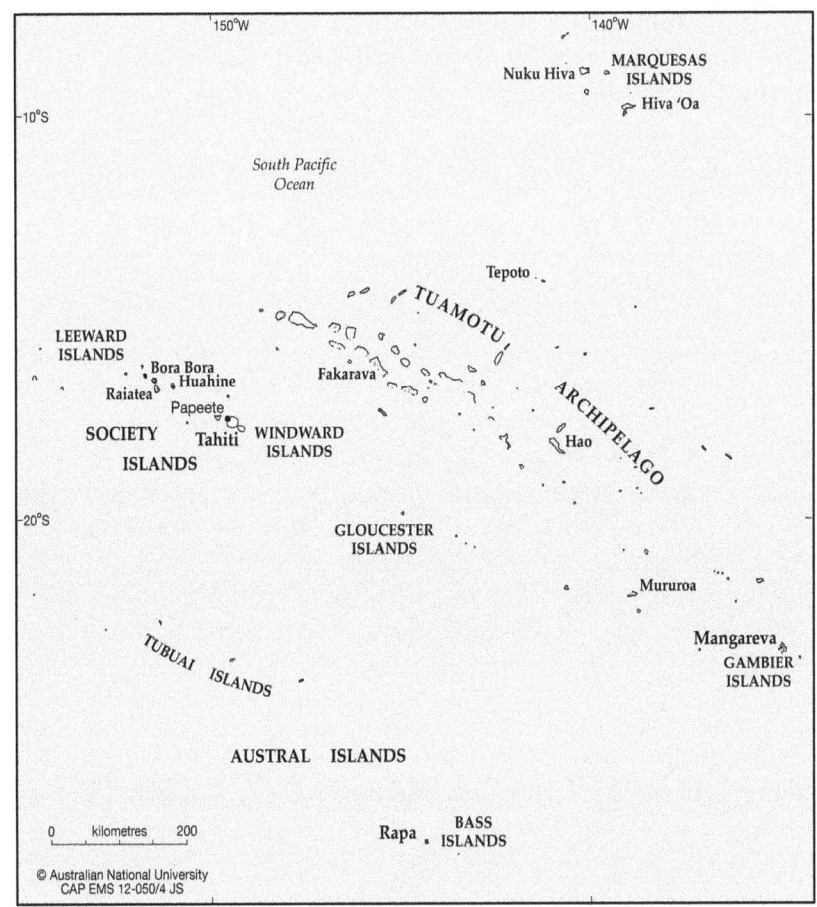

Figure 7: Map of French Polynesia
Source: © The Australian National University CAP EMS 12-050/4 JS

Yet, vested with the ancestral network's *mana* (sacred power), the chiefs and the sacred officiating priests are empowered to prohibit things that are dangerous for others only because these things run counter to their will. The practice of *kahui/rahui* provides an accurate definition of the scope of their power of coercion and initiative. Not heeding the prohibitions set by the chiefs and priests is tantamount to offending and arousing, through them, the wrath of the network's ancestors. There is always an extreme disproportion between the nature of the transgression — such as eating a forbidden fruit, for instance —

and the harshness of the penalty, which is often lethal. In this instance, it is less about punishing an individual fault than demonstrating the ancestral power of the network.

The history of the chiefdoms revolves around the distribution of hallowed domains, a relatively stable distribution, and on the indirect use of the sacred powers through *kahui*, provisional prohibitions that can be used as tools by an arbitrary power.

Polynesia does not comprise monotheistic societies, and an ancestral network is not safe from another network nor is it an invisible entity that is safe from the power of another entity. One chief's *mana* can always be counterbalanced by the growing power of another chief. This accounts for the fact that the temptation to abuse the tradition of *rahui/kahui* was great in the Marquesas, Hawai'i, in Rapa Nui or in Tahiti, which was expressed through those provisional *tapu* that are first and foremost the *kahui/rahui*. They also allowed the expression of a wise power, careful to act as the best manager of limited resources on behalf of the community. In this sense, we can understand how local governments nowadays wish to use this notion to promote sustainable development.

In any case, to understand *tapu* and the *kahui* in the Marquesas, the testimony provided by European observers describing Marquesan societies must be revisited, bearing in mind the distinction between *kahui* and *tapu*.

Tapu provide a structure for social organisation

The basic principles for the way in which prohibitions work, as they were canvassed by the French missionary and physician Father Chaulet, are presented in this way:

> *tapu* is a sort of veto that can be extended indefinitely, and whose power becomes time-honored through a religious prejudice. Sometimes *tapu* is absolute and applies to everybody. Sometimes it is relative and affects only one, or several clearly-identified persons … (Sometimes), *tapu* resulted from the fact that such and such an object had been touched by an animal viewed as a god, or by a *tau'a*. In other instances it resulted from the fact that an object had been

contaminated by a woman ... In others, it was because an object had been touched by a hallowed child ... Lacking direct means to enforce their orders, the chiefs — mostly — resorted to *tapus*. Whenever they wanted to keep troublesome or unwelcome visitors off their homes, their breadfruit trees and their coconut trees ... they imposed a *tapu* on their homes, their fruits ... The same applied to pigs, paths, etc.[1]

Many researchers use the notions of 'pollution' and 'contamination'. Contact between substances or persons, while they are charged with diverse energy and sacredness, favour the dreadful circulation of the most powerful energy toward bases that are not always able to withstand this energy. This is relevant to women's blood, chiefs' *mana* (which has also been phrased as the interdependence between *mana* and *tapu*)[2] and the female ancestral energy carried by young children.

Tapu is expressed as a sign of respect; it is cautious and marked with fear of sacred things, and its main aim seems to have been the avoidance of a dangerous imbalance in the relationships between men and gods: the world of the living — the visible world (*Ao*) — and the night world of invisible entities — the world of *Po*. *Tapu* was expressed in the form of multiple prohibitions, both religious and political (*tapu*)[3] under the control of priests and chiefs (*tau'a* and *haka'iki*); transgressing them led to a terrible punishment, regarded as the effect of powers originating in the *Po*.

On the Marquesas Islands, maybe more than in other areas, *tapu* determined behaviour in the face of material and immaterial requirements, toward places and objects, but also social relationships,

---

1   Chaulet, G., 1899. *Supplément*. Nuku Hiva; Archives of the Congregation of the Sacred Hearts of Jesus and Mary, Rome, p. 71. Father Chaulet had lived for 53 years on the Marquesas Islands until his death. He worked on documents collected by other missionaries and had exchanges with many researchers. He found that: 'Nowadays, *tapus* being things of the past on the islands ... ', and he specified: 'it is well known that woman is an impure being on account of her menses'. Similarly, he noted: 'Besides, they are as scared as can be of women's belts' (Chaulet, G., 1879. Manuscript. Nuku Hiva; Archives of the Congregation of the Sacred Hearts of Jesus and Mary, Rome).
2   Gell A., 1993. *Wrapping in Images, Tattooing in Polynesia*. Oxford Studies in Social and Cultural Anthropology — Cultural Forms. Oxford: Clarendon Press; Shore, B., 1989. '*Mana* and *Tapu*'. In A. Howard & R. Borofsky (eds), *Developments in Polynesian Ethnology*. Honolulu: University of Hawai'i Press, pp. 137–74; Thomas, N., 1987. 'Unstable categories: *Tapu* and gender in the Marquesas'. *Journal of Pacific History* 22(3–4): 123–38.
3   In 1791, Etienne Marchand defined *tabou* as to prohibit something, embargo something (2003. *Le voyage du capitaine Marchand, 1791: les Marquises et les îles de la Révolution, avec les Journaux de Marchand, Chanal et Roblet*, Odile Gannier & Cécile Picquoin (trans), Papeete: Au Vent des îles, p. 139).

more particularly in dealings with persons vested with a sacred character, be it permanent or temporary. This related mostly to women and people belonging to the '*tapu* class' — chiefs, priests, great warriors, and all those whose condition or activity made them part, more or less temporarily, of the sacred class.[4] While these persons were set apart from the rest of society, the head was always *tapu*.[5] It was the same for the first born in a family, people in contact with blood, those engaged in a 'dangerous' activity or one relating to the public interest, for example, preparations for war, preparing bodies for burial, preparing ink for tattoos, or fishing.[6]

Transgressing those multiple prohibitions meant being exposed to death or to serious diseases, such as leprosy and blindness, and it could disturb the community's existence by adversely affecting the normal

---

4   'When there was a major celebration in a tribe, by reason of some important occurrence, foreign guests were *tapu* for the whole duration of the feast, but as a precautionary measure, they came armed, for once the celebration was over and the *tapu* lifted, sometimes ambuscades were set to trap them on their way back home' (Rollin, L., 1974 (1929). *Moeurs et coutumes de anciens Maoris des îles Marquises* (*Les îles Marquises; Géographie, Ethnographie, Histoire, Colonisation et mise en valeur*). Papeete: Stepolde, p. 87). 'When there is some human victim to offer to the gods, the *moas*, or priests' servants, remaining permanently on the sacred grounds, could neither sleep with women nor have intercourse with them; nor were they allowed to enter secular huts, that is, islanders'; when they go for food to the natives' homes, they stay at the foot of the paving stones on which the huts are built. Behaving in any different way would invariably expose them to being killed by the gods' (Chaulet, 1873–1900. *Notices géographiques, ethnographiques et religieuses sur les îles Marquises*. Manuscript, Catholic diocese, Nuku Hiva; Archives of the Congregation of the Sacred Hearts of Jesus and Mary, Rome, p. 152).
5   'The head being very sacred, it must not be touched by hands or covered by anything whatsoever; nor was throwing anything over it allowed' (Chaulet, 1899, p. 73); K. von den Steinen illustrates through one of his observations the way implications were intertwined. He sought testimonies allowing him to follow the development of the island's arts. When he was in a position to study a complex headgear, he was very anxious to observe it with more precision and hoped to acquire it. The *paekea*, which 'from its style ... seemed to be ... the most ancient... was not for sale. I could take only two pictures of it before the woman yanked it off my hands. I made a gambit with the generous offer of a small piece of land ... this attempt failed miserably ... Because the land had been trampled by women's feet, and thus the head *tapu* would have been transgressed in an indirect way' (2005, 2008 (1925–28). *Die Marquesaner und ihre Kunst. Studien über die Entwicklung primitiver Südseeornamentik nach eigenen Reiseergebnissen und dem Material der Museen* vol. 2, *Plastik*, p. 20).
6   'The fisherman must fast three days and practice continence until the net goes to the sea for the first time. When it does, the fisherman's wife must fast and stay inside her hut. Those who go for reeds or bamboos to make torches for fishing *aku* must refrain from spitting and from relieving themselves on that location; otherwise they won't catch any *aku* and they would be wounded by this fish' (Chaulet, 1899, p. 74). The *aku* is the tropical needlefish, or garfish, belonging to the belonidae family; a fish with a long snout.

course of life. Oral literature, like travellers' testimonies, reveals that faith in *tapu*'s power was such that *tapu* could kill through the mere acceptance of this power.

Some resources, which could vary from tribe to tribe, and depending on locations, were the object of a long-term prohibition (turtles, sea rays, red animals or plants) or a short-term prohibition aimed at controlling their use or in anticipation of specific events, times of scarcity, building or any other decision. Thus, there were temporary *tapu* called *'ahui*,[7] or *kahui*, on fishing if fish became scarce, on breadfruit trees, whose fruit was supposed to fill up the silo pits (*'ua ma*), community reserves or, prior to major feasts, on some coconut trees, banana trees or other plants meant for a specific use.

As prohibitions ruled life, they were bound to be numberless, especially as they were complemented by many 'precautionary principles'; they dictated behaviour as surely as etiquette ruled life at the court of Louis XIV.

Social organisation and *tapu* were closely linked, as Testard de Marans, the government's representative, testifies:

> It is impossible to list even the major instances of *tabu* here; they vary from island to island, and even from valley to valley. We are seeking out only those that are common to all points in the Southeast and which are the best known. Some are not dependent on the chiefs' authority; others, which, they decided, are either everlasting or temporary, and

---

7   *'uhi'i te' ahui*: slap a *tapu*, a prohibition on' (Dordillon, R.I., 1904. *Grammaire et dictionnaire de la langue des îles Marquises*. 2 vols. Paris: Imprimerie Belin Frères). In response to questions posed in the 1970s by ethnologist H. Lavondès to the elders on Ua Pou Island, they answered: 'Many were the things that were *tapu* here on Ua Pou. For some people, white pigs were *tapu*, for others dogs were, for others still, it was the *kaki'oa* (the red-footed gannets); some fish were *tapu*, the *utu*, the *humu* … and the *puko'oko'o*. It was *tapu* to walk under a house. Numerous places were *tapu*. Nowadays, it's over, it's all over with those senseless *tapus*. Who is to credit for this? The missionaries, for thanks to them, who taught us the word of truth, the God of truth, Christian customs, the country has improved' (1975. 'Terre et mer; pour une lecture de quelques mythes polynésiens'. PhD thesis. Université Paris Descartes). Greg Dening mentions action by four *haka'iki* from Taiohae who, on 17 January 1834, taking the population by surprise, 'imposed *tapu* on Sunday, the Lord's Day. The whole valley hummed with the excitement of preparations, for on that day no fire was supposed to be built, and *tapa* was not supposed to be pounded. Old customs were of use to the new ones' (Dening, G., 1980. *Islands and Beaches: Discourse on a Silent Land: Marquesas 1774–1880*. Chicago: The Dorsey Press, p. 178). This action, certainly, is not to be disregarded as it seems to reveal support for the missionaries, since Sunday meetings, according to Dening 'caused great humiliation to the missionaries. They also suffered from not being able to lead a regular life and from lacking silence, which is conducive to meditation' (p. 178).

they have a general or private interest; finally, some apply specifically to women. Although the latter are less important now, they lived on despite the missionaries' endeavors and French occupation.[8]

Public *tapu*, which apply even to the chiefs, are those that made sacred woods and tombs inviolable, prevented the people from walking across the plantations before harvest and from touching certain trees before their fruits were ripe. They are perpetual or temporary depending on how important they are. The Marquesan chiefs and the European authorities themselves were sometimes slapped with a *tabu* as need be.

To these temporary *tabu* are linked the restrictions set on relations between people in good health and lepers (a French prohibition), and Marquesan prohibitions on contact with sick people who are fatally ill or regarded as such, women in childbirth or at the critical junction, the people who bury the dead,[9] and recently circumcised people.

---

8 Testard de Marans, A., 2004. *Souvenirs des îles Marquises. Groupe Sud-Est, 1887–1888*. Paris: Publication de la Société des Océanistes, no. 45, Musée de l'Homme, chap II.
9 Chaulet observed the following *tapu* related to death:
   Tapu which has to be observed when a corpse is being dried: *haka pa'a*.
   1. The women who manufacture cloths which must be used either to cover a corpse that has to be dried, either to wipe off its putrid humors, or to decorate its casket, must beat it while fasting. Besides, they must refrain from smoking a pipe, from putting on fragrances or pomade, from wearing a belt, from lust and from living in with their husbands.
   2. It is forbidden to take something from the hut where the corpse is being dried (such as a dish, fire, pipe, food).
   3. It is forbidden to take anything from one of those who are taking care of drying the corpse.
   4. Those who are taking care of drying the body are prohibited from any work (such as climbing up breadfruit trees, coconut trees, fishing, going for wood, lighting a fire, fixing or cooking food …).
   5. They are also prohibited from touching anything; thus, they must be fed; somebody must give them drinks or a smoke.
   6. They are also prohibited from putting on fragrances or pomade, and even more so from fornicating and from walking out of this hut to go somewhere else. (When they want to bathe, they must do it at night without anybody seeing them.)
   7. Libertines (*ka'ioi*) are prohibited from entering the hut where a corpse is being dried.
   8. Whenever the person who is drying a body breaks one of these *tapus*, the dead person's body bursts up and there no longer is any possibility of having it dried, and the dead person's spirit must inflict diseases on him/her as punishment for the lack of faithfulness.
   9. The person who is drying a body must observe these *tapus* for three months if the deceased is a chief (the same applies for big female chiefs), two months if the deceased is an ordinary chief, and one month if he is a commoner. But for this person to be allowed to touch a dish, a pipe or any other thing without prohibiting others from touching it, he/she must first purify himself/herself with water, taking a bath and ending *tapus*.
   (Chaulet, 1879, pp. 180–81)

Another temporary *tabu*, but a public one, is the *tabu* on picking *mei* (breadfruit fruit) from the breadfruit tree when it has been noticed that the amount of *mei* is decreasing and savings are required to avert scarcity.

Among perpetual *tabu* are those that protect priests, tribe chiefs and heads of families whose person was sacred, but nowadays these *tabu* are much less binding. Marriages between direct relatives are also prohibited by this law, which in this instance is in agreement with the French civil code. The enemy who has been invited to a *koika*, and who thus is inviolable, is *tabu* during the feast. Also *tabu* is a foreigner who has become a Marquesan's *inoa* by switching names with him, the hut of a *taua* when he nurses a sick person, and cemeteries and ancient burying places.

Private *tabu* can also be imposed by any individual and, in this way, he can, even for a trivial motive, such as access to his hut or to his enclosure, prohibit the use of some things belonging to him, or isolate another person from himself. For that purpose, it is enough to wrap the object in a bond made of a braided coconut leaf, a grass bouquet or *tapa* scraps. Such private *tabu* can be encountered regularly, especially on coconut trees and breadfruit trees whose fruits are forbidden to the general public.[10]

Many conventional *tabu* have lapsed now. The prohibition against wearing red *tapa* belts is no longer in force, as is the *tabu* that prohibited entering the places where offerings to the gods were made or the places where chiefs and priests had their meals. The *tabu* that prohibited going out after a chief or a high priest died before somebody had been offered as a sacrifice has also lapsed. Prohibitions relating to chiefs are losing their force by the day and respect due to their person is greatly weakened. It is not the same, however, of *tabu* relating to children; they are, with few exceptions,[11] still strictly observed by the

---

10   A man of around 60 years of age, Kohu, recollects that trees or shrubs, such as the lemon tree (*Citrus aurantifolia*), mango tree (*Mangifera indica*), or tamarind tree (*Tamarindus indica*), can be protected by a *kahui*. For that purpose, the tree was wrapped in a coconut tree leaf (testimony collected by Edgar Tetahiotupa).
11   Teupoo, a mother, explains that, when she was a young girl in the Marquesas, her mother insisted the children's clothes, whether boys or girls, had to be on top of the linen pile and that the boys' clothes always had to be on top of the girls (Tetahiotupa).

Marquesans. It is absolutely prohibited to touch a child's head[12] before he has reached adulthood, or to walk over him, even if he is lying in the way or across the threshold; only the mother is allowed to cut his hair, and it must be disposed of carefully by burial in a secret location. For Marquesans, hair is sacred and, regardless of the individual's age, the individual must pick it up when it is cut, wrap it in a piece of cloth and throw it into the sea as soon as possible.[13]

Tradition, represented by *tabu*, prohibits Marquesans from switching names with animals, from spitting in the middle of a hut, from dropping coconut milk on the ground while drinking and *popoi* while eating, from smoking a chief's pipe, from killing some birds, and from eating some fish.[14]

Tabu applying specifically to women are the most terrible. Initially, they must have been placed for sanitary reasons and inspired by ideas of cleanliness and purification. There are strong reasons to believe that they will survive for a very long time, for they are too strongly ingrained to become obsolete. Women are *tabu* for a period each month

---

12 Teupoo remembered that the head, in Marquesan culture, was sacred: 'There was a maid for the face and one for the rest of the body. Just like the head, the pillow had that sacred character; the most offensive thing for a person was the fact that somebody could sit on his or her pillow. The same applied to a baby being laid on a couch. Before doing that, it was necessary to cover the couch' (Tetahiotupa).

13 Father Delmas, writes, regarding hair: 'The father does not cut his daughter's hair and the daughter does not cut her father's hair. The wife does not cut the husband's hair but the husband can cut the wife's hair. The father can also cut the child's hair but not the daughter's. It is strictly forbidden. The mother does it.' (Manuscript. Archives of the Congregation of the Sacred Hearts of Jesus and Mary, Rome)

14 In 1884, Davin pointed out among the ways *tapu* applied: 'Birds are very rare in the Polynesians archipelagoes; in the forests on these islands there is a sort of nightingale called *komako* in the native language: a 15-franc fine was decreed against any individual convicted of having killed or taken one' (1886. *50 000 miles dans l'Océan Pacifique*. Paris: E. Plon, Nourrit & Cie, p. 237). In 1974, Jean-Claude Thibault also noticed during his research on birds that 'many places were sacred and prohibited, such as some sea bird colonies … '. Around 10 years later, Ottino-Garanger had the same findings relating to valley zones, for example, or for structures protected by reflexes, recommendations and precautions, as is the case for some gestures toward canoes, for example, or plants.

and regarded as impure by reason of her condition.[15] The Marquesans claim that he who touches, even inadvertently, a trace of blood, soon develops a disease contracting the joints, especially in the hands and feet. Such is the explanation propounded for leprosy. Only women, and only adult women, can touch what is part of a woman's outfit, and her clothes are *tabu* for children. In the past she was forbidden from sitting on the hut's threshold; she had a special mat to lie on and she ate alone. Except in very rare occasions, women were not allowed to enter canoes, for their presence was said to make the fish scamper. If women were ever allowed on a whaleboat, they had to refrain from sitting on or in it when the craft was towed from dry land.[16]

The community as a whole lived under the sway of some *tapu*, especially during certain periods or while performing specific activities, as Lavondès[17] notes: 'What could be called ceremonial *tapu* consisted in consecrating the whole tribe during tribal rites or tribal group activities such as fishing. In this kind of period, all usual everyday activities — work, food preparation, entertainment, trips in the valley and making any kind of noise — were prohibited.'

---

15   L. Tautain, doctor and administrator, wrote: 'calling a woman impure during childbirth, calling blood during menses specifically impure and a cause for leprosy, calling women generally impure *per se*, prohibiting sexual intercourse under some circumstances do not seem to us to run counter to the idea that there exists a genesis-related cult ... On the other hand, we must note that while the blood during menses is impure, it does not at all preclude living in the same place; nor does it preclude the fact that while a woman is impure during the days that precede and follow the baby's delivery, she can have intercourse with her husband soon after the baby is delivered. These issues relating to impurity are the result of myth-related attempts to account for some physiological phenomena: this is an explanation that occurs besides, and not against, the generation cult' (1896. 'Notes sur l'ethnographie des îles Marquises'. *L'Anthropologie* 7: 547–48). At this point a reminder is in order. It is important to remember to what extent the notion of impurity is relevant for our study: this blood is powerful — a lifeblood — and therefore dangerous, but not impure; otherwise, how could we understand this incredible Marquesan custom: 'While a high-society girl is giving birth for the first time, major male relatives prostrate themselves in such a way that the young woman is sitting on their heads as the baby is delivered; they are all covered with the same sheet' (Crook, P., 1990. *Life in the Marquesas Islands, Missionaries' Narratives, 1797–1842*. Uvea-Wallis, published by Te Fenua Foou, 1990, p. 13); 'If the sick woman is an *atapeïu*, a matron bites off the newborn's cord, those who attend the scene get the squirting blood on their heads, and the blood must touch only one sacred object' (that is, *ha'a-te-pei'u*, a woman of noble birth, Radiguet, M., 1978 (1860). *Les Derniers Sauvages: Souvenirs de l'occupation française aux îles Marquises, 1842–59*. Tahiti: Les Éditions du Pacifique, p. 126.) Blood could also be drunk and not a drop should fall on the ground (Tetahiotupa).
16   'Canoes are taboo for women, and women are prohibited from boarding them when they are afloat, and even from touching them when they are towed on dry land. The taboo extends to the masts, the outrigger, etc., although these objects can be collected in huts or under hangars (sic). People maintained that this taboo is still valid all over the islands' (de Roquefeuil, C., 1818. t.1, p. 324).
17   Lavondès, H., 1975, pp. 308–09. Lavondès worked in the Marquesas in 1963, up to 1971, and thereafter devoted several years to research on the subject.

According to Dordillon, the practices that were strictly forbidden during such periods were dabbing coconut oil and *'ena* (*Curcuma longa*) on the body, using weapons, playing the spinning top game, noisy laughter, raising one's arms above one's head, wearing coloured fabrics, eating *mei*, bathing'.

By contrast, in numerous other instances, prohibitions related to specific places, times, or categories of people. The conditions, or the spirit, under which prohibitions could be decreed are briefly described by Rollin:

> As the chief was inspired by the commonweal, after the council's opinion, he proclaimed temporary prohibitions on certain plants or animals which required protection and handling with care. This prohibition, called *kahui*, was signaled by a pole with some fruits from the forbidden tree[18] hanging and a shred of white fabric *(tapa)*. Violations were severely punished, more often than not by way of a punishment of the supernatural kind. The culprit, terrified by the punishment which he had courted, would unconsciously betray himself during the investigation and, when the time came, a priest secretly had him poisoned or bruised.[19]

---

18 Kohu recollected: 'In the past, when we wanted to do *ma*, we did a *kahui*. We took a shrub with many branches on it, and on the branches we stuck pieces of young aborted *mei* fruit which we had picked from the ground. We planted the shrub at the valley's entrance to indicate it was *tapu*, that *kahui* was imposed' (Tetahiotupa).

19 Rollin, 1974, p. 83. 'All diseases were viewed as sent by the gods, either as punishment for *tapu* breaking or as performance of an evil spell. Leprosy was perceived as a punishment for contact with menses blood. Insanity struck those who ate forbidden fruit — *tapu*. Abcesses occurred on those who ate fish reserved for the priests. Diarrhea was caused by *'jettatore'*. Babies' illnesses were caused by harmful ghosts ... ' (Rollin, L., 1928. 'La maladie et la mort chez les anciens Maoris des îles Marquises'. La Presse médicale, 1er décembre 1928, no. 96, pp. 3–4). Rollin was the islands' doctor from June 1923 through April 1928, and administrator from July 1929 through August 1930. In the 1840s, F.X. Caillet reported: 'I think at least half the Marquesas lands are 'tabooed' to women. Anywhere there were chiefs' corpses, women had to take long ways around, which made their trips in the mountain very long. Still, taboos were well observed, for poison punished them for their sacrileges, and this poison, called *Eva* [*Cerbera manghas* L], was, according to the *Tahua*, sent by God' (1930. 'Souvenirs de l'occupation des Marquises en 1843'. *Bulletin de la Sté des Études Océaniennes* (B.S.E.O.) 38(4): 95). Chaulet noted, among many other facts: 'Female commoners can be tattoed only in solitary and very thick places, for if, through bad luck the gods came to see this desecration, they would have to send either a big food scarcity or a big famine to punish them' (1873–1900).

De Marans describes the place of *tapu* in late nineteenth-century social dispensation:

> *Tabu* seems to have single-handedly made up the code that was used to rule the Maori tribes. This almighty word summed up both the moral law and the economic law that governed the peoples on the Marquesas Islands. *Tapu* was a decree relating to total prohibition and to less strict prohibitions, and it had negative virtues that imposed a host of deprivations on the natives. Its principle and its essence seemed to be either specific usefulness or general usefulness which shielded this prohibition that was valid for all. For that matter, *tabu* was deemed the expression of the gods' will conveyed to the people through the priests and the chiefs.
>
> Indeed, it was especially up to the priests and chiefs to impose *tabus*; in this valuable privilege they could find a way to control minds that were ignorant, naive and credulous, and to take unfair advantage of the simple-minded and the weak by imposing their wills, both good and bad. The priests and the chiefs used this right as a tool for despotism to the benefit of their passions and whims.
>
> Some *tabus* settled only issues relating to etiquette, which however, are too numerous to observe in the relationships between the *kikino* and the *hakaiki* on the one hand and the *taua* on the other hand. Other *tabus* were absolute orders outside the will of even the priests and chiefs. They themselves had to submit to those *tabus*. Finally, most *tabus* were relative and contingent only on the chiefs and priests who imposed them or lifted them at will, either for the public good or to increase their influence and their absolute domination. In such cases, *tabus* were imposed by proclamation either by the chief or by the high priest; they concerned a person or a piece of land, or prohibited the use of some objects.
>
> From this brief survey we can get a notion of the numberless *tabus* that existed in the past. There were so many of them that they were often violated unbeknownst to those who committed the violation. The violation, revealed to the public by way of huge disasters and heavenly wrath,[20] almost invariably led to the death of the individual deemed guilty of having transgressed the terrible prohibition. Revocation of prohibitions was very difficult and required big sacrifices. Children, however, kings of the Pacific, seemed to have had the right to lift *tabu* in some cases. Nowadays, a great number of *tabus*

---

20 It would be more accurate to say 'the wrath of the *Po* entities', as they have nothing to do with the Christian Heaven.

are still valid; if a stranger, who is not supposed to be familiar with them, got it into his head to violate them, he will not be bothered by the natives, but his relationships with them will become difficult, for he has deeply offended them.[21]

Navy doctor J. de Comeiras visited the area in the 1840s, noting:

> Generally speaking, *tapu*, among those peoples, is a substitute for laws and institutions ... *tapu*, or prohibition, usually has a purpose related to usefulness or hygiene; so it extends to fruits at certain periods; another example is the fact that a man cannot have intercourse with his wife until a long time after her baby is delivered ... *Tapus* extend to the most ordinary everyday things; they are invoked by the natives at every turn, and it seemed to us, laymen, that they were devised on purpose to inflict permanent torment on those children of nature ... The high priest, on all islands in the archipelago, has a great influence with individuals ... his ministers, who tend to the wounded during combat, are called *Moas*; they get orders from their chief, to whom they show total obedience. The high priest is also the one who imposes a taboo on food, on the season's fruits, etc. ... His jurisdiction, as we can see, is very extensive, and as his orders originate from the godhead, nobody would dare disobey them.[22]

Also during the 1840s, Admiral Dupetit-Thouars' secretary, Max Radiguet, noted: 'Each owner ... seems to have also the right to impose *tapu* on his home and on its contents, as shown by the grass bouquets and the white banners, *tapu* symbols which are used to mark huts, enclosures, canoes, and even trees ... '.

A few decades later, Chaulet recorded these details:

> When the Marquesans want to prohibit some people from taking up coconuts to a piece of land, they tie to one of the coconut trees on the land either a piece of native fabric or a piece of coconut leaf, to which they hang a coconut. They act in the same way when they want to prohibit taking breadfruit tree fruits and when they want to prohibit fishing in a certain place; on the very spot they plant a long pole adorned with banners. When they want to prohibit pig hunting in some place, they put a coconut tree leaf on a stone near the path and

---

21 Testard de Marans, 2004. At the time, the words *kikino* or *po'i kikino* referred to commoners, *haka'iki* referred to chief and *tau'a* referred to an eminently holy person whose opinions to a great extent ruled the community's life.
22 de Comeiras, J.R.A., 1846. *Topographie médicale de l'archipel de la Société et des Iles Marquises*. Montpellier, Printed by J. Martel ainé, pp. 64–65, 94.

cover it with another stone to keep it from being blown away by the wind. Such are, across the Marquesas Islands, Marquesan posters, called *'ahui* in the vernacular … When a chief wants to prevent his subjects from exporting *ma* to another district, he hallows the paths and the sea lanes and devotes them to the head of some important chief, and henceforth, communication is prohibited, or *tapu*. To have this *tapu* lapse, a hog must be offered to the gods: *mea papae 'a'anui*.[23]

As the Western presence increased, de Marans wrote in 1889:

> Private *tabus* may be imposed by any individual. In this way, he can, even for a futile motive, keep off others from his hut or his enclosure, prohibit the use of some objects belonging to him, or keep a person away from him. For that purpose, it is enough to wrap the object in a bond made of a braided coconut leaf, a grass bouquet or *tapa* scraps. Such private *tabus* can be encountered very often, especially on coconut trees and breadfruit trees whose fruits are off limits to the general public.

This ability to decide the fate of an object, a place or a person, came to be used by all, both Polynesians and Westerners.

Regarding the inevitable association, or agreement, in decision-making between the representatives of the religious world and the powers that be, de Roquefeuil, who was in the region during 1818–19, has this to say:

> One object is taboo in one valley and not in the neighboring one, one object is taboo today whereas it was not taboo a year ago. These prohibitions apply only at the priests' will; but to become valid all across a tribe, the priests' proposal must be agreed to by the chiefs. A priest declares he had got in touch with one of his colleagues or a deceased chief who became *etoua* (god) in the next world, by virtue of the rank he had here and now. The spirit told him that he would make the impact of its will felt by any individual who ate pork with such and such a brand, by any woman who touched a certain weapon or any other object meant to be used by men; henceforth, the animal or the object in question become taboo.[24]

---

23   Chaulet, 1873–1900, p. 96; see also Radiguet, 1978, pp. 116–17.
24   de Roquefeuil, C., 1823. *Journal d'un voyage autour du monde pendant les années 1816, 1817, 1818 et 1819*. 2 vols. Paris: Ponthieu, Lesage, Gide fils, pp. 325–26. P.A.

Regarding this power held by social and religious leaders on the islands, Rollin, on the basis of research and from what his Marquesan patients and the citizens under his administration told him, wrote this:

> Among the chief's functions was that of enforcing *tapus* ordained by the *taua*. He was the one to perform the routines, but the high priest pulled the wires. The *taua* and *hakaiki* were often relatives, but even when that was not the case, they were united by their common interests, and *tapus* were always favorable to them ... *Tapus* were the only law. Each acted as he pleased as long as he obeyed *tapus*. The *kikino* himself was free to change tribes at will, at his own risk, of course. *Tapus* were ordained by the *taua* and enforced by the chief, assisted by his *toa*; the *toa*, in peace time, acted as a club-happy police officer. Breaking *tapus* led to a terrible punishment, more often than not out of proportion with the fault ... In addition ... warriors, along with their *toas*, were united and *tapu* in wartime. During wars they lived separately. They were fed by the other tribe members, and they were forbidden to have any intercourse. It was the same for fishermen during fishing periods, for planters at crop time, for the tattooer, his aides and his patient during the operation, which brought them together for several weeks.[25]

'Contact' with death — in the case of warriors — and with life — women giving birth or having their periods — makes a person *tapu* per se as long as the contact is actual. This temporary *tapu* is not a *kahui*; it does not result from a decision but from the automatic effect of the contact. More often than not, rites are necessary to neutralise the sacred effect of this contact.

The large number of *tapu*

At the turn of the twentieth century, the missionary F.W. Christian recorded a list of *tapu*:

1. Formerly forbidden for women to eat together with men of bonito, squid, *popii*, and *koehi*.
2. Women might not go in a canoe.

---

25   Rollin, 1928, pp. 79, 82. A doctor, who was resident on the Marquesas in the 1840s wrote, '*tapus* are the only police on these islands. Lacking *tapus*, society would be impossible, for there is no other form of law enforcement' (Lesson, P.A., *Pylade*, 4e voyage, t. 3 et *Documents divers, Marquises*. unpublished documents. The Corderie de Rochefort archives).

3. Women might not climb on top of the platform of any sacred enclosure.
4. Red and dark blue clothes were prohibited.
5. Tobacco was not to be smoked inside the house.
6. Mats were not to be carried on the head or in the hands, but to be dragged along the ground.
7. Women might not eat bananas, fresh breadfruit, or coco-nuts.
8. Many sorts of fish were also *tapu* to women, also pigs of a brown colour, goats and fowls.
9. The *kuavena* fish was *tapu* to the fishermen, also the *peata*, a sort of shark.
10. Children might not carry one another pick-a-back.
11. Human hair when cut off was not to be thrown on the ground, for fear of being trodden on, or of any evil-minded person securing it for the purpose of uttering a curse over it.
12. Weeping was forbidden formerly.

The above list refers to the island of Nukuhiva; all *tapu* were abrogated when Te-moana married Vaekehu.

In South Marquesas:

13. There was a class of old men called '*taua*,' who were forbidden to do any kind of work, because of some sacred character attaching to them.
14. The *moko*, a species of shark, was *tapu* in Hekeani.
15. The *pukoko*, a small red fish, *tapu* in Uapou.
16. The *heimanu*, or sting-ray, *tapu* in Taipi Valley as the emblem of the god Upe-Ouoho.[26]

Numberless other *tapu* existed, including those regarding relations with the chiefs and priests, or *tauas*,[27] for example:

A Swedish officer, Adam Graaner, as he passed through Nuku Hiva in 1819 on the *Rebecca*, visited the bay, along with an American who lived there, and Graaner wrote: '… my interpreter Ross … tells me

---

26 Christian, F.W., 1895, 'Notes on the Marquesans'. *Journal of the Polynesian Society* 4(3):187–202. Christian authored *Eastern Pacific Lands; Tahiti and the Marquesas Islands*, 1910, London: Robert Scott. Christian arrived in the Marquesas in 1894, with letters of recommendation from R.L. Stevenson and in his work he is indebted to Th. Lawson (see N. Thomas).

27 Graaner, J.A., 1983. 'Nukuhiva in 1819', in 'Journal of a Swedish traveller' (unpublished), B. Akerren in *Institut for Polynesian Studies*, vol. 7, no. 1, pp. 34–58. There were many *tapu* slapped on *tapa* and clothes. Issues of contact relate directly to clothing, so it is not surprising to read this in de Roquefeuil (1818): 'Some clothes for one of the sexes are taboo for the other … '.

that they had priests and priestesses. One of them, who was highly respected, spent her days in Ross's home ... This priestess, who happened to be pregnant, and her husband were the valley's highest religious dignitaries, but their tasks were limited to tending diseases and wounds; ... They declared some objects, places or customs taboo.'

That is how all pink pigs were taboo and could not be served at the priests' table. A house could be declared taboo and thus uninhabitable although it was in good condition; the reason was that it had been desecrated by pig entrails as the pigs were slaughtered. All canoes were taboo for women, so much so that should a woman take it into her head to board a canoe, the canoe would become forever unusable for fishing or for war. ... The island's inhabitants used to manufacture their clothes themselves with the bark of a tree that resembled the mulberry tree. Now, for an unknown reason, the priests required that people discontinue the practice, and making fabric out of this tree was declared taboo. Since then, the fabric manufactured in Nuku Hiva has been made out of the breadfruit tree bark, and the other fabrics imported from Hiva Oa or from St Dominique ... The high-back chairs in public places are also taboo for the fair sex, which is not highly regarded on this island. Eating chicken is also taboo. As a matter of fact, the priests are lawmakers and physicians, and along with the chiefs, they wield a virtually unlimited power where superstition can influence the islanders' credulous minds.[28]

Regarding *tapu* decreed for the benefit of and by the priest, or *tau'a*, there is no shortage of testimonies. Chaulet cites some of those who became sacred (*hihi*), and consequently destined to die:

Those who 1) walk on their hair, on their shadow, on their mat, on their clothes, on their kitchen utensils, on the water meant for preparation of their food, on the place where they cook their food, on the wood meant to build their hut, etc. ... 2) All those who make no show of generosity toward them or take anything that is meant for them; 3) who pick fruits or coconuts from the trees that are reserved for them ...

In what he thereafter calls 'Human Victims' Statistics', Chaulet continues:

The *tau'as*, as members of the godhead, often claim human victims, thus: ... 4) Should they want to abrogate *tapus* that often go along with sacrifices, they still need a victim: *heaka mea puipui ia tau'a*,

---

28   Chaulet, 1879–1900, p. 150.

vel (or) *heaka mea ha'a meie ia tau'a*. ... 5) Should they want to make a sacred place secular for some time, they need a human victim: *heaka mea papae koika*. 6) Should they want to make a sacred hut secular, they need a human victim: *heaka mea papae ha'e* ...

This power, enjoyed by the chiefs and priests, while it may seem to make sense, did sometimes drift into perversions. Davin, while passing through in 1884, could only find, after others before him:

> Taboos were a powerful leverage in the hands of those who held power, the elder chiefs ... turned it into a tool for government, and the origin of property originated in taboos. When a ship dropped anchor in a cove, the chief held out his hand, uttered the two solemn syllables *ta-boo*, and this was enough to make him the only one to be eligible to exchange with strangers ... So the wise application of taboos may have one actual purpose; but what of the humiliating prohibitions preventing women from wearing white and red belts, or from lying on top of a dog?[29]

How a *tapu* is lifted

On the Marquesas Islands, the lifting of a *tapu* often consists in removing the sacred character from that which is *tabu* by, in simple situations, a seawater bath followed by a freshwater bath. Symbolic, 'dangerous' or polluting acts, performed, for example, in the complex framework of the family system, can also work towards the lifting of a *tabu*: acknowledgement by the father by placing the child above his head — as he carries the child on his shoulders — or other attitudes assumed by the *pahupahu*s — uncles or mother's brothers, paternal aunts, etc.

One of the most striking instances, reported by Chaulet, relates to the end of the one-year isolation period of a chief's child. The child grows up excluded from society because his birth makes him so *tapu* through the build-up of *mana* that he represents as a result of the series of generations he embodies:

> On the next day, a sixth ceremony starts; although it is the last one, it is the strangest of all ... In order to put an end to the *tapu*, they take the

---

29 Davin, 1886, pp. 237–38. Radiguet wrote: 'Other *tapus* have a sole purpose, namely personal advantage, or motives that are difficult to account for, such as the prohibition to lie on top of a dog, a hen or any *tapu* object ... ' (1978, p. 111).

young chief to a secular place, and as the latrines are the most secular of all, this is precisely where the *makuvaipu* leads him. When the child reaches the place, the *makuvaipu* walks him around the latrines to the beat of drums, *papo* chants and *papaki akau*. This ceremony goes by the name of *oho hava*, or *oho kotikoti*. After the ceremony, the child is no longer holy, and he can show himself freely and go wherever mortals are allowed to go. The same ceremony for princesses is called *ta'ata'a ha'e*.[30]

Von den Steinen relates another instance that, incidentally, underscores one of the roles that tattooing plays. It follows the shutting-out period that is reinforced by the *tapu* surrounding any major activity:

> Finally, we should keep in mind a remark by Wilson dating back to the eighteenth century. Body tattooing sessions ended with feasts accompanied by prayers and ceremonies — the *amoa*. The last *amoa* was designed to tattoo the head, if we don't take into account those meant for friendship and weddings ... Finally, a small mark on the inner side of the upper part of the arm of young boys and girls showed that the *tapu* affecting their relations with their parents was lifted, and they, at last, could have their meals with their parents.[31]

Desacralisation rites affect what is in the nature of a dangerous sacredness in itself, *amoa*.[32] They are not of the same nature as the lifting of a temporary prohibition, a *kahui*: what the chiefs' and *tau'a* have been able to do, the same will be enough to undo. This can be

---

30 Chaulet, 1873. In Tahiti, the inauguration of a new *ari'i nui* goes through a similar final step: 'The chief, or the king, was seated on mats, near the god's image, and he was paid what they labeled the final tribute from the people, namely most shockingly dirty dances and performances, marked by the grossest obscenity, in which several stark naked men and women surrounded the king and strove to touch him with the various parts of their bodies, to the extent that he had trouble staying away from their urine and their excrements, with which they tried to cover him. This lasted until the priests resumed sounding their trumpets and beating their drums, and that was the signal for withdrawal and the end of the pageant. At that point, the king walked back to his abode, along with his retinue' (Moerenhout, J-A., 1835. *Voyages aux îles du Grand Océan*. vol. 2. Paris: Maisonneuve, p. 27).

It seems that the first locus for sacralisation, even of re-sacralisation, is the sea, the first of the *marae* (Henry, T., 2004. *Tahiti aux temps anciens*, Paris: Société des Océanistes). That is where the future *ari'i nui* or *tahua* would dip into the water after a transgression. This reactivated or renewed sacredness had to be partly neutralised through contact with low matter which, precisely, serves as an energy reducer and enables the *ari'i* or *ariki* and the sacred child to enter into relationship with persons of more lowly extraction without endangering their safety.

31 von den Steinen, K., 2005, 2008 (1925–28), vol. 1, p. 76; Wilson, J., 1799, *A Missionary Visit to the Southern Pacific Ocean, Performed in the Years 1796, 1797, 1798, in the Ship Duff, Commanded by Captain James Wilson*. London, p. 399.

32 See Rigo, B., 2004. *Altérité polynésienne ou les métamorphoses de l'espace-temps*. Paris: CNRS Editions, pp. 242–62.

implemented by reminding ourselves of the sacred connections with the ancestors and the invisible entities. This does not stem from the neutralisation techniques of objects or entities that carry in themselves a formidable power and hence are sacred or *tapu*.

Relationships between men and women, the fact that all take part in activities, exchanges and, more broadly, anything that involves contact, even a merely visual one, was taken into account. Relation to food, whether cooked or raw, the use of fire but also, of course, anything surrounding death, was strictly regulated by prohibitions. Rather than digress at length around the innumerable fields that *tabu* touched, or the aspects that they assumed, we provide below additional testimony about the nature and practice of *tabu*.

Tapu affecting women and children

Regarding women, Stevenson sums up the situation thus: 'Many things were forbidden to men; to women we can say that few were permitted.'[33]

Women's lives laboured under a great number of restrictions, even though, Lesson remarked, 'Concerning *tapus*, I'll say a mother is something extremely sacred for her son: *mea tapu nui*, as Nu'uhivians say; the same goes for a sister;[34] a sister-in-law is also *tapu*, but less so ... '.

Thus, Radiguet observed:

> Women are barred from entering canoes, unless it is an exceptional situation, which happens very seldom. During a meal, they make up a separate group where some foods never appear. They are prohibited

---

33 Stevenson, R.L., 1995 (1880). *Dans les Mers du Sud*. Paris: Petite bibliothèque Payot/voyageurs, p. 69.
34 Teupoo explains that 'a brother always regarded his sister as *tapu*. That is why a brother would never take the liberty to lecture his sister in public' (Tetahiotupa). This relation among family members is born out by Teupoo's recollection of the complexity of the notion of *tapu* as played out in the 1980s: 'I was pregnant and my husband was supposed to find a home. Finally, we had an offer from a family member to sleep in his house. When my mother heard this, she said that I was strictly forbidden to sleep in her bed. This family member happened to be one of my nieces. Even though she is older than I am, she is still my niece, and therefore, I, her aunt, was not allowed to sleep in her bed. As a result, my husband had to go out to get a bed, which he found at one of my cousin's homes. A cousin is regarded as a sister, so I could sleep in her bed. A niece is viewed as a child (of mine)' (Tetahiotupa).

from touching their husband's or their father's head, to walk over them when they are lying ... Women must respect places hunted by men, their weapons, their fishing tackle, their tools, but men are not required to show the same respect; so men do not refrain from walking into women's huts, from eating their food, and they have no qualms about taking women's things whenever they feel like it.

Stevenson and others provide a lengthy list of women's obligations: 'Women could not sit in the *paepae*; they could not go there up the stairs; they were not allowed to eat pork ... '.

Chaulet lists *tapu* by life domains, including:

> *Tapu* relating to women: they were strictly forbidden to walk over the body of an individual, even his legs, to walk over men's clothes and mats,[35] to walk over household utensils, on places where food was cooked, on men's works, on wood brought by a man, on shavings, on the places where hair had been cut. They were forbidden to eat *popoi* beaten by a man,[36] even by his son, to hang their loincloth in the hut, to eat in places reserved for men ... etc.

As a doctor, in some ways Chaulet found that when a chief's son is born:

> As the mother cannot, in this situation, feed the new chief, nor even stay in the same hut, the *makuvaipu* priest gets her a nurse, and, in this situation, he carries with him the terrible god *etua vahi* so this nurse could under no circumstance refuse to complete this constraining chore, a refusal for which she could be — along with her husband — killed by the terrible god ... so both submitted to the chore with no possibility to retort. This nurse was strictly forbidden to touch any

---

35   Lesson P.A., *Marquises, Documents divers*, unpublished MS, Corderie de Rochefort, no. 8147, pp. 647–48. Teupoo still remembers the education she got from her mother: as a young girl she was never allowed to walk over a mat (except hers), she had to walk around it, and in this case she had to bring her skirt or dress against her legs, otherwise she had to fold the mat in order to clear the way, and then she returned the mat to its initial position.

36   Delmas noted about the *popoi*: 'The daughter should not eat the *popoi* beaten by her father; it is highly *tapu*. The father should not eat the *popoi* beaten by his daughter; that is strictly forbidden. The mother should not eat the *popoi* beaten by her daughter; that is strictly forbidden.'

secular object, to perform any work, to accept a puff of tobacco from anybody else's hand, to pomade her hair, to spread grease on her body, to get out of the *ha'e hakaiko* hut, to build a fire, etc.[37]

Regardless of whether they are boys or girls, children belong first and foremost to the women's space; as they are born of a mother's womb, they carry women's lifeblood. As they are descended from the *Po*, they are also closer to the ancestors, whose *mana* they perpetuate and, as such, they are sacred. That is why many *tapu* surround them as well, and more so when they are of prestigious high extraction.

> The hut in which a young child is fed is made *tapu*. The child is not taken to another person's hut. Anything that he touches is thrown into a sacred place. He can touch nothing secular, such as a mat, a belt, a loincloth or a bed sheet … He cannot walk under legs or under the mat, or under his parents' house. When the child is a chief's child, a *tau'a's* child, they keep his excrement for about ten days and usually they seek a human victim to throw this excrement onto a sacred place. Lacking human victims, they would make an offering to the gods. That was called *papae'i te tutae o te tama hou*. The droppings of a bird fed by a young child were also collected in a basket and thrown onto a sacred place. *Tapu* children could not wear anything on their shoulders; they were not even allowed to eat on their own; their mother had to feed them. The hut where a sacred child is fed is *tapu* and nothing inside it can be taken elsewhere … Even breadfruit fruits and coconuts that are close to it cannot be eaten.

Tapu food and fire

Anything to do with food preparation was strictly organised: categories and genders were separated, there were specific ways of eating food, specific places where food could be prepared, and what different individuals could eat was determined — for example, women could eat only the fish or shellfish that they caught on the seashore.

---

37   Chaulet, 1873–1900; see also Pallmann's annotation in the 1873 manuscript (p. 65): 'When a high priestess is nubile (Pallman: that is, when she feels for the first time what all women feel every month) they build her a specific hut where she can spend a few days (Pallman: 5, 6 or 7 days, that is, the whole duration of her purgations.) During all that time, the drum is beaten ceaselessly in her honor. Nobody but her husband, if she is married, can enter her hut, unless this person wishes to become a leper or go blind, but as nobody has this wish, they simply put the food at her door … '.

THE RAHUI

To provide an idea, Chaulet set up the following list:

> Food. The mother does not eat *popoï* with her children unless they are very young. A mother never eats octopus with her son; as for bananas, each person eats his/her bunch, but never another person's bunch, even though the other person were a parent or a relative. A man does not eat coconuts with his wife. Scraps should not be thrown away on the path, or on the paving stones — whether inside or outside — of the hut because if a women happens to walk over them, all those who ate this food would go blind or become lepers. The same goes for water, breadfruit fruit peels, the coals of the native lamp made from candle nut tree.[38]

Lesson wrote down the foods that were often tapu:

> the murena eel, called *ku'e'e*, hen eggs (*mamae*), *tatu'e* (a big sea fish), *patiotio* (bird), the hen (*moa*), *pukiki* and *uaua* pigs (red and yellow), bananas (*meika*), coconuts, in front of *tuukas* ... commoners could not eat them, *honu* turtles, that is, sacred and reserved for the big chiefs. I'm told elsewhere that *Eato*, king of Uapu (sic) Island, shut himself out in a special place to enjoy this food alone ... While fish is usually allowed to all, sometimes it should not be touched ... Women are the ones who sustain all hardships. Everything is prohibited, or off limits, for not only were they not allowed to eat some foods, they were also forbidden to touch the men's food, even their father's, brother's or male children's food. Likewise, big girls had to fix their own meals and eat them while separated from others. Even married women were not exempted.

> I was saying that there are many *tapus* imposed by the high priest. The *tapu ahui, tapu tuhia*. The *tapu ta te pua i te ahui* is imposed on pigs when there are no more of them. They wait for more or less a long predetermined period until the pigs' numbers increase. In order to break this *tapu*, a *koïka* (feast) is needed. The high priest orders one, called *koïka to te atua*. At that junction pigs are killed, and eating them and selling them are allowed. Even women can eat their meat. However, they are never all sold, and this happens only when they are all made *tuhia*. When the French arrived in Nuku Hiva, pigs were *tuhia* in Teii's tribe. The father of the Taua Veketu had made them so. This *tapu tuhia* is imposed under the following circumstances: The high priest is accused of theft, and he admits he stole pigs. In order to neutralise this charge and to wreak vengeance, he grabs a pig and raises him over his head, saying *ua hihi te puaka tuhia i te atua* ...! After these

---
38 *Aleurites moluccana, 'ama kukui*, tree nuts in Hawai'i.

words everybody is allowed to sell pigs and eat pork, except women, though, and all pigs must go (it is worth noting in passing that I clearly understood what I was told about this. It is easy to understand how pigs have so easily vanished from islands where they had been before ...) To put an end to this execration, now a human sacrifice is needed, and when it is performed, not only can women eat pork, but it becomes possible to raise pigs again. On April 12, 1844, the Taioa gave us an example of this, and a few months earlier the Taiipii [sic] had provided another one like it. The *ahui ehi* is the *tapu* on coconuts. The sign signifying it is a piece of dry coconut at the end of a long pole planted on a visible spot and meant to remind the people that they should not eat coconuts ... That is what Tamapu did when he saw Otooata coconuts being sold ... Often the pole is wrapped up in *tapa* flying in the wind. Nothing is more common than these poles, which have been noticed by all travelers and mean nothing but: The fruit of such trees (*mei, ehi,* etc.) are *tapu* for the people. The difference is that one relates to one fruit and the other to another one. Europeans need to get closer to tell one from the other, but the natives do not need to see them up close. For that matter, they do know that the *tapu* has been imposed on such and such an object.[39]

Quite specifically, some products were devoted to the members of the *tapu* class, which often included chiefs and priests. An officer from the Dupetit-Thouars expedition, Fl. Lefils, noted, for example:

> The taboo is imposed on anything that is reserved for the nourishment of higher-ups and priests; pork, poultry, turtles, bonito, sea breams are prohibited to commoners; they must eat only coconuts, fruit from the breadfruit tree and fish not under a taboo.[40]

It is worth noting that eating human flesh was strictly reserved for people whose *mana* allowed it; to this can be added the rules on cooked food, the relation to blood, the sacredness of bones (long bones and head bones). Von den Steinen says: 'Unlike men who are not tattoed and unlike women and children, all tattoed men had a major privilege, the right to eat human flesh which can be accounted for through the

---

39   Lesson, P.A., *Marquises, Documents divers*, unpublished MS, Corderie de Rochefort, pp. 643 à 645; *tatue*: parrot fish, *patiotio*: Marquesan monarch (*Pomarea* sp. *Muscicapidae*; *koika* means a ritual; *mei*: breadfruit tree fruit; *'ehi*: coconut tree).
40   Lefils, F., 1843. *Description des îles Marquises*. Paris: Prevot, pp. 27–28. Lefils goes on: 'the privileged classes' houses are also taboo, and nobody is allowed in, unless he is a priest or a high dignitary; a commoner who breaks this taboo would be chased to death.'

Marquesans' warrior temper and through religion.'[41] De Marans deals with this issue at length, according to the way it was viewed at the time in the West, and Testard de Marans remarks:

> If the number of prisoners that the victors were able to catch was considerable enough, they were led to the public square and offered as sacrifices to the gods to thank them, and to the tribe's protector genii. The victims almost invariably refused to utter a word or a complaint as they waited stoically for death, which they preferred to a demeaning adoption by the victor tribe. It was honorable for the vanquished to be devoured by the victor; the outcome of combat decided the fate of the man who had to succumb, and thus every warrior counted on it while fighting ...

Father Mathias Gracia, who lived on the islands between 1839 and 1842, and had a curious and intelligent view of Marquesan society, reported:

> During a war, prisoners must also become victims, *heaka*; but if they are caught alive, which often happens through horrendous deceptions, they are, at least for a few days, treated with extraordinary consideration; they are toasted. If they are women, all prohibitions women were usually submitted to are lifted, and everything is ready for the sacrifice which, for that matter, these prisoners expect, but they are not moved by it, and when they least expect it, they are hit to death, most often from behind, with a lance, or by a lace put around their neck. Everything that I am telling here happened almost before our very eyes to the five women taken together by the Teiis during the war they fought against the Taïoas.[42]

The role and the use of fire has a special place, which is evident in testimonies on *tapu* relating to its manufacturing, or to its purifying function, and even to the fact of smoking, touching a pipe, and more broadly what relates to tobacco.[43]

---

41 von den Steinen, 2005 (1925–28), vol. 1, p. 91.
42 Gracia, M., 1843. *Lettres sur les îles Marquises, ou mémoire pour servir à l'étude religieuse, morale, politique et statistique des îles Marquises*. Paris: Gaume frères, pp. 66–69.
43 Regarding tobacco, Delmas noted: 'A woman does not smoke tobacco which has been hanging round a man's neck, but the husband smokes the tobacco which has been hanging around the wife. The sister and her maternal uncle smoke it too. It is not forbidden. Women never smoke tobacco which has been hanging round a man's neck. There are no exceptions. Tobacco which touched the hands of a chief's son is not smoked. A female chief, however, or a chief's sister, can smoke it. Smoking is not allowed above a garment or a decoration (*hei*) on a garment ... '.

All Marquesans make *tapu* the fire that they build for themselves, that is, they do not give any to others, unless they want to go blind or become lepers, or wish to be killed by the gods ... No matter how well a husband and wife get along together, the woman will never get the least spark from the fire that he has built for himself. The wife, by contrast, has no reason, and in addition, it would not be appropriate for her, to refuse to give him any. It is forbidden to women not only to use the wood that men have brought but also the wood they cut (in the South-East group).[44]

Lesson remarked:

As we understand it, thanks to *tapu*, the priests on these islands, especially the high priest, know how to ... make their will appear to be the Gods' will. As a result, it is only natural that the major ceremony should be the one that takes place on the death of a high priest. Then, *tapu* is imposed on the fire ... The *tapu* on the fire is the thing we notice, as it proves that all prohibitions were made up by men, be they noblemen or not, only with the purpose of isolating them, making them distinct, and more particularly, from women. Thus, based on their beliefs, the men's fire is the nobler. It should not be confused with fire designed for cooking women's meals; at least, this used to be their belief.[45]

Tapu spaces and sacred plants

A fundamental portion of *tapu* rules was devoted to the setting where the islanders lived. Caillet emphasises how trips by individuals were determined by the places they had to avoid, either because the places were dangerous or because they were prohibited. As a result, people often had 'to take roundabout routes, which made the trip much longer in the mountains'. Lesson accurately noticed how islanders knew, thanks to their education and experience, how to naturally feel

---

44 Chaulet, 1879, p. 194. Chaulet also noted with regard to the birth rites of a chief's son: 'It is strictly forbidden to this nurse to touch anything secular, to work in any way, to accept a puff of smoke from anybody else, to pomade her hair, to oil her body, to leave the *ha'e hakaiko* hut (deep in the valley,) to build a fire, etc.' (1873–1900). We have also these remarks by Testard de Marans: 'Tradition, represented by *tabu*, forbids natives to switch names with animals, to spit in the middle of a hut, to drop coconut water while drinking and to drop *popoi* while eating, to smoke a chief's pipe, to kill certain birds, to eat certain fishes, etc.' (2004, pp. 170–71).
45 Lesson, P.A., *Marquises, Documents divers*, unpublished MS, Corderie de Rochefort, no. 8147, p. 649.

and recognise *tapu* signs. Handy indicates: 'The limits of sacred lands were well known among the tribe and marked, during ceremonies, by poles with *tapa* banners'.[46] Likewise, they knew, for example, that:

> All fruits near the hut where a corpse lies are prohibited to mortals, and for nobody to risk breaking this *tapu* unknowingly, they surround the place with stones walls, at least often so, and if there are only breadfruit trees, they surround the bark of those that are closest to the place where the body lies.[47]

Plants and trees were essential through their number and the amount they yielded: their substance, their fruits, even their shadow. The shadow was *tapu* on sacred places where it was forbidden to cut them, namely those belonging to each household or the community, but also deep in the valley, on the *me'ae* and in the *vao*, the space where the vitality or fertility of the island regenerates. Vitality or fertility determined the essence of places in the same way as the fixing fluid of fragrances in a perfume blend.

From banyan trees, which seem to link the sky and the earth thanks to their aerial roots,[48] to the breadfruit tree, which is so essential, prohibitions — *tapu* and *kahui* — relating to them were numberless.

W.P. Crook, a young Protestant missionary from the London Missionary Society, relates anecdotes regarding the breadfruit tree (*mei*) that occurred in Tahuata in the late eighteenth century and involved people related to chief Honu, from Vaitahu, whom Captain Cook met in 1774.[49] Oral tradition relates these incidents, which

---

46 Handy, E.S.C., 1971b (1923). *The Native Culture in the Marquesas*. Bulletin no. 9. Honolulu: Bernice P. Bishop Museum and New York: Kraus Reprint Co., p. 118.
47 Chaulet, 1879, p. 180.
48 The banyan tree is viewed as linking the earth to the sky. At the same time it represented the world and, more precisely, three worlds: the earth, the subterranean world (the *Po*), and the higher world. One account of this tree suggests that: 'Man is born of this tree; this tree protects him from the harmful effects of the outside world, just as a mother protects the child who is in her womb. When the baby is born, the tree continues to protect him, by offering him its bark in the form of *tapa*. And when the time comes to leave the earth world, man will come back home to his abode. That is why human skulls can be seen in banyan tree roots. For us Marquesans, the banyan tree is a human being, it walks, it moves like a human being. Look at its aerial roots; we have the feeling it's moving!' (Tetahiotupa). Thus, *tapa*'s sacred character, called *hiapo*, which can be obtained from this plant, can be largely accounted for by the assimilation of this tree to a human being through the image of an axis linking the three worlds. For that matter, this is the reason why we can often find it close to the *me'ae*. The word *hiapo* deserves special attention. Literally it means 'come out, come from the *po*', a word which can be found in the Tahitian word *matahiapo*, which means eldest. For that matter, *hiapo* was reserved for the chiefs' class (*haka'iki*).
49 Crook, 1800, p. 158.

conclude with the death of one of the protagonists, departures for faraway places or fierce fighting. The ancestor who founded a clan in Rotorua, on Maori land (Aotearoa New Zealand), left his native land with his people because of one of those misdemeanours.[50] A mother and her daughter had the same tragic end after they were suspected of stealing *mei* on the lands of Timotete's brother, Honu's nephew. Timotete was taken to England by members of the London Missionary Society.

The *Hibiscus tiliaceus* (called *hau* in the northern part of the archipelago, *fau* in the south) had multiple uses:[51] the bark was used during the offering of human victims, and the straightest, thinner branches were stripped. Their whiteness was reminiscent of the sacred character of a place. The *Pisonia grandis* (*pukatea*), whose bark and wood are very bright; the *mi'o* (*Thespesia populnea*), whose wood is, by contrast, red, like the *pua* (*Fagraea berteroana* var. *marquesensis*), whose white flowers are very fragrant; the *tou* (*Cordia subcordata*), whose flowers are orange-coloured; the ironwood casuarina (*toa*); and the banyan tree (*Ficus prolixa* var. *subcordata*, *ao'a*) could all be used as *tapu* signs, be *tapu* or *kahui* themselves. Chaulet, regarding the arrangements relating to the coming of a chief's newborn, reported:

> In order that no lay person should soil this place by his presence, they fence in the tank — the child's bath near the *ha'e hakaiko* — with stripped hibiscus and they decorate the whole with a great number of banners, tree branches and plants which are viewed as the strangest in the land.[52]

Another example from Chaulet relates that 'the trees against which they leaned the *me'ae's* drums are *tapu*, and so are those which stand near the dead's tombs'.[53]

---

50 This is Tamatekapua. Along with his brother, Whakaturia, he stole breadfruit tree fruits from a chief's enclosure. As they were caught, they had to fight Toi and Uenuku. Whakaturia and his father, Houmaitawhiti, died but Tamatekapua fled in a canoe with his family members. This is how the Arawas settled in the Rotorua area. On the Marquesas Islands it is possible to find, in the Pepei'u and Pepehau narrative, for example, facts that are reminiscent of those from which such an adventure originated, and this is not an isolated case.

51 Dening (1980, p. 195) relates the following scene: 'The girls were playing *pehi hua*, a ball game; the ball is made of hibiscus leaves which were *tapu* for the girls, for the leaves were used during drills for memorising their ancestries. When the Enatas whispered that those children and their actions would bring famine, the girls just answered by chanting with renewed ardor: "There is only one God, and his name is Jehovah".'

52 Chaulet, 1873–1900.

53 Chaulet, 1899, p. 73.

THE RAHUI

In this landscape there were buildings of all varieties; some were *tapu* to various degrees according to the sex and social class of the person, while others were clearly *paepae tapu* (prohibited) to all non-hallowed persons. That is the case for funeral sites. The biggest of these more or less *tapu* places were the communal sites, where the denizens of the valleys and their guests met year round. Roundabout, or in a section of the places, there was a more specifically *tapu* ensemble. Those places where feasts took place were called *taha koika, taha koina* or *tohua koika*. Stevenson wrote this about them around the 1880s:

> At length, the huge trunk of a banyan tree emerged, standing on what seemed to be the ruins of an ancient fort, and our guide, halting and pointing to it, announced that we had reached the *paepae tapu*. *Paepae*[54] means a platform, like those that supported the native huts; and even those — *paepae hae* — can be called *tapu* in a lesser sense, when they are abandoned and become the abode of the spirits; but the public high place, like the one I tramped at the time, was done on a grand scale. The forest ground was paved as far as the eye could see in the thick copse. A three-tiered terrace lay on the hillside; in the front, a parapet that had suffered a landslide locked the main area, whose paving was pocked with wells and divided into compartments by small fences. There was no trace left of the superstructure, and the layout of the amphitheater was hard to grasp. I visited another, smaller one, in Hiva Oa, but it was in better shape, and it was easier to follow the rows of terraces and to make out isolated honor seats reserved for eminent persons, and where, on the upper platform, a sole beam from the temple, or dead-person's house, was still there, with its richly-sculpted posts. Once, the high place had been well tended. No tree, except the sacred banyan, could encroach on its terraces, no dead leaf could rot on its paving. The stone groutings were smooth, and I was told that they were even lubricated. All around, in their ancillary

---

54 *Paepae* refers to a place to live in, with a protected space. It also refers to a headgear called *pa'eku'a*. This feathered headgear made of *kuku* (*Thouarsistreron leucocephala*) was worn by the big chiefs. An arrangement of horizontal feathers lined this headgear, another one of red feathers made up the horizontal band in the middle. In this word we can find *ku'a*, which means red, the sacred colour. The same colour was used on the stones making up the front of the upper platform of the Marquesan hut, called *pa'ehava 'oto*. P. Ottino-Garanger provides a clear drawing of this paving and explains the relation between the *pa'ehava'oto* and man's head: 'With this new threshold, which is raised and sheltered by a plant cover, we get into a more intimate and sacred place. Inside, the front part is paved; it leads to the sleeping place, which is the part furthest back in the lodging and the best protected. Marquesans used to sleep with their heads toward the back, that is, the most backward part, the best-sheltered one, their feet toward the front, and thus toward the less sacred part. The final space, between their heads and the back section of the rooftop, was reserved for the gods' (2006. *Archéologie chez les Taïpi, Hatiheu, un projet partagé aux îles Marquises*. Papeete: Aux vent des îles/IRD éditions, pp. 70–71).

huts, the guards in charge of watching and cleaning lived. No other human foot could get close. Only the priest, when he was on a tour, came there to sleep, maybe to dream of his impious task; now, on the feast's day, the clan gathered in groups on the high place and each had his/her predetermined seat. There were seats for the chiefs, the tambourine men, the dancers, the women, and the priests.[55]

Lesson visited and described other sacred places, including the interior of one of those buildings where the *tau'as* kept their valuables and *tapu* objects:

> Continuation of our visit to Haka'a'au, Uapu Island ... King Eato ... had a guide provided to us and permission to visit all sacred places ... On the way, he showed us, a few steps away ... the small case ... where the king retired alone to eat certain foods such as turtles, for example ... After this canvassing, we went to the sacred abode of the priests. I asked what the real name was, but got no answer. [It] was a *tapu* house, even <u>arch *tapu*</u> [sic]; that much was certain, and what was inside proved it. There was a mystery atmosphere all round it and we could see that commoners were not allowed to approach it knowingly. To access the interior it was also necessary to climb up the rungs of a ladder, as in the king's *paepae*, for like him, it was raised on a block of stones. We were surprised at the great number of ornaments and objects that it contained. The first ones that struck our eyes were the bracelets made of human hair, for the insteps (the ankle joint) and the wrists were wrapped in all ceremonies. Here and there we could see hanging on the walls of the house those big baskets made of flexible thin boughs designed for fitting the plumes made of rooster feathers, called *tavaha*, the plumes made of old men's beards, called *kumikumi*, those made with phaethons' tail feathers and other objects; these baskets are called *kete*, and they come in various colors ... a fairly wide variety of drums of various shapes ... were in this home. The generic name of these drums is *pahu*. On all sides, on a floor, or hanging, we could see victuals, *kava* root [*Piper methysticum*] vases to prepare this drink; they came in various shapes and colors, huge rolls of fabric probably meant for decoration during ceremonies, and finally a wealth of other objects such as priests' caps, fans, etc. What was remarkable there was a collection of godheads, set there apparently in a haphazard way and all life-size. Some, and actually most, were made of wood, others of stone. The stone one which drew our attention the most was the statue of the god Tiki. At least that was the name they gave me when

---

55 Stevenson, 1995 (1880). Stevenson visited a 'cannibal Mecca' in Hatiheu, on the island of Nuku Hiva. He was escorted by Father Siméon Delmas and a young guide.

I asked. It was a little less high than the others and sculpted exactly like the Tahitian statues which the author of *Polynesian Researches* showed in his books. Several wooden statues still showed traces of the *popoï* which was put in their mouths. Two or three priests only were present in this abode and they looked rather stern, but one of them could not help but smile when I showed him the heap of *kava* roots that were there. He seemed to understand that I meant they did not fail to indulge themselves. Not far from there was the casket meant for the king's (Eato) uncle, dead one month earlier, and still not buried ... Afterward, we went to see (in another place on the island) ... a vestige of a raised *paepae* ... a *paepae* is a high structure made of cut stones or roughly cut big blocks, square-shaped, ordinarily covered with a rooftop under which certain ceremonies took place and where there were permanent beds, a big amount of victuals, *pahu*, statues, etc; This is what I said about them when describing Eato's. This is what I think travelers called *maraï* on the Society Islands (and it should be spelled *marae* to be exact) but I think they mistakenly compared them to *paepae*, for the *marae* is just a place where the natives have pieces of consecrated coral devoted to the gods. From what I saw, the *paepae* on Uapu [note: Hakahau] might probably be a locale designed for religious ceremonies; yet, as I saw in Vaitahu piles of coral which looked like what elsewhere is called *marae*, it may be likely that the two words meant about the same thing.[56]

Transgressions and punishments

Punishments for having broken a *tapu* were most often ruthless, as described by Chaulet:

> The causes of droughts and famines are:
> - When women take it into their heads to have reeds run [sic], for these games are allowed only to men.
> - When women take it into their heads to walk on stilts or spin a top, for this recreation is allowed only to men.
> - When men take it into their heads to draw pictures with a string, to toss up walnuts and catch them, for these games are fit only for women.
> - When some people wear fragrances during a public *tapu*.

---

56   Lesson, P.A., *Pylade*, 4th voyage, unpublished MS, Corderie de Rochefort, no. 8137, vol. 3, Chapter 12, pp. 55, 60, 61, 62.

- When gods are blasphemed: *ia kupu 'i te mei ; e aha tatu'a tororo mei*.
- When people eat and drink what was sacred for the gods.
- When breadfruit trees fruit, coconuts are compared to secular or shameful things.
- When women climb up breadfruit trees.

On blindness:[57]

The causes of blindness are the same as those of leprosy, plus the following:

- When, to dress a wound, people use coconut oil which a woman has already used to rub her body.
- When a man rubs his body with coconut oil which a woman has used for the same purpose, and conversely for a woman.

On madness:

- When a child eats his mother's *popoi* or pork as well as the breadfruit tree fruit or coconuts she has reserved for herself.
- When one of his parents has blasphemed his belt or what was meant for him.[58]

Among all these circumstances where a child could break a *tapu*, there are, for example, those which surround the tattoo mentioned by Chaulet in various manuscripts:

> Tattooing the lower limbs of a noble woman or a female commoner is not only a huge disgrace for the tattoer but also a huge crime because … women are impure, and the gods must punish this act not only by making the tattoer blind or a leper, but also by slapping a big food shortage or a famine on the country; as a result, they refrain from that … female commoners cannot be tattoed except in isolated places with thick brush, for if through bad luck the gods get to see this desecration, they would have to send a big food shortage or a big famine as punishment.

---

57 Another instance asserts that 'The chiefs' tattooing was performed on the public arena, in the shade of holy trees; tattooing commoners, *kikinos*, was performed in the *vahi tapu* out of sight of women. Women on no account whatsoever could approach this holy place, for their presence would immediately result in the tattooed man's loss of weight and his going blind' (Testard de Marans, 2004, Chapter 2).

58 Chaulet, 1873–1900, p. 172; 1899. Sometimes poison was used, including the fruit of the *'eva*, which contains a violent poison, cerberine: 'Kanaks use it to kill the person among them who allegedly broke or divulged a secret' (Jardin, E., 1858. *Essai de l'Histoire Naturelle de l'archipel Mendana ou des Marquises*. Mémoires de la Société Impériale des Sciences Naturelles et Mathématiques de Cherbourg, p. 26).

What is striking is that it is not only the person who broke the *tapu* who is punished, but also the 'other party'. Everybody, often the whole community, has to suffer.

The fact that punishment is meted out to all stems from the notion of the primacy of the individual. The individual is perceived as a knot in the relations between the different elements in a network: both the *mana* — which can inform the whole community — and the adverse effects of transgression circulate through the punishment.

Assuredly, this permanent continuum between the visible and invisible members of the network, between the *Ao* and the *Po*, between the less sacred and the most sacred, involves extreme conductivity of energy among subjects and objects.

Conclusion

All testimonies by the early observers converge: Marquesan — and more broadly Polynesian — societies are structured on the basis of various *tapu*. Prior to canvassing these *tapu*, it is proper to remember that they are sacred.

This sacred character is the main thing to apprehend; we must understand its nature and peculiar features if we are to understand the logic at work in the past, and sometimes today in Polynesia. Invisible entities, ancestors or women's lifeblood, the nature of sacredness is always genealogical, and its peculiar feature is extreme conductivity. This accounts for the network structure of the communities and the obsession with contact: prohibition is necessarily the mark of a dangerous continuity. Dead people's space and women's space always adjoin men's space. The community represented by the chiefdom is that visible interval framed by these two poles.

The following distinctions must be made:

- The product of these two poles is *tapu* by nature: a funeral site or the hut for women giving birth, for example, but also a young child is still part of the female space, or the body of a *ariki/haka'iki* permeated with *mana* from the ancestors or guardianship entities.
- What has been in contact with these two poles is temporarily *tapu*, such as warriors who have killed enemies, embalming specialists,

or the servant of an *ariki nui/haka'iki nui*; just as in the case of nuclear irradiation, a more or less long period is needed for decontamination. This also explains why it is not safe to share the food meant for a woman or for an *ariki/haka'iki*.

- Anything that an *ariki/haka'iki* or a *tau'a* or any sacred authority has prohibited and which will remain prohibited for as long as the authority has decided. Examples provided by the various observers show that here prohibition is not controlled by the nature of the object but by strategies relating to political/sacred power. In this regard, every object is likely to be prohibited: a tree, a fruit, a sea bream, or a pink pig.

Only the last category is of the nature of *kahui*. The prohibition for women to stride over a dugout canoe belongs to the first two categories. Women's life power competes with men's *mana*. In this instance it is not a *kahui*.

It is also easy to understand that if there are rules that all must obey, there are also rules that can be made up — in this regard, the scope of initiative of the *ariki/haka'iki* and of their *tau'a* totally depends on their privilege to set *kahui*. While, as noted by the early European observers, the chief could base his action on public interest and, after the council's opinion, he could lay down a temporary prohibition on certain plants or animals that needed to be protected and looked after, it is also true that this privilege was 'a powerful lever in the hands of those who held power, the old chiefs, etc.'.

In some instances, this lever made it possible to strengthen societal domination by men over women, or to expand hierarchies and increase inequalities within the community to the utmost.

It is interesting to note Davin's remark: 'The origin of property is to be found in the taboo', which is illustrated by contemporary signs indicating private property. Still, we have to add in closing, the move from an exclusive right of use based upon a sacred filiation to a property right which is not dependent on use signals a recent history marked by evangelisation and market economy. The issue here, with the *tapu* sign at the entrance to a plot of land, is the problematic relation to the land. The *kahui*, most certainly, did not invent property but it has always been a useful tool for personal interests which adjusted to their respective eras.

Lastly, *tapu*'s efficiency is predicated on the punishment for transgression. The punishment may be automatic as soon as there is contact with a material that is hazardous in itself: madness, leprosy or blindness, for example. This idea is so deeply rooted that every plague is construed as punishment for a fault. Disease or drought don't necessarily originate in a transgression and it is important to identify its author. This logic can be found in many cultures: the Lisbon earthquake was regarded as the result of the wrath of the Christian god. When a *kahui* is involved, the transgression is perceived first as a challenge to the power of the *ariki/haka'iki* or the *tau'a*. Punishment first falls within their competence; it reflects flouted authority and, in the final analysis, the *ariki/haka'iki* or the *tau'a* is seen only as the privileged tool. It is not that the transgression of a perennial *tapu* cannot be punished inasmuch as the whole community is in danger; rather, punitive watchfulness involves first and foremost temporary prohibitions. Yet, as sacredness is the foundation of *tapu*, regardless of its nature, it is always dangerous to transgress a prohibition. Thus, the *rahui* slapped in 2010 on a sea area in Rapa is efficient only inasmuch as it reflects God's wrath, Yahweh henceforth replacing the ancestors' powers.

4

I uta i tai — a preliminary account of *ra'ui* on Mangaia, Cook Islands

Rod Dixon

Background

Mangaia is the most southerly of the Cook Islands with a land area of 52 square kilometres. It comprises the highly weathered remains of a volcanic cone that emerged from the Pacific some 20 million years ago and stands 15,600 feet (4,750 metres) above the ocean floor. In the late Pleistocene epoch, tectonic activity resulted in the elevation of the island and reef. Subsequent undercutting of the elevated reef by run off from the former volcanic core has helped create the current formation of the limestone *makatea* which surrounds the island, standing up to 200 feet (60 metres) above sea level.

As indicated in Figure 8, the island has a radial drainage system. From its central hill, Rangimoti'a, sediment is carried by rainwater down valley systems as far as the *makatea* wall, thus creating the current alluvial valleys and swamps.

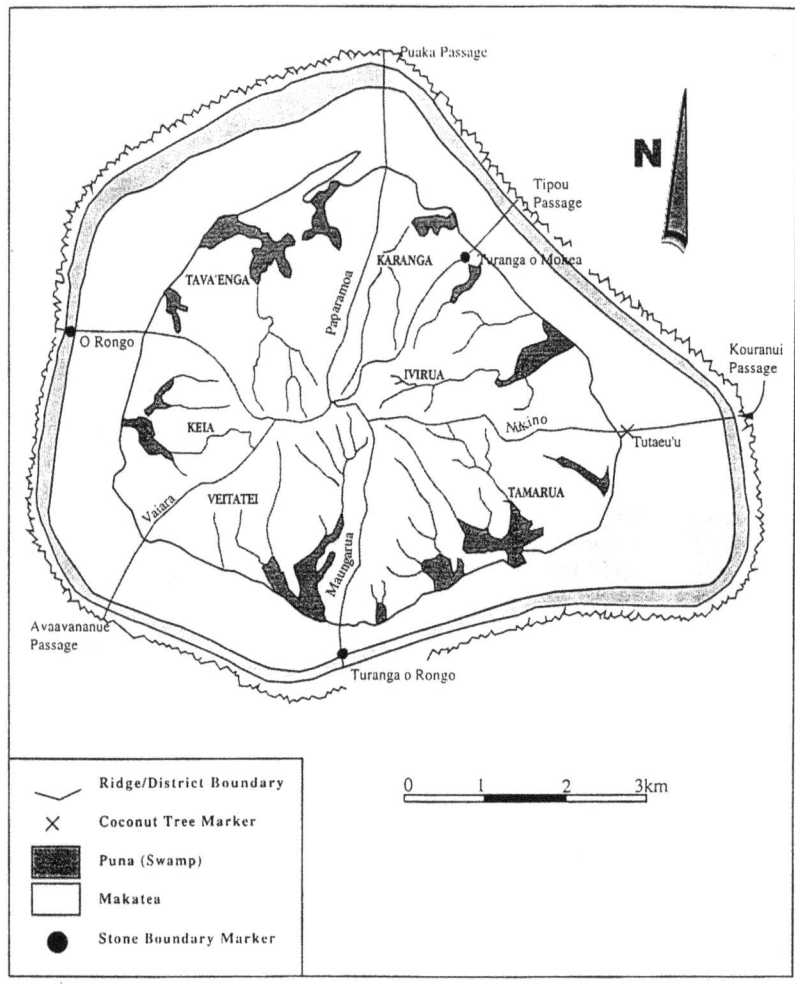

Figure 8: Mangaia Island, indicating *puna* divisions and taro swamps
Source: Rod Dixon

Kirch provides archaeological evidence that this erosion and deposition was accelerated by forest clearance and shifting cultivation of the inland hills somewhere between 1,000 and 500 years ago.[1]

---

1 Kirch, P.V., 1997. 'Changing landscapes and sociopolitical evolution in Mangaia, Central Polynesia'. In P.V. Kirch & T.L. Hunt (eds), *Historical Ecology in the Pacific Islands*. New Haven: Yale University Press, p. 163.

Political and economic zones

Mangaians divide the island into radial territories, pie-shaped slices based around each of the six main river valleys and swamps. Each of the six districts is known as a *puna*.[2] Each *puna* has access to each of the major resource zones: the ocean (*moana*), the lagoon (*roroka*), the beach side (*pae tai*), the *makatea*, the irrigated valleys (*kainga*), and the mountain (*maunga*).

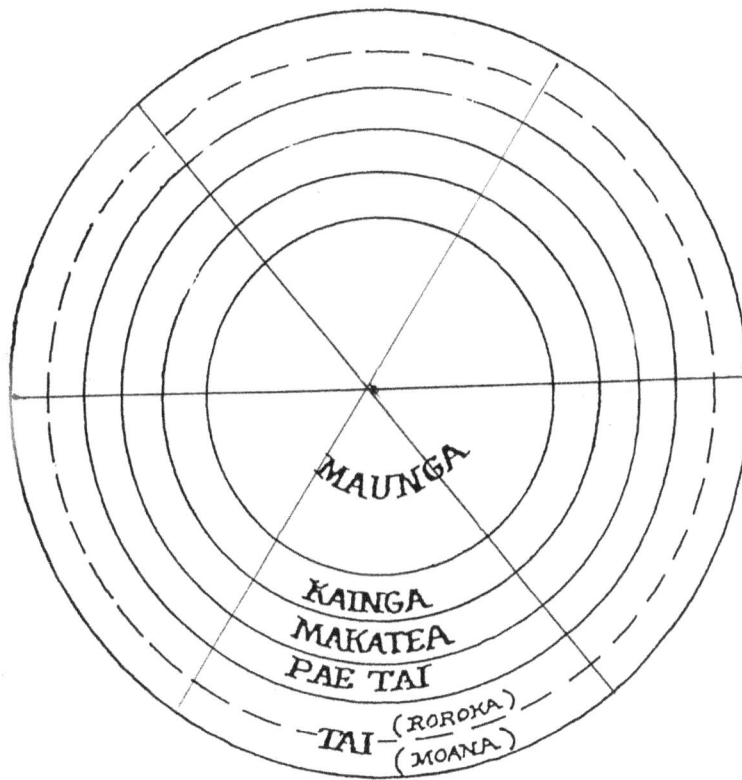

Figure 9: Mangaia as a series of concentric resource zones
Source: Mark, 1976

---

2   Literally, a river valley but also a family, a lineage, a tribe.

The *puna* are further divided into *tapere* or subdistricts — six *tapere* per *puna*, except in the *puna* Tamarua where there are 10. As far as possible these *tapere* boundaries also incorporate access to each of the major resource zones.

Directions

Mary V. Mark, who did research on Mangaia in the early 1970s, tells us that:

> From the *ngutu'are* [household] ... as the point of origin, one may go in any of four directions on Mangaia — *i tai, i uta, i runga,* or *i raro*. One goes from this point either *i tai* or *i uta* to pursue one or more of a variety of subsistence activities. It is to this point (... a particular household) that one returns with the fruits of his/her labours and where they are transformed, consumed or exchanged. Exchange occurs along the line of direction *runga/raro*.[3]

To travel *i tai/i uta* is to travel within the space or boundary of a *puna* (or *tapere*) — and across the concentrically organised resource zones that contribute to subsistence production.[4]

To travel *i raro/i runga*, a Mangaian moves out of the space of local reproduction and economic self-sufficiency, across the sociological boundaries of the *puna*, into inter-district (political and economic) relationships of alliance and exchange.

Subsistence production within the major subsistence zone (the pondfields)

Kirch outlines a number of different ways that water may be distributed to pondfields, as indicated in Figure 10.

---

3   Mark, M.V., 1976. 'The relationship between ecology and myth in Mangaia'. MA thesis. University of Otago, p. 47.
4   Mark, 1976, p. 46.

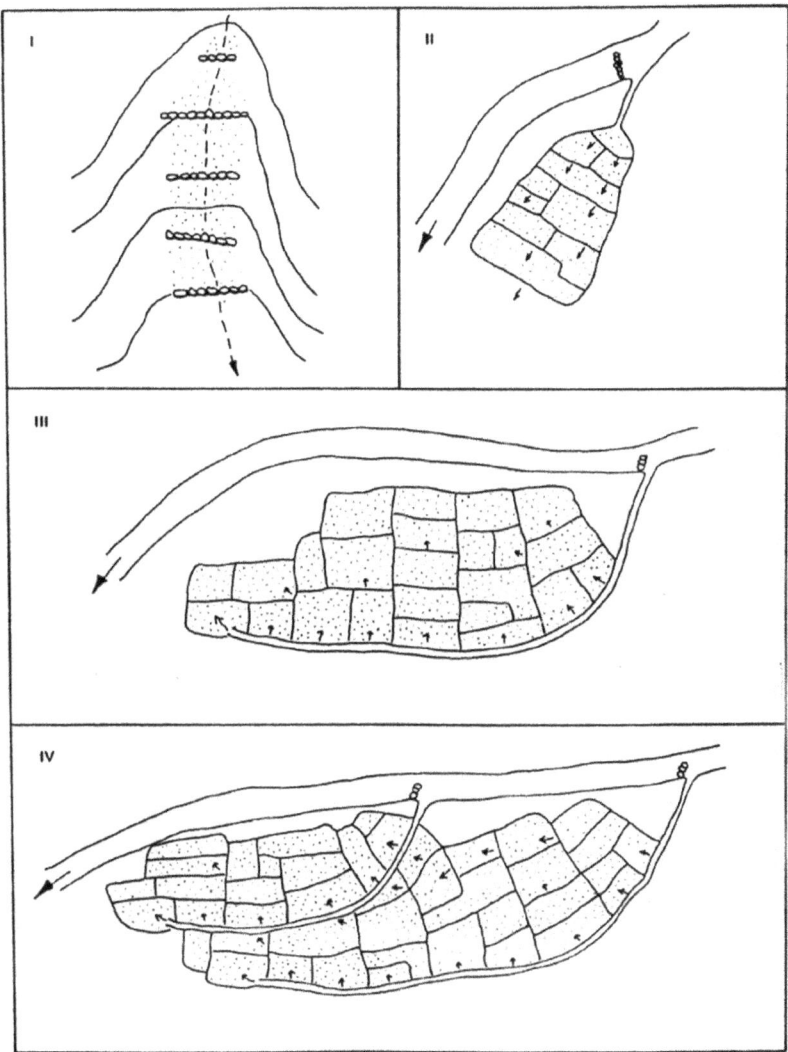

Figure 10: Types of pondfield organisation
Source: Kirch, 1977, p. 261

Type I systems of pondfield organisation consist of simple barrage terraces constructed across a narrow stream channel with no separate ditch. Type II systems comprise small groups of fields watered by a single ditch that feeds into the uppermost field. Water then flows from field to field through small gateways in the embankments. In Type III, the irrigation canal runs along the periphery of the field complex, allowing greater control of water distribution and allocation. The most complex systems, Type IV, have two irrigation ditches, with the lower ditch acting as both a drainage and irrigation device.[5]

Kirch's Type I and Type II of pondfield organisation are found on Mangaia — predominantly Type II with remnants of Type I in the upper valleys.

The manner in which the water is managed in its flow from inland (*uta*) to sea (*tai*) and through the pondfields illustrates something of the social, moral, political and religious life of Mangaia today and in the past.

In a Type II system water is drawn from the main channel to the first pondfield and then flows to all other farmers in the system. This places a high reliance, initially, on the farmer in the first field and subsequently on each farmer down through the valley system. (Interestingly, a farmer is responsible for only three of the four banks (*pae*) of his or her pondfield. The fourth bank belongs to the farmer above him in the water race.)

In a Type IV system, on the other hand, water can be drawn directly from the sub-channels by many farmers, which results in decreased reliance on the farmers in the first field and to the left and right side.

Each system reflects or results in a different social relationship between farmers and differing moral values. Type II involves high levels of mutual reliance and reciprocity. Type IV requires a lesser degree of mutuality and reciprocity and potentially greater individualism.

A map of the Tamarua swamp in Mangaia (Figure 11) indicates how the water travels along the main stream channel from its collection point in the hills (top centre) to its exit point at the inner *makatea* face (lower right). As the water descends through the valley system, it is collected into small dams (*pi'a vai*) along the way. Each of these dams distributes the water to a specially constructed terrace level.

---

5   Kirch, P.V., 1977. 'Valley agricultural systems in prehistoric Hawai'i: an archaeological consideration', *Asian Perspectives* 20: 246–80.

4. *I UTA I TAI* — A PRELIMINARY ACCOUNT OF *RA'UI* ON MANGAIA, COOK ISLANDS

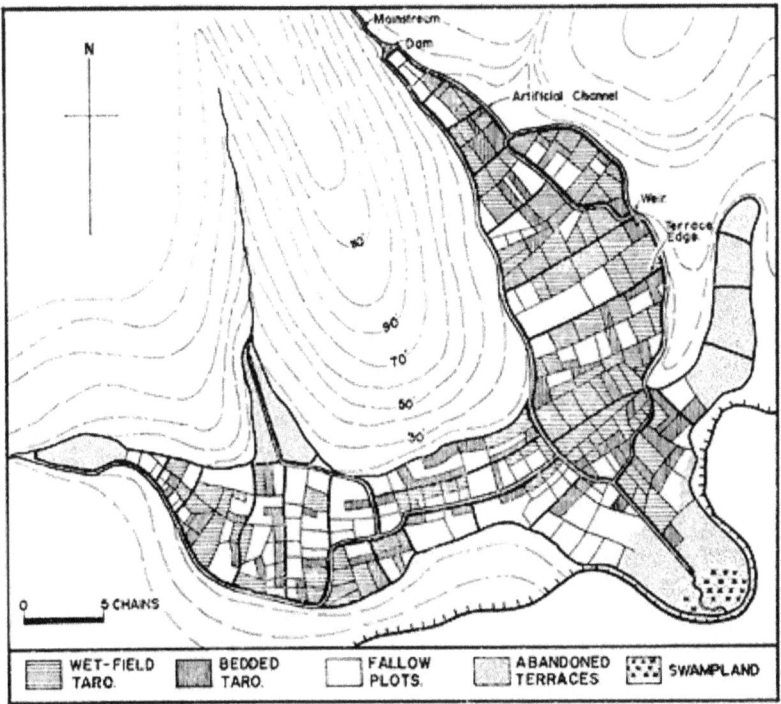

Figure 11: Water distribution through the Tamarua swamp
Source: Allen, 1972, p. 374

In the pre-Christian period, this system was overlaid by religious beliefs venerating water.

Figure 12 indicates the distribution of *marae* on the island. Historically, as the water descended from its origin in the *pito*[6] or navel of Mangaia (Rangimoti'a) or from springs (*pupu*) lower down the valley, it was stewarded through the lower valley system by priests located at *marae* proximate to the water race. The streams (*puna vai*) in this conception

---

6   Marshall notes that 'Rangimoti'a is called *Te Pito o Mangaia*, "the navel of Mangaia"; Mangaians clearly relate this term for the navel to the fact that this flat-topped mountain is the source of all water on Mangaia, that taro depends upon water for growth, and that Mangaians in turn depend on taro for their basic subsistence. Hence Rangimoti'a today is the "source" of Mangaian life' (1965. 'Descent, relationship and territorial groups, social categories relevant to the Mangaian Kopu discussion'. Unpublished paper. DS Marshall Archive, University of the South Pacific, Cook Islands, p. 25). According to Buck, 'The term *pito* was applied to both the navel cord and the navel depression' (1934. *Mangaian Society*. Bulletin no. 122. Honolulu: Bernice P. Bishop Museum, pp. 85–86).

were the *kauvai toto*, 'blood streams' or arteries that brought life to the swamps, an umbilicus from the *pito o te enua* (navel of the island) — the umbilicus being conceived as the *ara i'o* or pathway of the life spirit, activating growth in the swamps and giving life to the people.

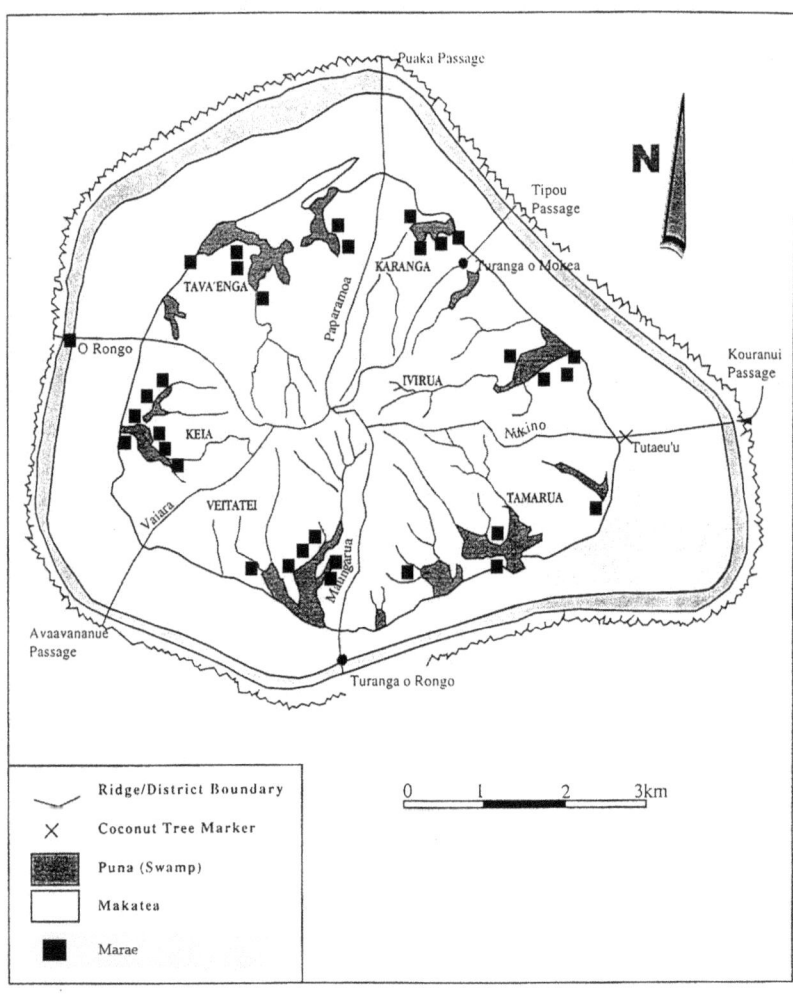

Figure 12: Map of Mangaia, indicating distribution of *marae*
Source: After Buck, 1934, Figure 1, and Bellwood, 1978, Figure 69

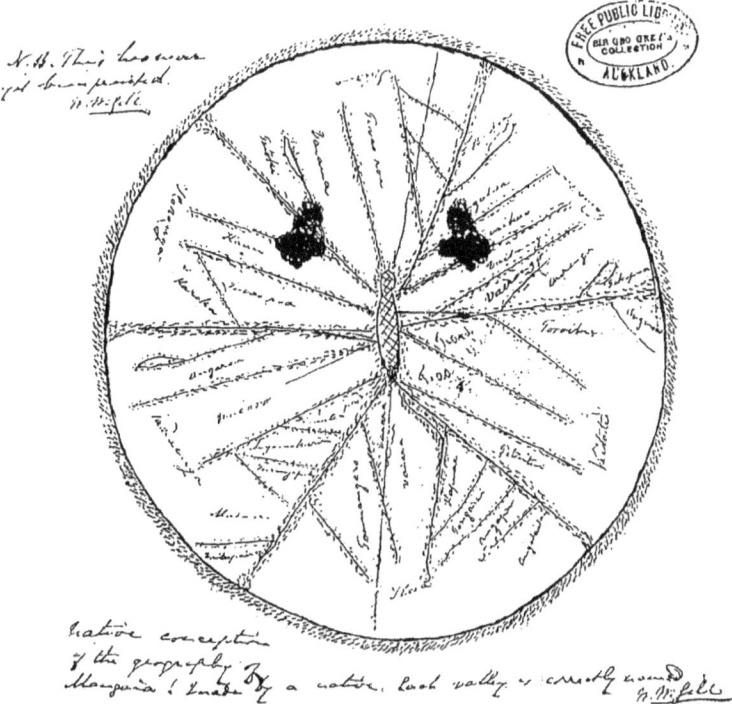

Figure 13: 'Native conception' of the island, recorded by the nineteenth-century missionary W. Wyatt Gill — with the fallen god Te Manavaroa at the *pito* or navel of the island (Rangimoti'a) and a series of streams radiating out from a 'sanctified core' to the valley swamps below.
Source: Image 45, Sir George Grey Special Collections, Auckland Libraries

Looking in more detail at the flow of water at each terrace level, water is fed from the dam (*pi'a vai*) to a single pondfield and then passed along the terrace horizontally and vertically from field to field through narrow channels broken in the banks of each pondfield.

Kirch's Type II, as the predominant system of irrigation on Mangaia, relies heavily on mutuality and reciprocity:

reciprocity — the flow of water from one field to the field horizontally or vertically adjacent;

mutual reliance — the need to ensure that the water flowing from one pondfield is passed to the next person in the manner it was received — weeded, virus free, and in sufficient quantity to ensure a cool growing environment for the taro tuber.

THE RAHUI

The Type II system, when applied to the Mangaian environment (which is subject to periodic drought), places an additional responsibility on the farmer at the head of the system and nearest the main water channel — that is the farmer in the pondfield known as the *matavai* (literally the 'eye' or source of the water).

Because the farmers at the front of the water (the *vai i mua*) are ensured year-round supplies of water, even during periods of severe low rainfall, the responsibility of the farmer in the *matavai* is to feed the rest of the farmers in times of drought. The *matavai* is allocated to a senior member of the family — the *rangatira* or sub-chief.

This hierarchy in the allocation of water from the first-born *kavana* (district chief) or *rangatira* (sub-chief) to their kinsmen and women — and the recognition of their reliance on him or her — is acknowledged every January in the annual ceremony known as the *takurua mata'iti*.[7]

At the *takurua mata'iti*, people bring food to their chief and the chief returns it to them ('the *kavana* feeding the people for the next year')[8] in a symbolic display of mutuality and reciprocity.

A well-regarded district chief ensures that all the people of his *puna* have watered pondfields that are able to produce a good crop of taro wherever they are located in the valley system, from *vai i mua* ('front water') to the *vai i miri* ('back waters') to the very end of the water run. This requires that the *kavana* and *rangatira* mobilise the *puna* as *tao'nga 'anga'anga*, or 'work supervisors', managing the water run, clearing the waterways and stream exits through the *makatea* and ensuring that the water catchment in the hills remains covered in vegetation and free from burning.

The ability to participate equally in the annual feast and put on a display of food at the *takurua mata'iti* and other feasts is evidence of *puna* prosperity and a public demonstration of the leadership and resource management skills of the *kavana* and *rangatira*.

---

7   The corollary on Rarotonga (though not on Mangaia) is that the entrance of water from a *matavai* may be blocked by the *rangatira* or *mataiapo* if this mutual reliance is not recognised by the annual presentation of a pig (see Buck, Field Notes, Rarotonga MS Staff Colletion, Box 3.03, Volume 1, Peter Buck Staff Archives, Bernice P. Bishop Museum: 55).
8   Marshall, 1958, DSM Archives, Box 7.3, Field notes of Third Expedition 1957/58: 641.

Figure 14: Mataora Harry *kavana* officiating at the *puna* Kei'a *takurua mata'iti*, January 2008
Source: Taoi Nooroa

Ra'ui and resource management on Mangaia

The widespread distribution of irrigation waters requires close management of the valley's resources, particularly land and waters in the irrigated terraces situated in the middle and lower valleys.

The middle and lower valley terrace systems are part of a larger ecological complex comprising:

- the *maunga* or central plateau — the water catchment;
- the *rautuanu'e* or inland hills — another vital area of water collection;
- the upper valleys with their *apua* (hollows) containing ancient taro reserves;[9]

---

9   Allen, B.J., 1971. 'Shorter communication; wet-field taro terraces on Mangaia, Cook Islands'. *Journal of the Polynesian Society* 80: 372.

- the middle and lower valley terraces with dams and *kauvai* and terraced pondfields; and
- the outflows beneath the *makatea*, which require regular maintenance to avoid valley flooding.

Damage to any one part of this complex is likely to place corresponding pressure on other parts. Accordingly, Mangaians observe a whole-of-island approach to resource management that is organised and executed at the valley level by the political head of each valley unit, the *kavana*, together with his *rangatira*.

Resource conservation on Mangaia is directed to ensuring the following outcomes, within each of the six valley systems.

(a) The unimpeded movement of water (*vai ta'e*) to pondfields across the terrace and from terrace level to terrace level

Permanent circulation is necessary to prevent water from stagnating (*vai taeta*) or warming, which provides favourable conditions for the growth of fungi and weeds (*nganga'ere*). Reduced water flow can generate corm rot (*pe*) with the infection flowing from one pondfield to others watered by its outflow. Permanent circulation also ensures reduced evaporation loss and thus water conservation.

Weeding (*vaere nganga'ere*) is critical to the circulation of water and tuber growth. As Allen notes, 'weed growth is rapid and stultifies the growth of the tuber, spoiling quality and taste'.[10]

Pondfields that are not weeded not only restrict the circulation of waters through the system, but also release weed seeds (*ua nganga'ere*) into fields that are fed by their outflow. In this case, a *rangatira* may take action to reallocate unweeded taro plots to another planter to protect the pondfields downstream.

In ensuring the permanent circulation of water to his *taro*, every Mangaian planter is reliant on all those ahead of him in the water race and, ultimately, on the holder of the *matavai*, the *puna vai* and

---

10   Allen, B.J., 1969. 'The development of commercial agriculture on Mangaia; social and economic change in a Polynesian community'. MA thesis. Massey University, p. 70.

the *pi'a vai*; i.e. the *rangatira*. Holders of the *taro* are consequently encouraged to take good care of their plots through attention to the bunds (*pae*) or risk losing them:

Tiakina a'ora te raupoto i te rauroa
I te 'apiki i te amenge
I te 'aanga taro a Tu-tavake

Look after — or lose — the short *pae*, the long *pae*
The bends, the corners
In the terrace swamps of Tu-tavake.[11]

In former times, the routine responsibilities of water flows and conservation were delegated by the chiefs to a *tao'nga ra'ui/tiaki ra'ui* (conservation guard) who 'looked after the *matavai* and the proper distribution of water'.[12] In particular, they ensured that conflict did not develop within their tribe or between tribal allies over matters such as the improper or careless diversion of water away from others for their own benefit.

(b) The conservation of water resources

The Mangaian irrigation system is predominantly fed by stream waters flowing from the rain catchment of the inland hills. Mangaia has a pronounced wet season (November to April) that accounts for around two-thirds of the mean annual rainfall of 1,967 millimetres. In the dry season the stream flow reduces, with some streams drying out or falling to a level that is too low to feed the irrigation systems, resulting in crop failure.[13] March and April are the favoured months for planting when the *i'i* (chestnut) is ripening. Critical months of water shortage for *taro vai* (wet swamp) cultivation are July to October, and in particular September, October and often November. During this season the *taro pa'i* (dry-land taro), with its reduced water requirement, has a better chance of survival.

---

11   Buck notes that 'Certain terraces in the *makatea* of Tava'enga are referred to as Tutavake's terraced taro patches' (Buck, Bishop Museum, MS Staff Collection, Box 4).
12   Buck, Bishop Museum MS Staff Collection, Box 4.15.
13   Facon, T., 1990. 'Irrigation and drainage development, Mangaia, Cook Islands'. Draft technical report. FAO Project TCP/CKI/8852. Rome: FAO, p. 5.

THE RAHUI

The capacity to increase water storage in the upper reaches of the water race is limited. An FAO project to facilitate water conservation found that 'the narrow shape of the valleys combined with their steep slopes prevent creating meaningful storage capacities economically ... Water storage to satisfy irrigation requirements, and even more so, to control flooding, is not practical'.[14] Since storage capacity is limited, conservation of the catchment and proper maintenance of the hydrological system of the pondfields is critical.

Traditional conservation measures that have been adopted to ensure that the rain catchments retain water for gradual release include a ban on land use in the *rautuanu'e* (fernlands), bans against burning the fernlands and, in former times, conservation of the *maunga* (the main watershed) as a *tapu*, or sacred, place. A *ra'ui vai* was also imposed on at least one of the springs in each valley system for domestic consumption during periods of drought.

(c) The prevention of flooding

A general *tapu* on agriculture and land clearing on the inland hills was historically important in preventing soil erosion (*one oro* — 'slipping soil' — and *nga'oro* — 'land slides').[15] Erosion contributes to the silting of stream beds, stream flooding and the blocking of drainage outlets.

In addition, irrigation channels must be kept clear of debris to ensure that stream waters are not blocked in periods of heavy rain. Stream flooding not only damages the terrace systems and crops but also draws the debris of the swamps into the subterranean *makatea* drainage outflows.

As Facon notes:

> A severe problem affecting the swamps of Mangaia is the flooding of the lower reaches of the swamps after a heavy rain. The plots may be drowned during several days under a depth of several feet of water, causing the crops to rot. As the risk of crop failure due to flooding is

---

14   Facon, 1990, p. 5.
15   This prohibition was ignored, in the name of agricultural modernisation, during the late colonial period when the inland hills became a locus of pineapple planting with serious soil erosion resulting (Sims, D., 1981. 'Erosion on Rarotonga, Mangaia and Atiu with recommendations and proposals'. Draft technical report. Rome: FAO).

very high, the lowest parts of the swamps have been abandoned for cultivation; as they are not weeded any more, the evacuation of flood water is slowed down, increasing the problem.[16]

The back-up of waters at the *makatea* outlets contributes to the existence of the permanent waters of Lake Tiriara and to swamp areas (*taro o'onu* — 'deep taro' — and *vai ngaere* — 'deep water swamps') that are unsuited to planting. These occur when silt-bearing waters from the irrigation terraces are trapped against the base of the *makatea*. Unless accumulations of silt are cleared through the *makatea* outlets, the *vai ngaere* increases in size, removing lower valley pondfields from production.

(d) Soil conservation

Resource conservation practices are also directed at maintaining ground cover to prevent soil erosion on the central hills. As well as bans on burning of the inland hills, planters are encouraged to plant sugar cane, bananas and coconut on *pae* and stream banks (*pae kauvai*) to hold soil and prevent its deposition into streams and channels. A general *ra'ui* is imposed on the tethering and feeding of animals (especially pigs) in the lower valleys and adjacent hillsides. Coconuts husked to feed pigs contribute to the flood debris blocking drainage outflows, while pigs (tethered or wandering) loosen the soil in rutting for food, contributing to soil erosion and siltation during heavy rains.

(e) Conservation of food reserves

Reserves of local *mamio* are grown untended under the shade of trees in small hollows (*apua*) in the upper reaches of the inland hills. These are watered by the first waters of the hillside catchments using a simple Type I irrigation system. These upland taro provide new taro shoots (*miko*) in the event that supplies in the middle and lower valleys are destroyed by flood, drought or disease. These reserves have been historically protected by a *ra'ui* and a general *tapu* on the inland hills. *Ra'ui* are also placed on the lagoons (usually for six months) and inland lakes to protect freshwater fish stocks, and on coconut and other food crops.

---

16   Facon, 1990, p. 11.

THE RAHUI

The valley irrigation systems require ongoing management involving the protection of the fernlands in the catchment areas (to prevent siltation of the streams, consequent freshet flooding and the deposition of silt and flood debris into drainage outflows), the clearance of irrigation channels, bund maintenance and weeding within the terraces themselves, and specific measures within and below the terraces directed at maintaining clear drainage outflows through the *makatea* and the protection of food reserves. The instigation and coordination of these activities is the responsibility of the valley's *kavana* and *rangatira* — supported by those appointed as *tiaki ra'ui*.

Buck notes that 'in ancient times' *ra'ui* was the responsibility of the 'Ruler of Food' (*ariki i te tapora kai*).[17] Subsequently:

> each district has acted independently. The district distributor of food is one of the sub-district chiefs who has been agreed upon by the district and sub-district chiefs … [this person] is termed the *rauaika*. It is the duty of the *rauaika* to inspect the cultivations within the district and take note of all vegetable food supplies. He also inspects the lagoon within the district boundaries to note whether the catches of fish are getting smaller. Should he think it necessary, he calls the district chief and sub-district chiefs (*'ui rangatira*) together in council. The matter is discussed and if a closed season is decided upon, the *ra'ui* is promulgated through the district, each *kairanga nuku* [*rangatira*] taking the word to his own sub-district. The news spread from mouth to mouth and the closed season commences on the date given out. The closed season affects the land food supplies (*'enua*) or the sea (*tai*); the two forms of closure are termed *ra'ui 'enua* and *ra'ui tai* respectively.

---

17   Buck, 1934, p. 141. According to Buck, taro, breadfruit, coconuts and bananas were the main land crops subjected to *ra'ui* and the *ra'ui* was 'promulgated by two special criers' each distinguished by 'a plaited coconut leaf suspended over the back and a leaflet tied to each arm. The coconut leaf so worn was termed a *tara ra'ui* (notice of a closed season)' (1934, pp. 141–42). The seaside *ra'ui* (*ra'ui tai*) was promulgated not just by word of mouth but by the striking of long poles set up on the beach or near fishing holes with the plaited coconut suspended from them. 'Men were [appointed] as rangers (*tiaki*) to make frequent patrols along the water front … Good rangers could tell from the appearance of the pools whether or not fish had been removed' (Buck, 1934, p. 142).

On Mangaia today, decisions on the management and conservation of valley resources continue to be made on a district by district basis, with each valley district meeting to discuss the *ra'ui* and other resource management issues a few days after the annual *takurua mata'iti* ceremony.

The *takurua mata'iti* occurs on a Saturday, the day before the end of the old Church year (Prayer Week — *'epetoma pure*). On the following Monday[18] the *uipa'anga mata'iti* (annual meeting), also referred to as the *uipa'anga ra'ui*, is held. In some districts this is also the occasion of the meeting of the *pūkuru* (hereditary leaders of a subdivision).[19]

At the *uipa'anga mata'iti*, the *kavana* and *rangatira* consult with their districts on the planting for the following year; including additional plantings to meet the requirements of feasts or visiting groups; the literal 'earmarking' of pigs for next year's *takurua mata'iti* and any intervening district feasts; the repair of *pi'a vai* and other infrastructure. The people of the district are encouraged to look after their livestock and plantings and make provision for their families and guests. Subsequently, at different times of the year, members of *tapere* work together under the direction of the *rangatira* to meet the goals set for the *tapere* at the *takurua mata'iti*.

---

18   'The Puna meeting on Monday is for the *kavana* and *rangatira* to put the *ra'ui* on cocoanuts … and to tell the people to plant, clean up their plantations, not to tie horses on the taro borders, to tether pigs and goats, — to give them the law' (Marshall, 1958, DSM Archives, Box 7.3, Field notes of Third Expedition 1957/58: 640).
19   Marshall (1953, DSM Archives, Box 7.1, Field notes of First Expedition 1951–53: 233) notes: 'Below these [the *rangatira*] are *Pūkuru* (10 of these in Pu'ati's own *tapere*). At the end of the year *Ui Rangatira* send to *Pūkuru* to collect money from all the people living in the district. (Office is handed down in families, but if die out *Ariki* appoints successor). Money is used either for church or to pay men and women who are chosen on the first of each year to look after plantations during the coming year — catching wandering livestock — *Tiaki Ra'ui*.'

Figure 15: *Uipa'anga ra'ui*, Veitatei district, *Ma'arona kavana*, setting out workplans for the coming year, 1954.
Source: D S Marshall Archives, University of the South Pacific, Cook Islands

At the *uipa'anga ra'ui*, harvesting, which is the second component of the agricultural year, is discussed to ensure the best use of resources for the benefit of families and the *puna* as a whole. This includes discussion of when the *ra'ui* will be, how long it will last, to what resources it will be applied, and its geographic boundaries. The *tiaki ra'ui* for the coming year are elected by nomination. The collected *ra'ui* fines for the year are brought to the *uipa'anga ra'ui*. Until recently, money collected from these fines was distributed among all the *tiaki ra'ui* and all those who came to the *uipa'anga ra'ui*, including the women who prepared the food and the children. In some districts the money collected from the *pūkuru* is used to pay the *tiaki ra'ui*.

Figure 16: The *kavana Ma'arona* with his *rauaika* (district distributor of food) at the division of food, *takurua mata'iti, puna Veitatei*, 1954. Foods distributed include pig, taro and *roiroi* or taro pudding.
Source: D S Marshall Archives, University of the South Pacific, Cook Islands

The role of the *pūkuru* of each *tapere* is to collect donations, or *'atinga*, from people on behalf of the *rangatira* of the *tapere* in which they are planting — the amount being 'up to you'. ('Giving money to the *rangatira* shows that you are still working under him.') A portion of the money collected by the *pūkuru* is used to pay for Church expenses and, in some cases, to supplement annual payments to the *tiaiki ra'ui*. Some of the money collected from fines against infringements of the *ra'ui* is deposited in a bank account in the name of the *aronga mana*, or leaders of the *puna*, to pay general community expenses.

Everyone is seen to benefit equally from the *ra'ui* and all are compensated for infringements of it. Only the *'orometua* (pastor) is exempt from the *ra'ui* according to the old belief: '*O tai kikau e topa na atua*' ('Only one coconut leaf will drop — that for the god').[20]

This distribution of fines at the *uipa'anga ra'ui* reflects the distribution of food at the *takurua mata'iti*, which in turn reflects the distribution of waters through the valley systems. Common to all is a basic ethic of egality, mutuality and reciprocity in the use of resources, as a means of ensuring peace and prosperity.

History of the *ra'ui* — initial suggestions

In an earlier period of Mangaian history, the irrigation system was differently organised and the current terraces result from agricultural intensification that occurred around 500 or 600 years ago.[21] The Type I irrigation system found in the *apua* of the upper valleys are possible remnants of this earlier period of Mangaian history (the 'Ngariki period').

The 'Ngariki period'

The 'Ngariki period' was a period of political and religious rule by a divine chief descended from the Mangaian founding ancestor, Rangi. In this period, the landscape of Mangaia was 'divinely' organised (predominantly on the vertical plane *uta/tai* —mountain to sea). The two divinely descended chiefs of Mangaia were *ariki pa uta* and *ariki pa tai* (guarding the flow of water from its origin inland to its exit at the shore — notably at Vairorongo — the bathing place of the *ariki pa tai* opposite the O Rongo *marae* at Tava'enga). Succession to land and titles was usually from the first-born son to the first-born son in a line of succession descending from Rangi.

---

20 Atingakau Tangatakino, 1992. Personal communication with the author. A coconut leaf tied to a tree is the symbol of the *ra'ui*. See also the chant '*E ra'ui tapu*' in Buck (1934, p. 142). Marshall records, 'there is not supposed to be a ra'ui in the village as it is "Te Oire No Te Evangeria" [The Village of God], and thus not within the domain of the chiefs' (DSM Archives, Box 7.3; Field notes of Third Expedition, 1957/58; 687).
21 Kirch, P.V., 1994. *The Wet and the Dry: Irrigation and Agricultural Intensification in Polynesia*. University of Chicago Press, p. 283.

In this 'divine' landscape, the hill (Rangimoti'a) was a 'heavenly mountain'. The sacred waters emanating from it were stewarded by the senior male descendants of the Ngariki in a vertical (*uta/tai*) descent from the mountain, paralleling the flow of the life force (*i'o*) from the sanctified core or *pito*: i.e. from founding gods to their descendants, the senior patriline of the Ngariki. From the sacred *puna vai* stream waters flowed into the *matavai* — the pondfields of the *mata mua* (the first-born) — thence down the patriline. At each stage in the water's descent, *marae* were erected.

Gill suggests that for the ancients:

> As an individual consists of two parts, viz. body and spirit, so the island has a sort of essence, or *spirit*, the secret name of which is Akatautika, i.e., The-well-poised, only used by the priests and kings of ancient days. When in after times the earthly form, or *body*, of Auau [Mangaia] was dragged up to the light, there remained behind in the obscurity of nether-world the ethereal form, or *spirit*, of [Akatautika] The-well-poised.[22]

A Mangaian gathering taro or catching fish in the upperworld routinely allocated a share to the gods in the underworld. Buck describes this as an act of propitiation to ensure continuing plenty.[23] Gill notes the phrase '*E mou Avaiki tena*' (that harvest for Avaiki), denoting luxuriant plant growth. In this context, *ra'ui* as an act of abstention in the upperworld could be seen as the allocation of forgone resources to the gods in the underworld. 'The gods', Buck notes of ritual offerings generally, 'were supposed to eat the shadow (*ata*) of the food'[24] leaving its substance.

In the Ngariki period, the *ra'ui* was presided over by the inherited priestly position of *Te ariki i te ua i te tapora kai* (translated by Buck as 'Ruler of Food'), a title which ran in the third, or junior, division of the Ngariki (the Vaeruarangi).[25]

---

22 Gill, 1876, p. 11.
23 Buck, 1934, p. 178.
24 Buck, 1934, p. 179.
25 'In olden times, the Ruler of Food had some influence as to the imposing of closed seasons (*ra'ui*) over districts and fishing grounds in order to let depleted food supplies recover. In time of peace, he exercised a ceremonial control over the distribution of food at public feasts' (Buck, 1934, p. 118).

THE RAHUI

The 'Tongaiti period'

The Ngariki organisation was abandoned for a variety or reasons, largely attributed by Kirch to environmental changes, particularly destruction of the original forest cover resulting in infertile fernlands of limited use to agriculture.[26] As a consequence, competition for the taro lands became intense, intertribal warfare resulted, with leadership passing from the hereditary *ariki* to a military dictator. In this period, Buck tells us a chief took control of the land in the name of his battle scars or wounds rather than through descent from the founding ancestor.[27] During this 'Tongaiti' period, which lasted for several centuries up to the period of first European contact, the *ariki* retained the spiritual link to the founding ancestor as 'High Priest' but the new head of government (*te ua mangaia*) came from the ranks of the leading warriors of the tribe(s) best able to assert and maintain dominance over the major resource of the island, the valley pondfields. The 'divine right' of the Ngariki to the land and waters, as Rangi's sacred descendants, was broken, although Ngariki chiefs (as *ariki pa tai* and *ariki pa uta*) continued to officiate at rituals accompanying the division of lands and waters following warfare.

In this new Tongaiti period, terraces and hydrological systems were constructed to intensify agricultural production and keep pace with the food requirements of a growing population. The need to maintain military strength meant political alliances across boundaries (*i raro/i runga*). This political reality was reflected in the newly intensified pondfield systems, with water running from kinsman to kinsman and political allies across the newly constructed terrace levels, following a horizontal *raro/runga* rather than the earlier *uta/tai* flow. Waters once allocated 'vertically', according to seniority of descent in the patriline, were now distributed 'laterally' to the *arutoa*,[28] the band or sodality of warriors who had achieved temporal power in battle, as a 'reward for service'.[29]

---

26   See Kirch, 1997.
27   Buck, 1934, p. 125.
28   The *arutoa* comprised the supporters or *toko* of the warrior who assumed, through victory in warfare, the position of Temporal Lord or *ua mangaia*.
29   Goldman, I., 1970. *Ancient Polynesian Society*. University of Chicago Press, p. 557.

4. I UTA I TAI — A PRELIMINARY ACCOUNT OF RA'UI ON MANGAIA, COOK ISLANDS

The 'divine' hierarchical, *uta/tai* organisation of Ngariki society and landscape was overlaid by the more intensely political *raro/runga* organisation of Tongaiti society and landscape. In this period, Buck notes, there was a gradual reduction in the role of the Ruler of Food in the organisation of the *ra'ui*,[30] and the localisation of his position among the successful *arutoa*, with both the *arutoa* and the Ruler of Food utilising *ra'ui* as a means of protecting food supplies for the future provisioning of their troops.[31] The position of *kairanga nuku tei a ia te rauaika* ('the subdistrict chief who has the banana leaf') — *rauaika* for short — with his role in declaring district *ra'ui*, and announcing the allotment of food at feasts, retains overtones of this district provisioning.

The 'mission period'

The arrival of Christian missionaries in 1823 meant an end to war and the introduction of the 'rule' or 'peace' of the Gospel (*te au o te evangeria*) and thus an end to the Tongaiti mechanism of land and water allocation via warfare. Existing resource allocations were frozen from the time the missionaries established ideological dominance. The *kavana* of today are the descendants of the warriors (*pava*) who fought at Araeva (c. 1821), where they succeeded in winning control of the pondfields. The *ariki* of today claims descent in a line of *ariki* stretching back to the founding ancestor Rangi. But, as a consequence of Tongaiti political organisation, the *ariki* has no privileged say in the allocation of land or water, and these decisions rest largely with the descendants of the last warriors (the *pava* or *kavana/Aronga Mana* of Mangaia).

With succession no longer decided by warfare, the old Ngariki principle of descent and succession through the patriline returned.[32] Looking into the pondfield system today, we can see evidence

---

30   Particularly in circumstances where the *ariki i te tapora kai* had become involved in politics and a combatant in war.
31   Buck, 1934, pp. 118–19.
32   Modified by the principle of the *pa metua* (agnatic seniority), a possible remnant of the warrior period. As Gill notes: 'The order of descent in regal (*ariki*) families was usually from father to son; but with great land or warrior chiefs it was different; the brothers of the deceased taking precedence over his sons, for the excellent reason that it was their strong arms that won or preserved the tribal lands' (Gill, W.W., 1979. *Cook Islands Custom*. Suva: Institute of Pacific Studies, University of the South Pacific, p. 10).

of patrilineal succession in the *uta/tai* allocation of waters — from the *kavana* to the *rangatira* down the water race, except that the *rangatira* today are descendants of warriors rather than direct descendants of the *ariki*. The *raro/runga* flow of waters across the valley terraces continues to reinforce family solidarity, and the values of mutuality and reciprocity, although no longer in the name of military strength.

In the mission period, as trade and commerce increased *ra'ui* provided a means by which chiefs, as 'single sellers', could maximise prices received from traders by interdicting the harvest and sale of crops below a set price. Colonial authorities, having initially recognised the rights of chiefs to impose the *ra'ui*,[33] acted in 1908 to limit its use, other than by the colonial island councils.[34] The island councils were charged by the colonial authority to 'use ... their power of *tapu* (or *ra'ui*) over crops to regulate the standard of produce for sale and to secure uniform prices from the traders'.[35] Needless to say, the ruling chiefs of Mangaia steadfastly ignored this attempt to strip their traditional powers.[36] Later, as the prosperity of the island came to rely on the mass export of oranges and pineapples, the *ra'ui* was used to schedule the harvesting of crops to coincide with the arrival of shipping.[37] In recent years, the practice of *ra'ui* has been subsumed under contemporary conservation and postcolonial paradigms, to reassert the legitimacy of traditional leaders as environmental managers (as suggested above and discussed elsewhere in this collection).

---

33   Laws of Mangaia, Law No. 2 1891— Section 7 provides for *ra'ui*.
34   *Te Mana Ra'ui* (The power of *ra'ui*) — Public Statement by Resident Commissioner, 1908: 'Asserted that the ancient right of *ra'ui* no longer existed in respect of any land which has been investigated by the Native Land Court. (Note: later Resident Commissioners varied in their practice in relation to *ra'ui*, some sanctioning them in relation to lands investigated by the Court and others not allowing them ...)' (Crocombe, R.G., 1964. *Land Tenure in the Cook Islands*, Oxford University Press, p. 325).
35   Gilson, R.P., 1952. 'Introduction to the administration of the Cook Islands (Rarotonga)'. MSc, University of London, p. 16.
36   For example, the resident agent's annual report for Mangaia, dated 1908, notes that the spokesman for the Mangaian *Aronga Mana* (chiefs), Miringatangi, denounced the new regulations governing *ra'ui*, just as the *Aronga Mana* had consistently rejected New Zealand colonial administration, saying that 'all he recognized was the [British] Protectorate flag'. He was summonsed by the resident agent for contempt and refused to appear (Box 19/1 Box 1 Cook Islands Administration, Resident Commissioner's Office, Correspondence with Resident Agents in the Outer Islands).
37   D.S. Marshall (1952) noted: 'The *Aronga Mana* [chiefs] has declared a *ra'ui* (economic *tapu*) on oranges in an attempt to bring up the size of the shipments'; that is, to accumulate sufficient tonnage to justify a ship calling at the island (DSM Archives, Box 7.4, Field Notes of Second Expedition 1954/55; 175).

Conclusion

In Mangaia, *ra'ui* as a short- or long-term limitation on resource zones or resource use, has been critical to maintaining the hydrological systems of the lower valley pondfields as well as the conservation of resources against overuse or stressful environmental events. The social organisation of *ra'ui* on Mangaia reflects the high level of mutuality and reciprocity inherent in the organisation of irrigation water flows. While contexts and practices of *ra'ui* have changed over time, common to all has been the deployment of divine and/or political power to the guarantee of plenty.

5
Technical exploitation and 'ritual' management of resources in Napuka and Tepoto (Tuamotu Archipelago)

Eric Conte

From 1981, the atolls of Napuka and Tepoto in the Tuamotu Archipelago have been the site of an ethno-archaeological research project on the exploitation of the marine environment.[1] The study, covering a long time span and set in a period of economic and cultural alterations, makes it possible to analyse how the fishermen of the atoll reacted to upheavals and technical innovations. The length and continuity of this project allowed a detailed study to bring to light problems resulting from the contradictions between traditional mentalities and the use of a new technology.

---

1   Conte, E., 1988. 'La pêche pré-européenne et ses survivances. L'exploitation traditionnelle des ressources marines à Napuka (Tuamotu-Polynésie française)' PhD thesis, Université Paris.

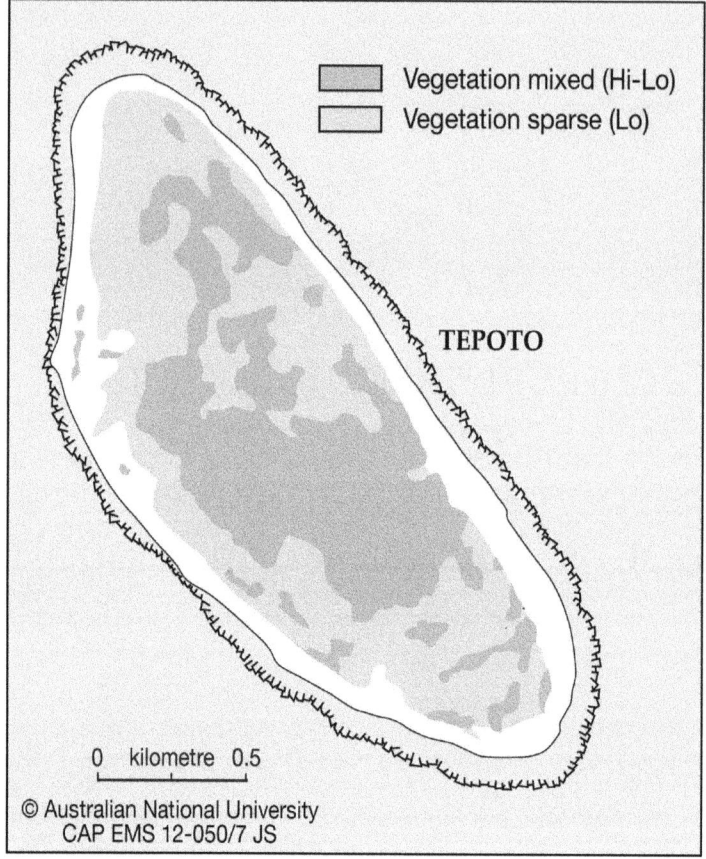

Figure 17: Map of Tepoto
Source: © The Australian National University CAP EMS 12-050/7 JS

Napuka — a Polynesian atoll

Traditional lifestyles in the Tuamotu Archipelago, including material and spiritual culture (except perhaps religious beliefs), were less severely modified post-European contact than in the other island groups of French Polynesia for reasons ranging from navigational hazards to the minimal economic importance of these islands for European colonisers. The eastern atolls, and Napuka and Tepoto in particular, can be considered as extremes in this general situation of isolation and conservatism since, in addition to the usual navigational dangers, their relative distance and isolation from Tahiti meant that European penetration of Napuka and Tepoto occurred later than in the majority of atolls in the area. These islands were not really influenced by Catholicism until after 1878, colonial control was unable to take hold at all until the beginning of the twentieth century, and copra — that determinative source of social and economic transformations — was not exploited until after 1925. For these reasons in Napuka and Tepoto, as in other isles of the eastern Tuamotus, lifestyles that had undergone only slight changes due to Tahitian and European influence persisted until recently. These characteristics motivated the research conducted by K.P. Emory of the Bernice P. Bishop Museum in the 1930s,[2] and were especially conducive to the implementation of the ethno-archaeological approach that was adopted in the 1981 project. This ethno-archaeological research project on the exploitation of the marine environment as part of a doctoral thesis focused on four major research avenues.[3]

---

2   Emory, K.P., 1934. *Tuamotuan Stone Structures*. Bulletin no. 118. Bernice P. Bishop Museum; Emory, K.P., 1947. *Tuamotuan Religious Structures and Ceremonies*. Bulletin no. 191. Honululu: Bernice P. Bishop Museum; Emory, K.P., 1975. *The Material Culture of the Tuamotu Archipelago*. Pacific Anthropological Records 22. Honolulu: Bernice P. Bishop Museum.
3   First of all, it was concerned with the analysis of fishing techniques. Present-day practices, both traditional and modern, were studied and, in some cases, filmed. Fishing techniques that are no longer in use were the subject of oral inquires made among the elderly people and the necessary materials were fabricated for practical research. Sometimes these were redone for the occasion, as with the capture of sharks. In general, for each technique the information collection began with preparation through to the consumption of the catch. The fact that more than 100 fishing techniques were examined allowed, for the first time in French Polynesia, a study of all of the techniques that were traditionally used in the exploitation of an atoll's marine environment.
Secondly, the ecological milieu and fishes were studied. In inserting the whole array of techniques into the ecological milieu of the atoll, we emphasised the fishermen's knowledge of their marine and terrestrial environment, their interpretation of the influence of the moon, the tides and the seasons on the behaviour of fish and on the conditions of their capture.
Thirdly, a general ethno-historical inquiry was undertaken. The techniques mentioned above were placed in their social and cultural contexts as they have evolved since the end of the nineteenth century, the period that has been recorded in historical and ethnological sources. The distribution of products, the types of preparation and the culinary practices applied to them were examined in detail as well as the former rituals intended to ensure good catches, and the forms these rituals took after the introduction of Christianity.
Fourthly, archaeological research was undertaken with the aim of extending the ethnographic inquiry in order to give it historical depth. Thus, considering only the exploitation of the marine world, a given type of mother-of-pearl fishhook that has been discovered may be related to a limited range of techniques and species, but also to a certain period of the year, a kind of fishing organisation (collective, individual, by men or women), culinary practices and rituals. An identical approach was taken for icthyological remains (fishbones), which are the other main types of archaeological evidence relating to fishing. The project also sought to identify all ceremonial sites (*marae*) that ethnographic information indicated were used in ceremonies related to marine life, including the ones for turtles caught during their season. Some of these sites were also the focus of excavations (*marae* Marokau at Napuka and, especially, *marae* Te Tahata at Tepoto) (Conte, E. & Dennison, K.J., 2009. 'Te Tahata. Étude d'un marae de Tepoto (Nord). Archipel des Tuamotu, Polynésie Française'. *Cahiers du CIRAP* 1).

These four complementary approaches make it possible for us to apprehend, to some degree, the adaptive connections linking the particular environment of an atoll with the men who peopled it, and the techniques that allowed them to take advantage of its resources. After looking into the way the exploitation of marine resources affects the daily existence of people, this essay discusses traditional resource management and its underlying logic. Lastly, it provides examples of the negative effects of technological advances on a society in which a traditional conception of man's relation with the natural milieu still persists.

Subsistence cycles and life rhythms

Several natural rhythms of variable duration influence the lives of the atoll's inhabitants as well as their marine prey: seasons, periods of northerly or southerly swells, lunar cycles, tides, and day and night. Other rhythms that are unique to fish impose certain constraints on men, as fishers, and women as gatherers, and offer certain opportunities as to available species and the means with which they can be caught. The conjunction of these elements determines what may be called 'the exploitation cycle of the marine environment'. Atoll dwellers define this cycle in terms of the opposition of two great periods: they distinguish between *tau tapiko* (the best season) from May to November, and *tau ati* (the bad season) from December to March. The period between March and May has no particular name but covers the transition between the end of the bad season and the beginning of the season of abundance. Taking into account the lack of food resources offered by the land, this cycle of marine exploitation is also the true cycle of subsistence of the group and of the individuals whose lives are entwined within this yearly cycle.

Tau tapiko (the best season, from May to November)

This season, which corresponds to the southern winter, is the coolest, driest and sunniest season. At this time of year the southern swells are not strong, the turtles come onshore to lay their eggs, the fish in the lagoon reproduce, and large schools of bonito cruise close to the atoll.

5. TECHNICAL EXPLOITATION AND 'RITUAL' MANAGEMENT OF RESOURCES

From May to September, the men devote themselves to the primary task of capturing turtles, which are highly prized on Napuka and Tepoto for their flesh and their fat. Turtles are taken either by diving into the deep waters close to shore during their mating season, or on land when they come onshore to lay their eggs. The research identified five ancient and modern methods of capture. Until recently, the turtle was the object of special consumption rules and vestiges of ancient rituals, which can be traced to various sources that refer to the era prior to European contact.[4]

In August, the lagoon fish enter their spawning period. This time is known as *tau hanu* (season in which the fish run) because the majority of fish assemble in schools of sometimes considerable size and circulate in the lagoon before moving on to the deep waters offshore where they spawn. The project identified 28 fishing techniques designed to catch these schools of fish as they make their way through the lagoon before heading out to sea. For instance, schools of fish can be caught in the lagoon by means of wreaths made with coconut palms, or with coral traps set in channels leading from the lagoon to the outer sea. The techniques for catching sharks while standing on the reef[5] and to encircle schools of fish that swam on to the reef were also recorded.

From October to December, bonito fishing is carried out from canoes in the deep waters close to shore with a rod and pearl-shell lure. Due to their number, the quality of their flesh and their seasonal character, bonitos are important to the economy of these islands and are also the object of specific alimentary practices and restrictions.[6]

Tau ati (the bad season, from December to March)

Beginning in November/December, the weak swell that normally comes from the south turns northwards and increases. It renders fishing difficult or impossible on the reef or in the deep water near shore. In addition, fish in the open sea and in the lagoon are rare and often underweight. During this period, 48 fishing techniques were utilised: 36 in the lagoon or while standing on the reef platform, and 12 from

---

4   Emory, 1947; Conte, 1988, pp. 50–77.
5   Conte, E., 1987. 'Pêche ancienne au requin à Napuka (Tuamotu)'. *Bulletin de la Société des Études Océaniennes* 238: 13–29.
6   Conte, 1988, pp. 245–90.

canoes offshore. Most of these techniques involve using use baits for fishing on the surface or in deep water (as with tuna). During this bad period, driven by the necessity of finding food, men are prepared to undertake more difficult and less profitable types of fishing. Most of the techniques, whether offshore or on the reef, are carried out on the south side of the atoll, which is protected from the swell. This has an influence on the distribution of settlements at this time of the year.

The gathering of shellfish, in particular giant clams (*Tridacna maxima*), also occurs at this time. Throughout the year, the giant clam is one of the food staples of the Napuka people, but during the bad days it becomes of prime importance and is often the essence of a meal.[7]

The intermediate period (March to May)

Around March, the swell changes direction and once again comes in from the south. It is not as strong as that from the north, and this allows fishing on the reef and offshore. The techniques employed during the bad season are still practiced, but with greater ease. If sea conditions allow, rod fishing on the reef can be productive as the fish live close by, probably because of the calmer seas, and are able to feed better and go through a season in which they have more fat than usual. This more abundant period is also the season of the *makoto*,[8] a fish that is much appreciated in Napuka. Besides techniques used during the off season, 18 techniques of rod and handline fishing are known and utilised for reef fish and *makoto*, offshore as well as in the lagoon.

Traditional management of marine resources

As with most of the atolls of the eastern Tuamotus, Napuka and Tepoto are not rich in fish resources and there are many difficulties encountered in obtaining fish. This relative scarcity raises the issue of whether there existed any real management of the marine environment, including measures to protect and, possibly, renew and augment these resources.

---

7   Conte, 1988, pp. 479–92.
8   Black-spotted perch (*Lutjanus monostignus*).

5. TECHNICAL EXPLOITATION AND 'RITUAL' MANAGEMENT OF RESOURCES

Elderly people on Napuka remember certain coral clusters in the lagoon known as *kahui ngaiere*,[9] which, not many generations ago, constituted reserves of clams where it was possible to take clams for important occasions (collective feasts).[10] The chief (*ariki*) controlled these zones, prohibiting access to them or regulating their exploitation. This is a good example of conservation of an area, but only with respect to deferred exploitation, the coral beds being to clams what holding cages are to fish. Therefore, the principle of *rahui*, which was generalised throughout Polynesia and which is commonly presented as a traditional measure for protecting the environment was actually, in the form described here, a simple way to organise resource exploitation.

It must be pointed out that a zone depopulated by the use of an especially deadly technique (for instance poison) would be left to rest till such time as it was once again colonised by fish. If this form of 'fallowing' appears to be an effort to regulate marine exploitation, it can also be ascribed to the impossibility of obtaining good catches in these areas and not just a true concern for ensuring renewal of the fauna.

In the case of *pati* (milkfish),[11] which lives in the brackish waters at the edge of the lagoon and offshore, interventions are intended to assist in the reproduction of the species. The Napuka fishermen believe that the fish reproduces thanks to its scales and to *vare*, which is a secretion of its skin. Fishermen clean their catches immediately after having caught them, at the edge of the sea, where they throw the scales back into the water so that they give birth to new *pati*. This tentative form of stock management, regardless of whether its underlying assumptions are true, is not the common attitude amongst the islands' fishermen, which is not generally characterised by a sense of proportion or by foresight. Of course, the capture of a number of fish in excess of personal needs explains the necessity to distribute food to those who cannot fish, but cases of waste are frequent during

---

9 *Kahui* has the same value as *rahui*, which is better known in French Polynesia. In the areas known as *kahui ngaiere* it is prohibited to harvest clams (*ngaiere*).
10 In the twentieth century there was no prohibition on the harvesting of clams. Yet people still knew about *kahui ngaiere* and access to those ancient reservations was forbidden to menstruating women who were not allowed to harvest giant clams for fear that the remaining ones would become too lean.
11 Milkfish (*Chanos chanos*).

the season when fish are abundant, as if to compensate for the hardships endured during the southern winter, when resources were few. Contrary to logic, the spawning season is the main time for fishing on the atoll, and the fish are captured even before they have spawned.

The same contradictory logic applies to the harvesting of turtles (*Chelonia mydas*), which occurs during the mating period and, for females, at the time they lay eggs. Fishermen take advantage of this occasion to immobilise the females by turning them upside down on their shell, without waiting for them to lay their eggs. Moreover, the eggs were avidly sought to be eaten. Yet complex rituals existed, in particular for the first turtles of the season, together with certain practices and strict rules of consumption — some of which have persisted until recently — in order to guarantee that the turtles return on a seasonal basis and to ensure their abundance. Therefore, there seems to be a contradiction between the desire and the interventions to obtain numbers of turtles and the conditions of capture, which directly jeopardise the reproduction of the species. This apparent paradox, however, gives insight into the concepts that govern the relationship between men and their marine environment. For the people of the archipelago, there is no causal link between the reproduction of turtles under good conditions and their return the following year — the arrival of turtles, their number and their quality depends solely on the good will of the ancestors. As the ancestors grow turtles in the hereafter, they send them to earth as gifts to their descendants. Prior to the arrival of the missionaries, the rituals that were performed on the *marae* symbolically associated ancestors with the consumption of the first tortoises of the season.[12] If they were satisfied with the strict observance of the rituals, the living had proved themselves worthy descendants who fully merited their gifts. Therefore, through ceremonies, one engaged the ancestors to offer turtles in large quantities. Various more recent practices, less 'pagan' amongst the now devoutly Catholic population, derive from these same concepts. As with turtles, all fish are more or less considered as presents from the ancestors who were the subject of various individual and collective rituals, and were invested with important powers over the world of the living. Therefore, if one can speak of a form of management of marine

---

12   Emory, 1947.

resources amongst the fishermen of these islands, this did not consist in actions taken to manage or protect the environment, but in rituals that today have become 'superstitious' practices.

Environmental protection through measured exploitation is in opposition to another concept of the men of these islands: to make the maximum use of the resources offered by the ancestors ostensibly demonstrates one's interest in them and one's need for them. For instance, if the fishermen who had captured a school of fish let part of it go free to keep only what they strictly needed, would not their gesture be interpreted by the ancestors as contempt towards their gift or proof that it had been too generous? Their fear was that in response, their ancestors would be deeply hurt by their descendants' attitude and might deprive them forever of those species of fish for which they had shown such little appreciation.

Therefore, in order to get more of a marine resource, it is necessary to harvest all that is available at any one time; the intensive or, even, excessive exploitation of marine resources is, then, paradoxically viewed as a determinative factor in the renewal of resources.

As far as we know, however, for all these concepts and acts of extreme predation, there has not been any significant decrease in resources in the past, or even the disappearance of certain species due to overfishing. Such changes have occurred only recently. It is also significant that these ritual practices in regard to the marine environment were not an attempt to preserve men from the disasters of diminished supply, in fact, they purported to bring about abundance, conserve the taste and quality of fish, and ensure their return the following year. One must remember that the limited needs of a reduced population and the relatively weak destructive capacities of these traditional fishing techniques have never placed the marine environment in peril. As the available resources have not been depleted, the practical management of the said stock did not prove necessary.

Damage to the milieu and men

Two examples will demonstrate how this predatory mentality resulted in detrimental consequences when it was underwritten by the more efficient technology introduced by Europeans.

In the 1930s the method of catching turtles at sea with bare hands (*tango*) was replaced by a method using a metal hook (*takatu*), which the men would attach to the turtle as it started to dive towards the bottom of the ocean. The hook was tied to a rope and allowed the fisherman, once he returned to his canoe, to haul up the animal to the surface. As this new method requires less strength, breath and know-how than the traditional one, more people on the atoll were able to employ it. The number of captures increased considerably, all the more so since this type of fishing could be done from a canoe. A fisherman was now able to catch up to four turtles, which he would attach to the canoe as he captured them. In the 1950s, lifestyle and attitude changes resulted in transgressions of the consumption rules for turtles, especially that of sharing with the entire population. A merchant from Tahiti encouraged people to sell turtle meat and, with the introduction of this commercial aspect, an increasing number of turtles were caught. It was probably as a reaction to this excessive fishing that, since 1955, turtles have practically deserted Napuka and Tepoto and now reproduce on more hospitable islands. Today, even in the best years, captures are limited to only a few turtles.

The fishermen propose other reasons for the disappearance of the turtles. They trace the origin of this phenomenon, described as a catastrophe, to the abandonment of former customs, which has caused the ancestors to cease bestowing their gifts,[13] or to sorcery practices attributed to the population of the neighbouring atoll, or else to a curse placed by a visiting Catholic missionary who, in the heat of a dispute with the community, threatened to cause all turtles to disappear from the island.

Through these explanations, one can ascertain that, for these men, the causes of abundance or dearth are not of a material nature, or man-made, but of a spiritual and religious order and determined by supernatural forces. The mentality of the fishermen who first made use of metal hooks did not prepare them to foresee such disastrous consequences. Their habit of exploiting the environment with little concern for its depletion, their management of resources through rituals alone, the sense of excitement created by new fishing facilities and greed drove them into a hitherto unknown situation, which they perceive in non-material terms even today.

---

13   According to the fishermen, individual rather than collective consumption, as well as the sale of turtle meat, represented a considerable departure from traditions.

5. TECHNICAL EXPLOITATION AND 'RITUAL' MANAGEMENT OF RESOURCES

More recently, the use of the underwater spear gun has also had debatable effects. As underwater fishing is linked with sports requiring certain physical characteristics, young people have turned away from the practice of several fishing methods, especially the deep-line fishing that is traditionally carried out where the seaward edge of the reef drops off into deeper water. For these young people, the spear gun made it possible to catch several types of fish easily, quickly and using a single technique whereas, in the past, several methods were required to obtain a similar catch. The gradual displacement of such fishing techniques by a better performing one is a normal process if taken from the point of view of technical progress, even though one may regret the resulting loss of memory of ancient methods.

More significantly, underwater fishing, which causes fish to bleed profusely, has attracted many sharks to the atolls. This endangers the fishermen themselves and hinders or even prevents certain types of fishing in deep waters (for instance tuna fishing) as the catches are almost always ripped away by the sharks even before they are brought to the surface. The fish that are captured by these techniques are generally of larger size and better quality than the ones caught with a spear gun and, thus, inhabitants of the atolls suffer indirect harm from this practice.

Easy and seductive technical innovations sometimes have negative consequences for those who were ill-prepared to foresee all their implications. In addition, technical transformations induce a new relationship with animals and, beyond that, a change in the way that men view themselves in nature. With regard to the turtle, catching and subduing it, bringing it to the surface, and restraining it on the ground, implies a close fight, a struggle between equals the outcome of which remains uncertain. The fisherman has some form of intimacy with the animal, and a great sensitivity to its reactions. Indeed, man's rapport with the turtle — a prey to be killed — was paradoxically enough in the sphere of affectivity: it was offered to him by his ancestors and it was described as gentle-natured and feminine, regardless of its sex.

Moreover, in several settings, turtles were identified with fishermen's wives and were, thus, to be treated with due care. It should be noted that the positions (*tango*) used to keep control of the animal were named like the postures of a man lying on a woman (Figure 18). Thus, in gripping a turtle, the fisherman mimicked having sexual intercourse with his wife and, by the same token, acted like a male turtle impregnating the female. This form of symbiosis with the turtle is a compelling illustration of man's broader relationship with nature.

The adoption of new fishing techniques has shattered the deep empathy with the animal. The use of metal hooks has made the struggle unequal, tipping it in favour of man; it is no longer a man-to-man fight, as it were. The animal, now an inferior at the fisherman's mercy, has been demeaned. Flesh-piercing hooks are a form of violence that is not in the least reflected in ancient methods of bodily capture. The new aggressiveness foreshadowed the arrows of the spear gun.

Physical distance from the animal and unequal struggle has created an affective distance, and the memory of the past sacredness of the turtle has diminished in the minds of people who have turned to Christianity. The turtle has become little more than a prey, a source of meat. It is hardly surprising, then, that individual consumption of shared or sold pieces of flesh has supplanted the collective consumption of an animal that was once viewed as the ancestors' gift to the community. The export of turtle meat from Napuka to Tahiti, as has occurred, would have once been unthinkable.

Technical changes have a broad impact on society, be it on material practices or ideas. In small island communities, their effects are sometimes harmful, especially when innovations brought in from outside conflict with traditional usages and conceptions. Traditional methods of managing resources, whether they are practical (as with the conservation of giant clams) or based on alimentary taboos or rituals, are no longer observed these days. Conversion to Catholicism and opening up to the twentieth-century world has gradually, albeit at an uneven pace, eroded the old ways of thinking and acting. The broad transformation of society encompasses technical changes and the shedding of some taboos and practices as part of a process in which the people of the archipelago are indissolubly both the agents and the products.[14]

---

14 I would like to thank my friends, Pr. Pat Kirch and Dr Léopold Mu Si Yan for translating the French version of this text into English.

5. TECHNICAL EXPLOITATION AND 'RITUAL' MANAGEMENT OF RESOURCES

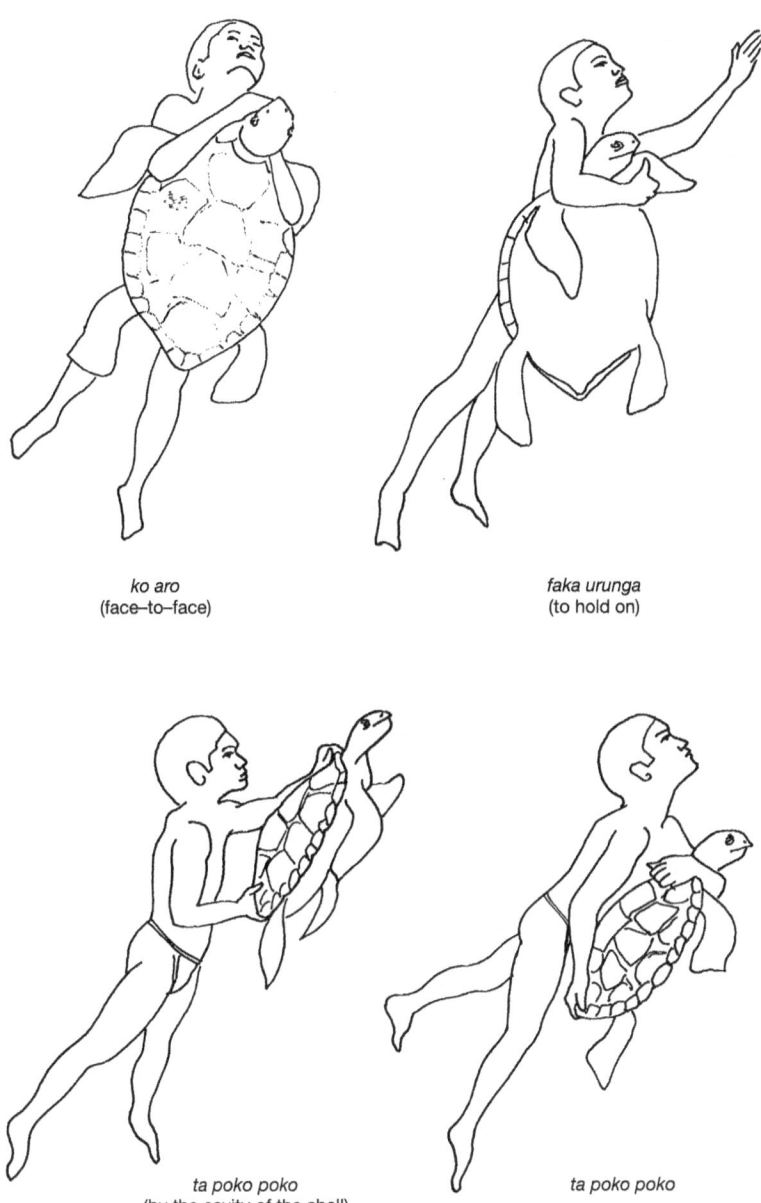

ko aro
(face–to–face)

faka urunga
(to hold on)

ta poko poko
(by the cavity of the shell)

ta poko poko

Figure 18: Various turtle-catching methods used by divers (the two in the lower part are variants with a similar name)
Source: Conte, 1988, Part 2, Vol. 1, p. 24

6

The law of *rahui* in the Society Islands

Tamatoa Bambridge

Scholars consider *tapu* and the *rahui* to be fundamental institutions in pre-European societies across all parts of the Polynesian Triangle.[1] Yet very little is known about them in contemporary Polynesia as far as legal and organisational issues are concerned. *Tapu* is a term that signifies an object, person or location that was 'marked', 'contained', 'restricted', or 'put aside'. In one sense, *tapu* is the state of a person, a thing, a place where *mana* (divine power) is present. A second meaning signifies 'forbidden to certain categories of persons in certain contexts'. This term may have been translated as 'sacred', but we need to question this assertion given that Western intellectual schema posing oppositions between sacred and profane elements cannot explain categories of the Polynesian cosmogonies.[2] If *tapu* has been

---

1 Smith, J., 1974. *Tapu Removal in Maori Religion*, Memoir no. 40. Wellington: The Polynesian Society; Best, E., 1904. 'Notes on the custom of Rahui, its application and manipulation, as also its supposed powers, its rites, invocations and superstitions'. *Journal of the Polynesian Society* 13(2): 83–88; Oliver, D., 1974. *Ancient Tahitian Society*. 3 vols. Honolulu: The University Press of Hawai'i; Devatine, F., 1992. *Tapu et Rahui*. Assises de la Recherche en Polynésie française, Document dactylographié, non publié. Papeete: Académie tahitienne.
2 Rigo, B., 2004. *Altérité polynésienne ou les métamorphoses de l'espace-temps*. Paris: CNRS Editions.

extensively analysed in the secondary literature,[3] it is not the case with *rahui*. *Rahui* generally refers to the ability of a chief to order a *tapu* on a specific place or a particular resource, for a limited period of time.[4]

The relative wealth of descriptions of *rahui* in primary sources and comparatively limited attention in secondary modern sources has resulted in the misrepresentation of *rahui* and related concepts such as *mana* and *tapu*, which, in turn, has resulted in an overly structural understanding of Polynesian sociopolitical chieftainship. Theoretical approaches advocated by Sahlins,[5] and more recently by Hviding,[6] imply a model of chieftainship based on a structural and functional model of society. On the contrary, the careful analysis of primary sources from the Society Islands shows a more varied use of *tapu* and *rahui* that depends on contexts and network relationships of one chief ramage with others and across sociopolitical groups. For these reasons, it is useful to return to the primary sources in order to fill the gaps and revise modern representations of *rahui*.

Rahui is often represented as having a supreme authority.[7] Fraselle[8] and Oliver[9] described — in Aotearoa New Zealand and Tahiti respectively — some manifestations of *rahui* during the nineteenth century. The traditions of *rahui* were as rich and diverse as the different regions of Polynesia. For example, in the Society Islands alone, it has been noted that a leader would establish a *rahui* on the *marae*

---

3   Hocart A.M., 1914. 'Mana'. *Man* 14: 97–101; Firth, R., 1940. 'The analysis of mana: an empirical approach'. *Journal of the Polynesian Society*, 49: 483–510; Keesing, R.M., 1984. 'Rethinking mana'. *Journal of Anthropological Research* 40(1): 137–56; Hooper S.J.P., 1996. 'Who are the chiefs? Chiefship in Lau, Eastern Fiji'. In R. Feinberg & K. Watson-Gegeo (eds), *Leadership and Change in the Western Pacific: Essays presented to Sir Raymond Firth on the Occasion of his Ninetieth Birthday*, LES Monographs on Social Anthropology 66. Athlone Press, pp. 239–71; Shore, B., 1989. 'Mana and Tapu: a new synthesis'. In A. Howard & R. Borofsky (eds), *Developments in Polynesian Ethnology*. Honolulu: University of Hawai'i Press, pp. 137–74; Rainbird, P., 2003. 'Taking the Tapu. Defining Micronesia by absence'. *Journal of the Pacific History* 38(2): 237–50.
4   Oliver, D., 1974.
5   Sahlins, M.D., 1958. *Social Stratification in Polynesia*. Seattle: University of Washington Press, pp. 140–49.
6   Hviding, E,. 1996. *Guardians of Marovo Lagoon: Practice, Place, and Politics in Maritime Melanesia*. Honolulu: University of Hawai'i Press.
7   Ellis, W., 1829. *Polynesian Researches*. vol. 2. London: Fisher, Son and Jackson; Morrison, J., 1966. *Le Journal de James Morrison, second maître à bord le la Bounty*. Traduit de l'anglais par B. JAUNEZ. Paris: Musée de l'Homme.
8   Fraser, 1892. 'Notes and queries'. *Journal of the Polynesian Society* 1(4): 273–76.
9   Oliver, D., 1974.

(temple) on a child's birth,[10] after a bloody war, or during ceremonies such as *pai atua* (god worship) and *taurua ari'i* (chief feast). On these occasions, the production of common resources was brought to a standstill for a short period. According to French nineteenth-century ethnographer De Bovis,[11] the *rahui* embodied a new form of *tapu* in the Society Islands. The English missionary William Ellis,[12] however, recalled that *tapu* operated on a spiritual and religious level whereas the *rahui* applied mostly to material elements.

The breadth and diversity of the traditions of *rahui* makes it interesting and necessary to address the phenomenon more closely, especially in the field of legal anthropology.

The literature involving the Society Islands is often vague and contradictory in regard to *rahui*. How the population came to justify the implementation of a *rahui* on a specific territory, and how leaders brought legitimacy to the sanctions they imposed are still unclear. As to the decision to impose a *rahui*, the majority of primary sources attribute the responsibility to the *ari'i* (chief). These sources include published observations made by nineteenth-century European witnesses,[13] sources based on recollections of traditional authorities,[14] and secondary works that utilise references from both of the former categories.[15]

The purpose of this chapter is to describe, in legal anthropological terms, the numerous traditions of pre-European *rahui* within various contexts. Three difficulties arise in producing such a categorisation.

---

10 Adams, H., 1964. *Mémoires d'Ari'i Tamai*, Paris: Publication de la Société des Océanistes no. 12, Musée de l'Homme, p. 27.
11 de Bovis, E., 1978. *Etat de la société tahitienne à l'arrivée des européens*. Publication no. 4. Tahiti: Société des Études Océaniennes.
12 Ellis, 1829.
13 Rodriguez, M., 1995. *Les Espagnols à Tahiti (1772–1776)*. Publication de la société des Océanistes no. 45. Paris: Musée de l'Homme; Ellis, 1829; de Bovis, 1978; Tyerman, D., & Bennet, G., 1832. *Journal of Travel and Voyages by Rev. Bennet and Tyerman*. 3 vols. Boston: Croker and Brewster; Davies, J., 1851. *A Tahitian and English Dictionary with Introductory Remarks on the Polynesian Language and a Short Grammar of the Tahitian Dialect*. Tahiti, printed at the London Missionary Society's Press; Morrison, 1966.
14 Adams, 1964; Henry, T., 1928. *Ancient Tahiti*, Bulletin no. 48. Honolulu: Bernice P. Bishop Museum; Pomare, T., 1971. *Mémoires de Marau Taaroa, dernière reine de Tahiti, traduits par sa fille, la princesse Takau Pomare*. Publication de la Société des Océanistes no. 27. Paris: Musée de l'Homme.
15 Handy, E.S.C., 1971b (1923). *The Native Culture in the Marquesas*. Bulletin no. 9. Bernice P. Bishop Museum, Honolulu, New York: Kraus Reprint Co; Oliver, 1974.

First, many reports were based on romanticised stories rather than practical observations of everyday life. Moreover, in these accounts, *rahui* was described as a set of rules laid out and obeyed uniformly, instead of as a process defined by enactment and subject to important variation across sociopolitical groups. Second, reports from the early period of European contact were influenced by the historical context in which the authors participated. The most significant examples may be those of Takau Pomare,[16] the daughter of Pomare IV, the last queen who ruled Tahiti and its dependences in the late nineteenth century, and the English missionary William Ellis,[17] a member of the London Missionary Society. In many instances, both describe the *rahui* as they experienced it as a monopoly of the *ari'i* (chief). Third, the researcher is challenged by the abstract and somewhat confusing descriptions of *rahui*, so that it is difficult to grasp the reality of the 'living law'.[18] The temptation to describe the *rahui* in terms of English common law (especially in the descriptions made in the early nineteenth century), and French civil law as interpreted by the high judiciary court in the second half of the nineteenth century, contradicts the description of *rahui* as a process determined by enactment of the chief and sociopolitical groups.

There has been a major paradigm shift in legal anthropology towards analysing law as a process[19] instead of a static system of rules, especially among oral and non-centralised societies where legal pluralism was part of the social structure.[20] Prior to European colonisation, with the notable exception of Tonga, Polynesian society did not know any centralisation of power, even if the possibility was a preoccupation of certain Polynesian chiefs. Legal pluralism did not exist because of the presence of a centralised state power in the late nineteenth century, but existed within and beyond such centralised polities because of the

---

16   Pomare, 1971.
17   Ellis, 1829, vol. 2, p. 557.
18   Ehrlich, E., 2001 (1913). *Fundamental Principles of the Sociology of Law*. New Brunswick: Transaction Publishers.
19   Moore, S.F., 1978. 'Law and social change: the semi-autonomous field as an appropriate subject of study'. In L. Nader (ed.), *Law as Process. An Anthropological Approach*. London: Routledge and Kegan Paul, pp. 54–81; Griffith, J., 1986. 'What is legal pluralism?' *Journal of Legal Pluralism* 24: 1–53.
20   Bambridge, T., 2005. 'Cosmogonies et juridicité en Océanie'. In *Anthropologies et Droits, état des savoirs*. Paris: Association française d'Anthropologie du Droit, PUF, pp. 392–95; Bambridge, Tamatoa, 2009. *La terre dans l'archipel des îles Australes. Étude du pluralisme juridique et culturel en matière foncière*. Institut de Recherche pour le Développement (IRD) et Aux Vents des îles.

plural authorities that continued to enforce a set of rules and sanctions that might defer from one sociopolitical group to another and according to status of the sociopolitical group or groups involved.[21]

Most of the literature introduces the *rahui* as the exclusive power of a leader. Yet, in order to contextualise the tradition of *rahui* properly, one must take into account the structure of a non-centralised society, the social organisation, the ramage and lineages as fundamental sociopolitical institutions for understanding Oceanian societies.[22] In the specific context of the Society Islands, it is important to take into account the influence of these ramages through the study of the extended families (the *opu*), which were often affiliated to one another. Thus, each leader could have their own form of *rahui* established in various designated territories. This important point has *implications* for core debates in Oceanic anthropology on leadership, as it moderates a structural perspective on chiefly leadership defined as 'conical clans', where absolute differentiation of the eldest brother from his younger brothers is recognised.[23]

After discussing the authority of the *rahui* on land (part I) and at sea (part II) in the Society Islands, we will analyse the extent to which the *rahui* seems to have been a ramified institution (part III), that is to say, an institution managed by a plurality of statuses, including the lesser status category of this Polynesian society: the *manahune*.

Rahui: A monopoly of the *ari'i*?

Discussing the term *mana* in a broad sense, Keesing[24] indicates that it signifies efficiency of endeavour derived from divine origin, the capacity to produce an effect that goes beyond human contingencies. *Mana* is associated with the power of the chief.[25] Shore specifies that for understanding a concept like *mana*, one also needs to understand

---

21 Bambridge, 2009.
22 Firth, R., 1965. *Essays on Social Organization and Values.* Monograph on Social Anthropology no. 28. University of London, London School of Economics: The Athlone Press; Petersen, G., 2007. 'Hambruch's colonial narrative.' *Journal of Pacific History* 42(3): 317–30.
23 Sahlins, M.D., 1958. *Social Stratification in Polynesia.* Seattle: University of Washington Press, p. 150.
24 Keesing, 1984.
25 Firth, 1940, p. 508.

related concepts such as *tapu* and *noa*.[26] Neither Keesing, Shore nor Firth mentions the concept of *rahui*, despite its obvious importance in the primary sources. In all cases, it is not clear how the concepts of *mana* and *tapu* are enacted across sociopolitical groups and related to higher or minor chiefs. For example, Firth calls for an empirical approach in the analysis of *mana*,[27] but most of his work was done with the *ariki* (the highest statute of chief) on Tikopia, in such a way that it is never clear which chiefs are concerned with *mana*.[28]

The notion of *rahui* is usually classified with other sacred notions of the Polynesian cosmogony such as *raa* or *mo'a*.[29] According to Oliver, the word *rahui* is used to 'to denote the restrictions, usually spiritually sanctioned, periodically laid on hogs, fruit, fish and so forth, for conservation and other purposes'.[30] D. Oliver insists on the political character of the institution rather than on it having an ecological purpose to preserve resources.[31]

In her mother's memoirs, Takau Pomare points out that the earliest Tahitian traditions about *rahui* concern Tetunae, who was the first legislator; indeed, he was called 'Tetunae, the legislator'.[32] Pomare recalls his precepts of *rahui*, transmitted to her mother:

> All that is rahui must not be eaten: the turtle, the *urupiti* [a large fish], all the big fish of the sea and the lagoon, breast and tenderloin of pork, the first fruits of earth. All of this is reserved. These foods are banned. The *rahui*, prohibition of food for the *arii*, must be honoured by all, except one who disobeys will be punished by death.

Actually, Pomare aimed at establishing the genealogical history of her family in relation to Tetunae and, at the same time, to underline that the *rahui* was an institution where the *ari'i* had exclusive rights. Nevertheless, her recollection does not specify whether the authority of the *rahui* encompassed all the territories or only those linked to the *ari'i* family members.

---

26   Shore, 1989.
27   Firth, 1940, pp. 482–507.
28   See also Petersen G., 1999. 'Sociopolitical rank and conical clanship in the Caroline Islands'. *Journal of the Polynesian Society* 108(4): 367–410; 368–69 for Micronesia.
29   Davies, 1851; Ellis, 1829.
30   Oliver, 1974, pp. 65–67.
31   Oliver, 1974, p. 1073.
32   Pomare, 1971, pp. 98–100.

According to the American historian Henry Adams, who first came to Tahiti in 1891 and recorded the memories of the elderly female chief Arii Taimai:

> Tavi's direct and full authority extended only over his own chiefery of Tautira, but by rank or courtesy, through his family connection or his influence, it extended over the whole island, and only Eimeo or Moorea was exempt. A *rahui* was a form of corvee to which other great chiefs seldom willingly submitted; but even if a chief were himself anxious to avoid a war, which was the penalty of breaking it, his wife or his sisters or his relations were always ready to urge him to conspire against it.[33]

This description is interesting since it portrays a complex process that goes beyond the idea, often prevalent in current literature, that the *rahui* was the exclusive monopoly of the *ari'i* or even of a secondary chief. Moreover, this passage seems to imply that no one could impose a *rahui* outside the territory he directly controlled. In this instance Tavi, the chief of Tautira, established a *rahui* on the entire island of Tahiti thanks to his family ties. At that time, the nearby island of Moorea was ruled by an *ari'i* of equal status called Marama. The issue of kinship was not always clear, all the more so because extended families had numerous members, including some with equal social status and therefore potentially contestable rights and obligations.

Although Takau Pomare described the *rahui* as an institution for the exclusive benefit of the *ari'i*, she notes that the implementation was more complex:

> The *rahui* of the broken branch prelude the *rahui* of the products of land. When the *uru*, the fruit of the breadfruit tree, had reached full maturity, administrators informed the *arii* who communicated it to the priest. This latter decided the day of *avari* (its end). Criers, carrying lighted torches, went from house to house to make the announcement, and as soon as the torches were burned out, delegations of men gathered around the feet of the breadfruit. They did not take the first fruits, but broke the branches or took a couple of these fruits and brought it as a special offering to the *arii* and god represented by the *arii* and the high priest.[34]

---

33   Adams, 1964, pp. 27–30.
34   Pomare, 1971, p. 100.

In other words, while Pomare notes the idea that the *rahui* was declared or lifted by the *ari'i*, she also describes a procedure that required the consent of several other authorities such as 'administrators' and a 'priest'.

According to Handy, the criers mentioned by Pomare are the *vea* (messengers of the *ari'i*).[35] Nevertheless, Pomare's descriptions are ambiguous. Does what she describe apply to the exclusive territory of a chief or to several larger territories, including those on which the chief has indirect control, as Adams maintains? The sources remain coherent on the first issue, but diverge on the second.

The idea of a plurality of authority in the establishment of a *rahui* is mostly recognised by the eighteenth-century English beachcomber J. Morrison. An unusually astute and perceptive foreign observer of Tahitian culture, his testimony is all the more important and relevant as he was the direct witness of the traditions he described:

> The chiefs, *toofa* and *raatira*, may declare at their pleasure the *rahui* on such and such provisions, livestock, fish, within their jurisdiction and where they consider necessary to prevent excessive consumption of pigs, they decree a *rahui* in the entire district. The King may decree the *rahui* in several districts and sends instructions accordingly to the chiefs, *toofa* and *raatira* to prohibit the consumption or transportation of such or such food in such and such districts or properties for a specified time.[36]

Morrison's words seem more explicit: all types of leaders (*ari'i*, *toofa*, *raatira*) may declare a *rahui* only on territories under their control. The implementation of a *rahui* on territories they did not directly control required the consent of other leaders who also directly controlled their own territory. This testimony concurs with that of Adams[37] and casts doubt on Takau Pomare's assertion about the *rahui* as the exclusive privilege of the *ari'i*.[38] Besides, the social organisation in which the *rahui* was implemented is congruent with what we know about land tenure in Polynesian societies in the pre-European period.[39]

---

35   Handy, 1971, p. 74.
36   Morrison, 1966, p. 161.
37   Adams, 1964.
38   Pomare, 1971.
39   Oliver, 1974; Crocombe, R., 1987. *Land Tenure in the Pacific*. 3rd edn. Suva, Fiji: University of the South Pacific; Oliver, D., 1989. *Oceania: The Native Culture of Australia and the Pacific Islands*. University of Hawai'i Press.

As a matter of fact, the idea that the *ari'i* had a monopoly on control over land — an idea often defended by informants with high political status in traditional Polynesian society (priest or *ari'i*) — appears to have its origin in European colonial ideology. Missionaries and colonial administrators apprehended Polynesian society through the categories of the European feudal model of land tenure. The theory of the 'eminent domain', taken from ancient French law, was a tool with which to substitute the theoretical power of Polynesian chiefs on land for the power of the colonial state. When this reform was completed, the state could establish individualised tenure, which opened the way for fragmented ownership among local and absentee landowners.[40] Last but not least, it is noteworthy that Adams[41] and Morrison[42] evoke the tradition of the *rahui* in which only the highest ranked individuals of society are involved. A lower social status, such as the *manahune*, is omitted. As suggested below, this omission is not justified in the traditions.

Before proceeding further with analysis of sources on *rahui*, it is vital to establish the real meaning of the notion of 'territory'. In particular, are marine territories included in territories where the *rahui* is implemented? What are the specificities of the *rahui* in this type of territory?

The *rahui* of the lagoon: What are the differences?

As paradoxical as it may seem, marine tenure has not received much attention in the anthropology of Oceania, whereas it was and remains a major concern of local populations.[43] In particular, the question of the nature of user rights associated with lagoons has not been addressed in detail, as compared to research into user rights on land.

Did the same rules of the *rahui* have to be observed on land and at sea? If so, were there any differences between the two types of territory? Customary law on cultural continuity between land and sea

---

40   Bambridge, 2009.
41   Adams, 1964.
42   Morrison, 1966.
43   Hvding, 1996.

may lead us to conclude that the appropriation of land was enacted the same way as that of the lagoon. In reality, however, there were distinct characteristics between the two types of territory. The lagoon might be seen only as a natural resource — as would be the case for a coconut tree or a pig — and, therefore, customary norms might only allow some privilege in guardianship and access. This is a significant distinction that emphasises the larger framework of existing rights of use involving land and sea. Were these rights similar? Did they have the same effect? Was there any continuity between the laws of appropriation or were there discontinuities between the two areas so that the rights of use on land might differ to those at sea?

Morrison describes the establishment of a *rahui* on the lagoon during the visit of some foreigners:

> The rahui on reefs is indicated by placing shrubs along the forbidden part with small pieces of cloth and from their appearance no one would dare to fish for fear of losing their land but they can fish with nets, hooks, etc … in their canoes, the beach is prohibited if they can use their boat, under any pretext. But this only happens when the royal flags go through a territory.[44]

Various reports can be found as to the implementation of *rahui* on the reef or on the coast.

Certain principles seem to have operated, depending on the context. On the one hand, a *rahui* on fish would not differ from a *rahui* imposed on pigs, for they were considered a resource in both cases. The status of the coral reef was more ambiguous. Was the coral reef viewed as a prolongation of land, or as a natural resource? In this respect, Ellis's report is informative in its description of the territorial categorisation of the lagoon:

> if the proprietors of the land on the coast wish to preserve the fish of the adjacent sea, they *rahui*, or restrict, the ground, by fixing up a pole on the reef or shore, with a bunch of bamboo leaves attached to it. By this mark it is understood that the fish are tabu, and fishing prohibited; and no person will trespass on these parts, without the consent of the proprietor.[45]

---

44   Morrison, 1966, p. 167.
45   Ellis, 1829, p. 286.

According to Ellis's description, the portion of sea close to land was considered the same way as if it was land. Nevertheless, in a traditional Polynesian context, it would be incorrect to speak of 'property rights' in a Western sense, as far as land and sea are concerned. Actually, the type of ownership that some Polynesians could enjoy refers to some privileged control or mastering of land or of a resource. Therefore, it appears that the coral reef should be treated as both a resource and as a marine area subject to certain appropriations. Indeed, the reef appears to be a resource in the sense that it contained crustaceans and fish. By analogy, the reef is no different than a tree that bears fruit and could have a *rahui* placed on it. Furthermore, the reef was bounded (whereas the tree was marked). According to Morrison:

> The *rahui* on reefs is indicated by placing shrubs along the forbidden part with small pieces of cloth. Thus, the prohibition of these resources took some general rather than some specific character: all resources located in the designated area were subject to a *rahui*. Finally, according to several testimonies, the political status of the person who implemented the *rahui* might vary from the *arii* to the mere landholder. In both case it extends to the beach.[46]

There is limited detail on the establishment of a *rahui* at sea and the sanctions behind this process, but it is likely that there were some local differences in both respects. In some cases, a *rahui* could apply to everyone, including the leaders of the extended family, while in other cases, it excluded outsiders or it could be exempt from it by individuals who got the chief's permission. As far as sanctions involving a marine territory are concerned, some of their descriptions are similar to those applied to land.[47] In some instances, the chief's influence or coercive physical power could suffice to obtain compliance, but it is likely that the chief's intimate or tutelary spirit was frequently invoked. A second respect in which limitations were put upon fishing involved the *rahui* that was imposed throughout whole districts on specific occasions or during certain periods of the year (*taurua arii, pae atua*). For example, some restriction could be imposed on some subsistence activities — such as fishing — during the mourning period for a person of high status. Indeed, Pomare recalls a prohibition on fishing bonito and

---

46   Morrison, 1966.
47   Morrison, 1966; Ellis, 1829.

albacore at the beginning of the open-sea season until several different rituals had been performed.[48] Infringing such a *rahui* would result in individuals being subjected to political or religious sanctions.

As previously noted, *rahui* on land and at sea embodied several kinds of rights, depending on the chief's status. The decision of a leader to remove a *rahui* on resources implied organisational changes that affected the labour structure. The leader was not the sole decision-maker concerning *rahui*. His followers and other chiefs had to be included in the numerous debates. Some of the literature on the Society Islands intimates that the *rahui* at sea might not be as different as the one on land. Albacore, coral reefs and the first fish could be subject to *rahui*, as well as the whole lagoon in terms of territory delimited by poles on the reef or on the shore.

The political economy of Tahiti was based on a ramified organisation. A chieftainship could encompass one or more ramages. The elder of the senior ramage was normally the chief, not only of his ramage, but of the whole chieftainship. But, as a ramified organisation, each elder of each ramage was recognised as chief over its own extended family on its own territory. Such recognition implies a recognition of distinctive rights over the control of the land and the lagoon attached to its territory. Among these rights, one must emphasise the power to implement a *rahui* on the land and the marine territory of its ramage. Such use rights were associated with *rahui* held by ramages, and were more relative than absolute. On certain occasions and in different contexts, a major chief may have formal rights of *rahui* on a territory he does not control directly (in terms of the first fruit or the first fish). On other occasions, the right to implement a *rahui* by a lesser chief of ramages was independent from the privilege of the major chief. Such rights did not only concern land rights but also lagoon territories, as part of the overall territory controlled by ramages in a context of overlapping duties and responsibilities.

This review of the traditions of *rahui* in a dynamic perspective makes it clear that *rahui* could be implemented by a plurality of statuses and not only by the mere authority of the *ari'i*. Another issue, however,

---

48 Pomare, 1971.

involves the rights of individuals of lower political status — especially the *manahune* — and asks whether these groups had any right to impose a *rahui* on their territory.

The *rahui*: A ramified institution?

At least two major questions have still not been addressed concerning the status of those able to impose and police *rahui*. First, what were the relationships between *rahui* and the main territorial structure? Second, what were the relationships between *rahui* and the main familial structure? Answering these questions reveals the extent to which *rahui* conformed to each social stratum — see the structural concept expressed by Lévi-Strauss[49] — or, on the contrary, defied all hierarchies, therefore conforming to the concept of society as one large network.

Morrison's names for territorial divisions — districts (*fenua*), subdistricts (chief shares, *patu*) and lesser divisions (squire shares, *bahooe* — probably *rahui*) — raises the issue of the relationships between the types of territories and *rahui*.[50] It is important to note that the former (the territorial division in Morrison's terminology) referred to the residential centre of an extended family gathered around the *marae*, and the latter (the lesser divisions in Morrison's terminology) referred to a territorial treaty — including land and lagoon — subject to one's individual control. The former could be a political and religious centre whereas the latter could be a territorial division. None of the available sources contradict the idea that both elements might represent two different kinds of territorial units. Consequently, the *rahui* might have been established on a tract of land and lagoon — the former with no households — in areas that were not subject to unitary control.

To better understand Tahitian *rahui*, it is important to consider the relations between extended families and the *rahui*. In *Social Stratification in Polynesia*, Sahlins considered that 'every brother is differentiated to every other in accordance with the respective order

---

49 Lévi-Strauss, C., 1958. *Anthropologie structurale*. Paris: Plon.
50 Morrison, 1966.

of birth'.[51] In such a view, the *rahui* is implemented by the chiefs according to the 'closeness of their relationship to the main line of descent'.[52] Oliver tackled this question by trying to figure out the extent to which the normative right to *rahui* affected the relations between extended families affiliated to others and assembled around a *marae* and the *rahui*.[53] Oliver asserts:

> Let us suppose, that all four units (ABCD) are subdivisions of what was formerly a single kin-congregation, whose ancestral 'temple' was marae A ... In the first place, I believe that the chief of kin-congregation A would have had the right of *rahui* over B, C, and D as well. Also, I am inclined to believe, but by no means certain, that in term of the ideology of consanguinity, this right of *rahui* was normatively executed through 'channels', that is, when imposing a general *rahui*, the chief of A included B by asking the latter's chief to impose it, and not by direct order to B's whole congregation.[54]

If Oliver's general assumption about the process of social organisation and the *rahui* as a ramified institution is accepted, many questions still remain. First of all, little evidence is available as to the obligation for a chief — for example, A — to go through another chief — say B — when imposing a *rahui* on a specific chief — say D. Since Polynesian social organisation is, in practice, functioning through a network of relationships, we may wonder whether or not *rahui* rights paralleled consanguineous relationships. Actually, in some instances, chief A could impose a *rahui* on chief C's territory but not on chief B's even though chief A's own ancestor may have been an 'elder brother' of B, 'which among blood relations would have embodied some authority over a younger brother'.[55] According to Oliver's hypothesis on social and political hierarchy, it is clear that high status in Polynesian society involved clever negotiations between privileged individuals in order to impose a *rahui* on a territory — at sea or on land — they did not control directly. According to Petersen, Sahlins is implicitly conscious of this issue observing that 'a certain inconsistency in the application

---

51 Sahlins, 1958, pp. 147–49.
52 Sahlins, 1958, pp. 147–49.
53 Oliver, 1974, pp. 650–52.
54 Oliver, 1974, p. 651.
55 Oliver, 1974, pp. 650–52.

of the rule of stratification'.[56] As a result, 'it does not follow that all members of the highest standing large ramage outrank all members of all other ramages'.[57]

Therefore, the *rahui* was less based on a ramified social organisation than on a network of consanguineous relationships and depended on political hierarchy, various local circumstances and opportunity for decision making.

The above discussion on the institution of *rahui* implies a conceptual model of authority over the control of land, sea and resources based on a network of privileged consanguineous relationships where political status is the basis of the network. Petersen's analysis of power and kava use in the Caroline Islands shares this position. Because of cross-cutting principles of rank 'the character of political power in Pohnpeian society is vague, ambivalent, contradictory, and virtually impossible to observe'.[58]

Utilisation of this non-structural approach to consanguineous relationships, contradicts Lévi-Strauss's perspective by inferring that all statuses may have had some degree of authority on a *rahui*, including lower status such as the *manahune*.[59] Evidence is limited to categorically support this viewpoint and only Ellis alludes to it in his work.[60] Of course, it is likely that only the chief of the congregation, whether he is an *ari'i*, a *raatira* (secondary chief) or a *manahune*, could have the authority to enforce a *rahui* on his land or the sea adjacent to the land he controls, as a family land.

A careful review of the literature around the issue of *rahui* in the Society Islands before European influence confirms the idea that the *rahui* was indeed a fundamental political institution in Polynesian society. The above survey supports the hypothesis that the *rahui* was an institution deeply linked to the social organisation, in such a way that a plurality of statuses was engaged in *rahui* implementation and sanction. *Rahui* was not the monopoly of the *ari'i*, but rather an institution shared among all chiefly congregations. One consequence

---

56 Petersen, 1999, p. 386.
57 Sahlins, 1958, p. 142.
58 Petersen, 2005; Petersen, 1999, p. 386.
59 Lévi-Strauss, 1958; Lévi-Strauss, C., 1964. *Le cru et le cuit*. Paris: Plon.
60 Ellis, 1829, p. 286.

of this finding is that a more complete understanding of *rahui* requires more detailed discussion of social and political organisation in Society Islands, and Polynesia in general, about the relations between chiefs and the responsibilities, like the *rahui*, associated with rank. Similarly, Petersen wonders whether other supposedly chiefly societies within the Austronesian sphere lack 'chiefs' as well.[61]

In terms of legal pluralism theory, the facts observed in Tahiti demonstrate why and how an institution such as the *rahui* was deeply embedded into the social organisation and did not obey any absolute stratification of the society. The plurality and the network of relationships paralleled the political and religious hierarchy. In so doing, it provided a great number of opportunities for decision-making within and between kin-congregations. This accounts for the profound plurality of Polynesian society, and because social organisation was pluralistic, a legal pluralistic approach is not only efficacious, but vital.

This analysis has major implications for understanding Polynesian sociopolitical structures of power, especially the strength and status of ramages. It is also a contribution to the better understating of the relationships between religious power and what might crudely be coined secular power, a problematic dichotomy for Polynesian societies. This essay not only demonstrates more variation across space in rights to apply *rahui* than is commonly recognised in the secondary literature, but also a wider range of sociopolitical groups able to apply *rahui* than is commonly acknowledged. *Rahui* is seen as an evolving process defined by enactment rather than as a static set of rules along the lines of Hviding's account for marine tenure in Marovo lagoon, and Sahlins's account of conical clans.[62]

The restitution of a rich and nuanced account of *rahui* in the Society Islands shows it as a varied and diverse institution, able to be deployed by different individuals and groups in different contexts. This analysis represents a major departure from the standard

---

61   Petersen, 1999, p. 401.
62   Sahlins, 1958.

interpretations popularised by Firth,[63] Sahlins,[64] Keesing,[65] and Shore[66] in Oceanian anthropology, according to which only higher chiefs could implement *tapu* through their *mana*. *Rahui*, like *tapu* and *mana*, appear much more localised in application and power source, but also tied to sociopolitical alliances and linkages for wider application. The methodological implications of this conclusion are the need for more local archival work and primary research as well as familiarity with secondary debates and current themes of Polynesian sociopolitical societies.

---

63 Firth, 1940.
64 Sahlins, 1958.
65 Keesing, 1984.
66 Shore, 1989.

PART II
Rahui today as state-custom pluralism

7

Protection of natural resources through a sacred prohibition: The *rahui* on Rapa iti

Christian Ghasarian

The management of natural resources implies conceptions of ownership and property that provide precious information on the way a society perceives itself. Established moralities on the matter are sometimes sustained by a sacredness that reinforces the values and principles at stake. In the case of ideological and environmental change, the sacred conceptions most of the time adjust to new circumstances and become part of the cultural dynamics. An invisible and superior force, associated with the past and the ancestors, legitimates the new social order.[1] Therefore, compliance with sacred models can ensure protection in the present life. In this essay, I address how these representations can be mobilised to enforce a new set of rules and a set of associated practices defined as 'good' for the whole community. Interestingly, although in the Polynesian society studied here these representations refer to a pre-European past, they are today expressed through the medium of the adopted Christian religion. This hybrid

---

1   Nielsen, D., 1999. *Three Faces of God. Society, Religion, and the Category of Totality in the Philosophie of Emile Durkheim*. Albany: State University of New York.

situation offers a fascinating example of how, with pragmatic logic, societies combine innovations and continuities to give meaning to their members.

The case study presented here is that of Rapa iti, a small and isolated island in the Austral Archipelago (Tuhaa Pae) in French Polynesia. Located approximately 550 kilometres south-east of the closest island of Raivavae, Rapa iti, which is around 40 km² with a population of only 500 inhabitants, is the southernmost island in the area. The population's collective management of land and marine resources is unique in French Polynesia as it takes place in a political context in which the French laws are applicable only in theory. In fact, the local society regulates individual and community access to the land and to the sea through two customary councils whose members are respected elders. My research on this island began in 2001 and is focused on understanding how global models and institutions are dealt with and reformulated locally. I approach the local dynamics that take place in terms of 'dialogical processes'[2] rather than acculturative ones, in which dominant external models would simply be imposed on a social space that integrates them as they are. Cultural and social realities are always a matter of construction, even if sometimes a negotiated one, notably when political and technological powers are at stake.

This essay focuses on the institution of the *rahui*, which combines different structures of meaning and agencies to deal with the marine environment.[3] It describes an ancient version of *rahui* on Rapa iti, before addressing the reasons why it was reinstituted a few decades ago on the island and its current principles and related practices. I then show that this institution is part of a local strategy aimed to deal collectively with ownership — a key issue of everyday life in a small community. Subsequently, I explore how the people of Rapa iti carefully manage this consensual, self-imposed prohibition through a form of moral restraint built on a sense of the sacred — a pre-European sacred ideology that engages each socialised individual to consider that any infraction of this prohibition can expose him/her to both social and supernatural sanctions. The last part relates

---

2   Bakhtin, M., 1985. *The Dialogic Imagination: Four Essays*. Austin: University of Texas Press.
3   Giddens, A., 1984. *The Constitution of Society*. Cambridge: Polity Press.

7. PROTECTION OF NATURAL RESOURCES THROUGH A SACRED PROHIBITION

local laws to global stakes, and analyses the *rahui* as an expression of an underlying consensual Rapa project to construct and maintain collective local cohesion.

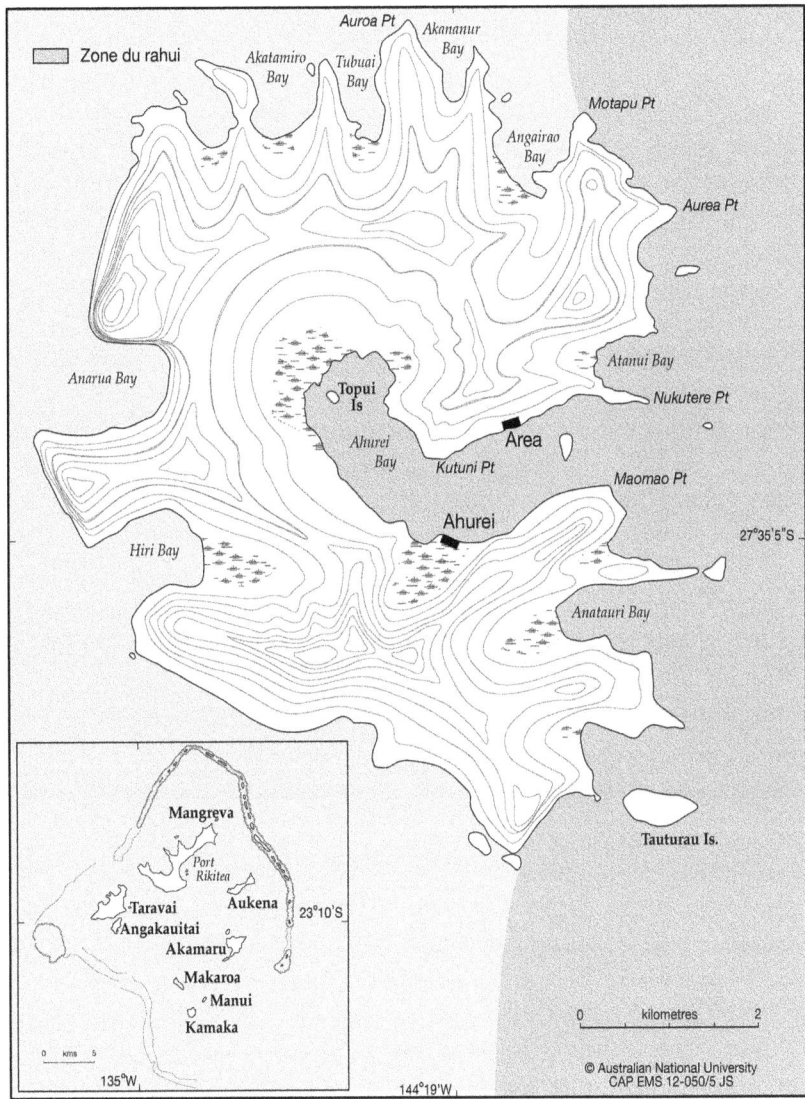

Figure 19: Map of Rapa with the *rahui* zone
Source: © The Australian National University CAP EMS 12-050/5 JS

THE RAHUI

Rahui and fishing regulations

As it is implemented on Rapa iti today, the *rahui* placed during a defined period on some designated coastal spaces is a prohibition on fishing aimed at allowing the marine fauna to increase for a period without human predation. It is part of a general desire for maintaining natural resources to ensure the community's food supply and, therefore, its survival. However, although there is a *rahui* on Rapa iti today, *rahui* is not a Rapa word but a Tahitian one. The Rapa word to qualify prohibitions on some natural resources is *iki*. Due to lack of historical data, it is difficult to ascertain how the system worked in pre-Christian times. Elders, however, gave me some information about the types of *iki* they have known on the island. According to them, there was a sacred dimension to the ancient *iki*, which was established, for instance, to forbid the gathering of some grey birds of Rapa iti (*kea*) to allow them to incubate their eggs, to protect a plant (*kiekie*) that was used for making basket weave (a means for getting money) and, today, to collect mangoes in a given bay of the island only at certain times. All these prohibitions have been implemented to allow resources to grow again in sufficient or larger quantity for a future usage and for its sharing among the population. Interestingly, the substantive *iki* was (and still is) also associated with the one of 'danger'. As noted, the term *rahui* is used on Rapa iti today rather than *iki*. The word *rahui* is polysemous and combines meanings such as 'the prohibition', 'the prohibited areas', 'the day of the collective fishing', and 'the products of the fishing in the *rahui*'.

Before describing the form that the *rahui* currently takes on Rapa iti, I address the reasons behind its implementation. Interestingly, the project to launch it on the island came from the municipal council (a French institution: Conseil municipal or *Tomite oire*) almost three decades ago to protect the local marine fauna in a context of technological and social changes. Prior to the setting up of the *rahui* on Rapa iti, fish were abundant and the fishing modes were not excessively predatory, therefore there was no special prohibition on fishing. In the 1980s, new technologies and fishing techniques were adopted, such as outboard motors, that allowed fishermen to easily catch a large number of fish in a short time. People remember, for instance, that with a simple torch at night they could harvest around 300 lobsters in three hours! New fishing methods (such as using a trap to catch lobsters) were then prohibited by the members of the municipal council as they were rapidly depleting some marine food resources. Today, any type of fishing at night is prohibited in the *rahui* (while, outside the *rahui*, only fishing underwater is prohibited at night). The prohibition was also extended to fishing with a net everywhere around the island and with an underwater spear gun in some defined areas. Fishing with a harpoon or with a rod, two much less efficient techniques, remained — and still are — authorised everywhere around the island. At the same time that the *rahui* was set up, an association of fishermen was created to make sure that people respected and understood the new fishing principles.

The existing *rahui* ban is placed on the 800-metre-wide and two-kilometre-long main bay that separates the two villages of the island (Haurei and Area) and on the first three bays on each side of this big bay, extending to the spot called Tematapu in the north and Karapoo koio in the south. Interestingly, the limits are not marked, but are perfectly known by all the fishermen. The system obliges the approximately 80 skilled fishermen of the island to go fishing further away in other bays. The prohibition is at work the whole year, apart from one day, when collective fishing and sharing is organised. Usually, that day is between Christmas and New Year's Eve — two European feasts that have become meaningful on the island. Community events (games, songs, dances and banquets) are organised during that week which marks a special —not only religious — time in local life. In some cases, such as an official government visit, a marriage (which is a collective matter on Rapa iti), or a religious celebration, the *rahui* can also be reopen. The day to engage the collective fishing is determined by observing the weather in the early morning, and confirming if the sea is peaceful. Everybody, and especially the fishermen, wake up at dawn (usually between 4 am and 5 am) to be ready to go fishing after watching the quiet sea. Men and women then spontaneously go to the dock where the community gathers for the *rahui*. The opening of the prohibition of fishing takes place after the singing of a traditional hymn (*himene*) by the fishermen and people present, followed by a special prayer recited by the pastor of the island who then suspends the *rahui* prohibition. During this liminal ritual, everybody present humbly stands motionless with heads bent.

THE RAHUI

Following the prayer (which takes around five minutes) and the suspension of the sacred prohibition (*tatara te rahui*), the collective fishing can start for eight hours only, from 6 am to 2 pm. All the fishermen must have returned to the village by 2 pm at the latest. With their fishing gear, they leave in small or bigger groups according to the size of the boats, all of them ready to fish in the *rahui*, the areas that have been, until then, prohibited for fishing. During the authorised time for catching fish, the men ignore discomfort, diving down, coming up to the boat with a fish, diving down and coming up, again and again. Although this continuous fishing is exhausting, the possibility of catching as many fish as one wants in the previously forbidden areas produces an excitement that wipes out the fatigue. Hour after hour, each boat fills up with more and more fish.

As they return to the village (before 2 pm), the boats are so heavy with fish that they almost sink into the sea. Just after coming to shore, and before the fishermen take the fish out of the boats and return home to rest, the pastor prays again in the company of everybody present on the dock. That second prayer (which also lasts for approximately five minutes) puts an end to the temporary suspension of the *rahui* and reinstates it (*tamau te rahui*). From that moment, fishing in the *rahui* area is prohibited until it is opened again the following year. The fishermen place their catch on the dock, cover it with big green leaves to protect it from flies, and return to their home by foot or by boat. A dozen men who participated to the fishing then take charge of the second part of the *rahui* day: the distribution of the catch. They first place each type of fish in a specific pile and then create mixed piles of approximately 100 fish.

Two hours later, an animated crowd gathers on the dock as each family sends a 'representative' to get its share. In company of some of their relatives, these delegates patiently wait their turn with plastic bags and/or barrows until they are called, one after another, to get their several kilos of fish; each family getting an amount based on its size. Some families decide to scale the fish they received directly on the shore near the dock while others take it straight home. Some fish will be consumed the same day and the following days, and the remainder will be placed in freezers for later. Some part of it can also be sent in plastic freezer boxes on the next boat to family members (*fetii*) in Tahiti, a practice that is part of the Polynesian system of reciprocity.[4] The end of the distribution of the *rahui* to the entire population and the desertion of the dock as night falls marks the end of the *rahui*. Let us now examine the logic behind that institution.

Ownership and collective cohesion

The collective dimension of the *rahui* is palpable and can be related to a larger model of communal management of the island. As mentioned earlier, the use of sea and land on Rapa iti is regulated by the entire community through two customary institutions: the council of the elders and the committee of the fishing. The first one, the Conseil des Sages or Toohitu, implemented by the French administration at the end of the nineteenth century, ceased to be in existence in the mid-twentieth century and was re-established by the municipal council three decades ago. It includes representative members of different cognatic descent groups (*kopu*) on the island and is aimed at distributing land for houses and cultivation.[5] The second institution that deals with natural resources is the local fishing association, the Comité des pêches or *Tomite taià*. This committee is also sometimes called the *Tomite rahui* as it is also in charge of the implementation of the prohibition to fish in certain areas, which is ritually lifted from time to time. It is composed of eight persons who are elected annually by the population (previous members cannot be re-elected). As with the Toohitu, it was also created by the municipal council when it instituted the *rahui*.

These two customary institutions work on the basis of local principles. They have an elected president and a revolving membership composed of elders whose moral status is locally acknowledged (*taata paari*). As I have mentioned, they are both supported by the municipal council and by the entire the population. That significant participation of a French institution — the most important locally — in the insular collective authority on the management of the land and the sea

---

4   Robineau, C., 1978. 'Réciprocité, redistribution et prestige, chez les Polynésiens des îles de la société'. *Journal des Océanistes* 61.
5   Hanson, A. & Ghasarian, C., 2007. 'The land belongs to everyone. The unstable dynamic of unrestricted cognatic descent in Rapa, French Polynesia'. *Journal the Polynesian Society* 116(1): 59–72.

informs us about the preponderant role the mayor and the members of the municipal council play in reinforcing local autonomy. In a way, it could be said that the official Rapa representatives to the French administration use the power given to them from outside to empower the insular community in its management of the land and the sea. A new tradition has been invented locally for concrete purposes and has taken a pre-European value that continues to increase in strength in the minds of the people.[6]

The customary collective system of ownership as it has been developed on Rapa iti remains fragile as more and more individualistic outlooks and strategies have developed in recent years. These mostly come from people of Rapa ancestry who are not full-time residents but who come back to the island from time to time to claim land rights, as the system of cognatic unrestricted descent includes them in collective ownership. In the meantime, some residents, wishing to improve their future and that of their close relatives on their own terms, try to appropriate some 'mobile goods' on the land, such as the wild cattle (cows and goats) that roam freely over the hills of the island. They do so by marking the animals they catch in a specific way on their ears. In an identity process that emerges from situations that favour one's own difference,[7] most local residents denounce these individualistic attitudes and are even more inclined to protect the communal interest.

To get a bigger picture of the situation, I should mention that the cattle are collectively owned and managed by another institution: the Coopérative of Rapa iti. Established in 1928 to collectively manage a dozen cows imported from New Zealand, the Coopérative (which is also in charge of the importation of basic goods such as powdered milk, soap, flour, sugar, petrol and tobacco) has 66 members, one from each family unit (*utuafare*), whose ancestors decided that the increasing number of wild cattle would be the collective property of all the members of the Coopérative, and therefore of all the population

---

6   Hobsbawm, R. & Ranger, T., 1983. *The Invention of Tradition*. Cambridge University Press; Hanson, A., 1989, 'The making of the Maori: culture invention and its logic'. *American Anthropologist* 91: 890–902.
7   Barth, F.,1969. *Ethnic Groups and Boundaries: The Social Organization of Culture Difference*. Bergen: Oslo; London: George Allen & Unwin.

of the island at that time. Although some current households do not have a representative member in the Coopérative, everyone still has close relatives who are members by ancestry.[8]

Although it was considerably weakened on the other islands of French Polynesia because of the French *code civil*, the Polynesian distinction between the right of exploitation and the right of ownership remains operational on Rapa iti.[9] On the island, collective goods, such as the land and the sea, can be used — and in a way appropriated — temporarily but not definitely. The exploitation of the land (for a house and/or a plantation) is of course more durable than that of the sea, on which people just come and go. Through this logic, according to which the main resources of the island can only be temporarily used, individual fishing enclosures (to keep the fish alive in the sea after being caught) are still not allowed today on Rapa iti as that would constitute a private and durable appropriation of the common sea. The policy of the *rahui* expresses a common desire to collectively manage ocean resources, through the preservation of some areas of the marine ecosystem around the island, but still needs widely agreed principles to be effective. I address these principles in the following section.

A local strategy between social and sacred control

Elders on the islands have memories of painful periods when food was in short supply. They have also heard of difficult times earlier on in the island's history involving starvation, which sometimes led their ancestors to fight to the death for the limited land and resources available on this small island. In people's minds, regulating the distribution of the land through the Toohitu is a way to maintain the unity of the population in the present day. The control of the usage of the sea derives from the same logic: the sea is considered as a food resource that can become limited and so has to be used with care. By voluntarily preventing themselves from fishing in the areas that are

---
8   Hanson, A., 1970. *Rapan Lifeways. Society and History on a Polynesian Island.* Boston: Little, Brown.
9   Ottino, P., 1972. *Rangiroa. Parenté étendue, residence et terres dans un atoll polynésien.* Paris: Editions Cujas.

closest to and easiest to access from the villages, local residents allow the fish in these areas to reproduce in number without any threat from human predators, which makes them easy preys in case of urgent need or for special community feasts.

I do have not enough data to say that this contemporary concern about a possible difficult time to come — therefore a sense of life in the future — is something new on Rapa iti, but this clearly sustains the institution of the *rahui*. My anthropological research on Rapa iti over the last 13 years has revealed that the protection of the island is a recurrent idea that is often explicitly expressed by the population.[10] The respect for the *rahui* prohibition is perceived by everybody as a mutual act of responsibility towards the whole community (including past and future generations). The self-imposed rule to not appropriate more land than what is allowed and to not fish in certain marine spaces with certain fishing equipment definitely plays a role in social cohesion — which, as we know, is not a given but a dynamic and constantly challenged process. Being established by the population, the Toohitu and the *rahui* committee constitute a unifying strength in the local community. Behind them, people imagine and represent themselves through a sense of duty and care for their natural resources.[11]

If the respect for the *rahui* first takes place in individuals' consciousness, in their constructed sense of morality, the people of Rapa iti have nevertheless developed a social system of control to implement it. In relation to responsibility for one's self (in people's minds and belief systems), this form of control is simply realised by people's watching others' actions and places of fishing. Due to the size of the island, it is rare for a fisherman to go fishing out of sight of other fishermen. Therefore, everybody is potentially obliged to comply with the rules by the simple presence of other people involved in the same sphere of activity. Besides this social control system, fully supported by the municipal council, the *Tomite rahui* responsible for everything related to fishing (security matters, rescuing of fishermen, and so on) is also supposed to intervene by boat if the rules are broken (including those committed by fishing boats from off the island).

---

10 Ghasarian, C., 2014. *Rapa. Île du bout du monde, île dans le monde*. Paris: Demopolis.
11 Anderson, B., 1989. *Imagined Communities. Reflections on the Origin and Spread of Nationalism*. London: Verso.

7. PROTECTION OF NATURAL RESOURCES THROUGH A SACRED PROHIBITION

Social sanction, ranging from moral condemnation and the threat of social ostracism to concrete punishment, is always possible when the prohibitions of the *rahui* are not respected. Everybody remembers for instance what happened around 20 years ago to a family of the village of Area whose son went to fish in the *rahui*. He was seen — therefore caught in the act — and the mayor of the island at that time (reputed to be quite a tough person) decided with the municipal council to cut off for one week the electricity in his family household. This situation is extreme and, although the possibility of social coercion is present (through the *Tomite rahui*, for instance), this control system has up to now been only rarely enforced. Nonetheless, elders remember that at the beginning of the implementation of the *rahui* on the island in the early 1980s, cases of infringement of the *rahui* could be observed. This is why, a few years after having set up the *rahui*, the people most willing to have it respected resorted to a strategy to give more strength to this institution: they enhanced respect for the prohibition through giving it a religious dimension. Consequently, the pastor was asked to participate in the *rahui* by opening and closing it. Apparently, the succeeding pastors on Rapa iti (each one staying on the island for only four years) have enthusiastically endorsed the responsibility to bring God — and the awe that it entails — into the *rahui*. As one would expect, these pastors have since been among the strongest advocates of that institution.

As it works today, the *rahui* seeks to prevent transgressions, perpetrated individually or not, through a sacred prohibition. It is sustained by a collective representation of the natural environment as a door to an invisible power of the imperceptible world. The idea of a sacred power beyond oneself and what is visible and tangible is clearly behind the system and the respect for the *rahui*. The dramatisation of the moment, with public prayers, implicates each individual who is considered to be fully responsible for acting in accordance with what is defined as a common good. As the *rahui* is about fishing, it concerns only men who, in the local gender division of labour, are the ones who go fishing. The compliance with the ban is mainly based on a self-imposed avoidance of an act that would be perceived as inauspicious if realised. In local conceptions, infringing the prohibition places the individual in a dangerous situation. All the fishermen consider that a problem, an accident or a disease can hit them and their close ones if they fish in the *rahui*. Collective stories point out the misfortunes that have befallen those fishermen suspected of having violated the *rahui*, for instance, trouble with their motor boats, a situation that prevented them from going fishing on their own for a time.

People also consider that the punishments can be much bigger than such technical damages, as the *rahui* involves a dimension beyond human understanding. The underlying presence of sacred forces, associated with *mana* and ancestors supervising their descendants' deeds towards the island and the community, reinforces the deference to the system. Any fishing in the *rahui* outside its official and temporary opening exposes offenders to social reprobation and supernatural sanction; two strong reasons for local people to comply with the prohibition. In a way, a sense of *tapu* — and the consequent fear of its violation — is associated with the *rahui*. Yet, people of Rapa iti do not consider the *rahui* exactly as a *tapu*, as it is initiated by a collective decision aimed at dealing with natural resources and it does not have a definitive character that they normally associate with things marked as *tapu* (like the inconceivable act of moving an *ofai fenua*, a stone separating the clan land units in the previous land tenure system).

Local laws, global stakes

I would like to conclude this chapter by viewing Rapa customary institutions from the French legal perspective, as Rapa iti, along with more than 100 other islands, belongs to the political and administrative entity called 'French Polynesia'. With regard to the French jurisdiction, all the islands of French Polynesia (their land and their surrounding sea) are subjected to the same rules. Based on the Roman law, the French *code civil* does not sustain the idea of the land as collective property, but highlights private rights. Therefore, the customary system of collective management of the land of Rapa iti is a contradiction of French laws. The same can be said about the population's implementation of the *rahui* prohibition that has no legal validity in French law. As the marine space between the Polynesian Islands is the property of the French state, anybody who is a French citizen — Polynesian or not — can theoretically fish wherever he or she chooses. Therefore, the French jurisdiction makes it legal for non-

Rapa people — and also for Rapa residents on or off the island — (as long as they are French) to fish in the *rahui* of Rapa iti, even if the islanders themselves have decided not to do it.

A few years ago, a boat from Tahiti came at night to place some traps around the island to harvest big red lobsters. This incident expresses a classic case of cultural–juridical pluralism[12] and also exemplifies a collision of moralities. A Rapa iti fisherman who happened to be fishing at night saw the Tahitian boat crew placing traps in the *rahui*. He ran back to the village and informed everybody. A moment later, almost all the able-bodied men of the island were in their boats, removing these traps from the sea. Someone was delegated to go to the Tahitian boat (which had taken anchor some distance from the shore after placing its traps) to tell its captain to come to the harbour of the island the next morning to meet the population. When the captain and its team arrived at the meeting place, the mayor and the Rapa iti fishermen explained to them that they had done something that the islanders do not even allow themselves to do, that is, fishing in their *rahui*. Having stated that this act was locally forbidden, the Rapa people gave back the empty traps to the Tahitian fishermen. A few weeks later, however, that same boat came back to fish again around the shores of Rapa iti, this time on a Sunday morning, when most people do not go fishing but are in church or stay at home. By good fortune for the islanders, a young boy walking in the hills saw the Tahitian boat furtively fishing in the *rahui*. Again, the alarm was given and, led by the *Tomite rahui*, all the able-bodied men of the island jumped into their boats to collect the newly deposited traps. They brought them back to the dock and made a bonfire out of almost all of them, while some were kept as a private 'war treasure'. The Tahitian boat did not dare to come ashore to ask for these traps but instead returned to Tahiti.

It is impossible to say for sure that this Tahitian boat, or any other boat, did not come back again to fish in the *rahui*, unnoticed by the islanders. Besides, the striking point of this story is that, under the current jurisdiction, any fishing company located in Tahiti and whose interests are external to the island has the right to fish in the places that the people of Rapa iti try to preserve. If the case was brought to court, the current law would be on the side of the Tahitian boat,

---

12   Bambridge, T. & Neuffer, P., 2002. 'Pluralisme culturel et juridique: la question foncière en Polynésie française'. *Hermès* 32/33: 307–16.

and the judges would probably be very embarrassed to have to justify outsiders' administrative rights as superior to the islanders' moral rights. Fortunately, the fishing company did not dare to go to court to claim the right to fish around the island of Rapa iti, as the risk of highlighting such a sensitive matter was too great. This sad but interesting example shows the contradictions and the collision of global, or at least external, logics with local stakes.

In Appadurai's formulation, these experiences bring the Rapa people face to face with new imaginary and techno scapes that have reinforced a local feeling about external threats.[13] The imaginary impels residents to find collective ways to protect their island. They thus deal with global processes through constructed cultural answers,[14] of which the Toohitu and the *rahui* institutions are among the most important. A form of protectionism of local resources is thus at work on Rapa iti, which also reveals some contemporary dynamics of insular societies.[15]

The *rahui* system at work on Rapa iti shows how a local community, being primarily concerned for the maintenance of its food resources, thinks and institutes original ways of dealing with its natural properties in relation to possible future emergency needs. Using the same logic, the population of Rapa iti manages the land (to live on and cultivate), the marine fauna and the wild animals that constitute a food resource on the island. It considers that its primary rights in dealing with everyday life should be respected by external institutions and policies. The ancient Polynesian sense of continuity between the land and the sea — two exploitable spaces — is clearly at work here. The term *fenua* encapsulates all the material dimension of the island: what is on and around it.[16] It also implicitly refers to the ancestors and to God (*Atua*) — whose powers are much beyond that of the Christian God, although the formal prayers are Christians — who is constantly mentioned by people when addressing land and sea issues. As agriculture and fishing are long-established activities that insure everyday subsistence on the island, the population is sensitive to the

---

13   Appadurai, A., 1996. *Modernity at Large: Dimensions of Globalization*. Minneapolis: University of Minnesota Press.
14   Friedman, J., 1996. *Culture Identity and Global Process*. London: Sage Publications.
15   Bernardie, N. & Taglioni, F., 2005. *Les dynamiques contemporaines des petits espaces insulaires*. Paris: Karthala.
16   Saura, B., 2005. *Entre nature et culture. La mise en terre du placenta en Polynésie française*. Tahiti: Edition haere Po.

idea of preservation of its terrestrial and marine environment. This is why the people of the small island of Rapa iti today strongly value a communal relationship with the natural environment, as a condition of their well-being and peace.

The people of Rapa iti value self-management of their resources, based on solidarity and sharing, as their ancestors in all probability also did — although perhaps in a more clannish and exclusive manner (when they did not simply fight against each other). Regulated management of natural resources is possible because the demographic pressure of the population on the environment is not too heavy. Besides, there is little exportation of the local production as the economy is mostly one of subsistence, and the island does not face many external influences (there is no airport and a supply boat arrives every two months). While it is fragile, the system of collective management of the marine fauna described here shows how a small, insular community, remote from the world, values and implements sharing and equity of access to available goods on the land and in the sea.[17]

The *rahui* on Rapa iti is thus part of a local underlying project aimed at constructing and maintaining a collective local cohesion to face the always possible adversity related to being a very isolated island. It also invites people to be responsible in the protection of the space they have inherited. What makes this *rahui* policy interesting anthropologically is that it pragmatically combines different dimensions: religion and sacredness, environment and food resources, new techniques and community solidarity, state, territorial and local institutions. Through the geographical distance to Tahiti — and therefore to France — and the will to master their insular destiny, the people of Rapa iti are constructing a kind of 'third space'[18] in which they successfully conjugate customary principles and practices with Western (here French) institutional frameworks. At a time when collective ownership of natural resources is a matter of growing interest in many societies, this forgotten island in a neglected archipelago offers a remarkable model of successful local management of resources in a small community.

---

17   Doumenge, J-P., 2002. 'Diversité culturelle et constructions des identités collectives outre-mer'. In D. Wolton et al. (eds), *La France et les outre-mers: L'enjeu multiculturel. Hermès* 32–33, CNRS Editions.
18   Bhabha, H., 1994. *The Location of Culture*. New York; London: Routledge.

8
From traditional to modern management in Fakarava

Lorin Thorax

Fakarava: A protected atoll

Fakarava is the second largest atoll of the Tuamotu Archipelago in French Polynesia. The atoll encompasses a 60-kilometre-long and 25-kilometre-wide lagoon. The surrounding reef only forms a barrier to the ocean in the north-east and the south-east. The rest of the periphery consists of a partially emerged coral plate, which leaves the lagoon in direct contact with the ocean by many *hoa* (small passages between the coral plates). The atoll contains two reef passes (deep and wide openings of the reef, where the most important flow between the lagoon and the ocean occurs). The first one, Garuae, in the north-west, is relatively closely located to the main village Rotoava. The Tumakohua pass, in the south, is much smaller and is located near the old village of Tetamanu, which housed the atoll's first inhabitants. Inhabited by about 600 people in 2007, the atoll is considered by the Polynesians as an authentic and natural destination, populated by the traditional *Paumotu* (inhabitants of the Tuamotu Archipelago) and their culture. Spared from mass tourism, the local population has preserved the environment by using it in a sustainable and conscientious way. This exemplary behaviour has resulted in international recognition, in particular, when the atoll was declared a biosphere reserve by UNESCO in November 2006. Thus, management and exploitation of natural heritage today is governed by official institutions that work closely with the population.

The main economic activities on the atoll are tourism (particularly tourism related to scuba diving), pearl culture, copra (dried coconut flesh) and, to a lesser extent, fishing (which remains a means of subsistence that is rooted in the local micro-economy). Recently put on the global map by the construction of an airport and a new port, Fakarava attracts an increasingly high number of tourists, which provides new opportunities for residents, but also new issues related to exploitation of the lagoon. Anthropogenic pressure on atoll ecosystems is growing and management models set up by UNESCO and the PGEM (Plan de Gestion de l'Espace Maritime, or Marine Space Management Plan) have been employed to optimise operation and natural-resource management. They do so by involving the population in the decision-making process and by raising awareness of the environmental issues arising from the introduction of modern and Western concepts.

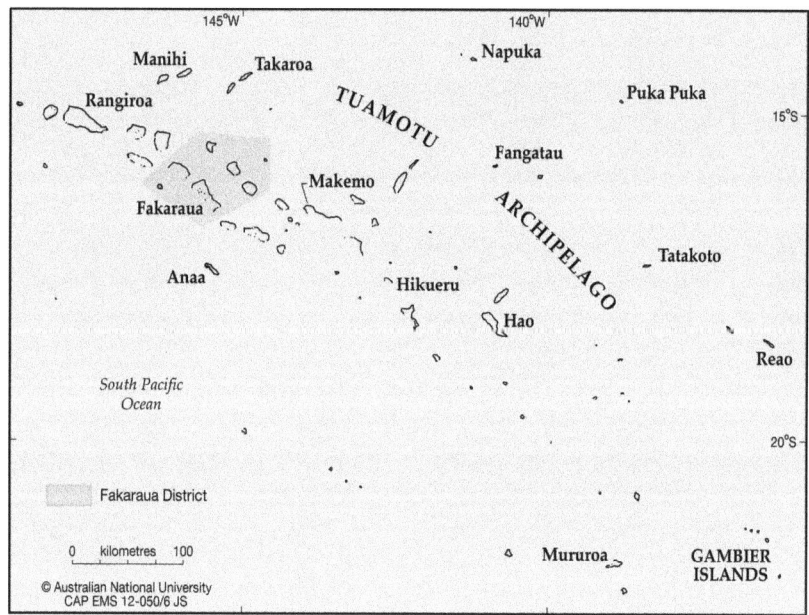

Figure 20: Map of Fakarava in the Tuamotu Archipelago
Source: © The Australian National University CAP EMS 12-050/6 JS

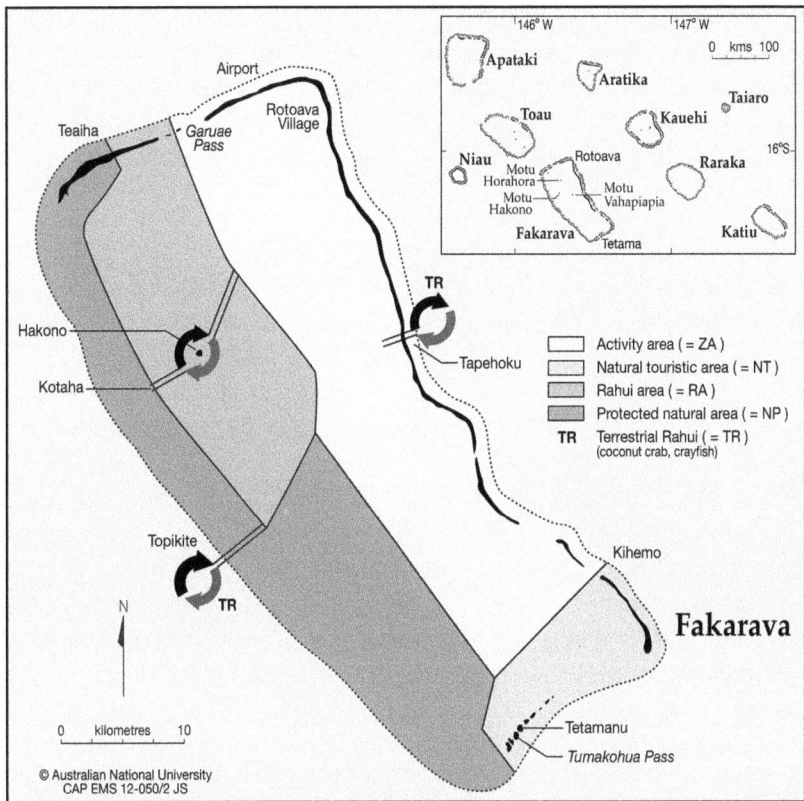

Figure 21: Map of Fakarava with the *rahui* areas
Source: © The Australian National University CAP EMS 12-050/2 JS

The remaining question is whether these models are adapted to the local culture and the way of life on an atoll. The study of traditional farms and representations of nature by the *Paumotu* is essential for assessing the degree to which locals and their culture have adapted to these changing circumstances. It is important to understand how the circumstances of life on an atoll can affect the social, economic and environmental development of the local community or, in other words, to understand the cultural impact it has. Insularity is strong in Polynesia and isolation is especially felt in the Tuamotu Archipelago and other outer islands.

Another aspect that influences life on an atoll is its limited land area. Resources are restricted and demand can only be modified by demography or opportunities for travel. These constraints cause complex social issues and the emergence of cultural specificities that are related to the phenomenon of isolation and inherently associated with the life on an island. Thus, the limitation of resources inevitably leads to social adjustments and cultural events, such as specific forms of *rahui* that are the main topic of discussion in this chapter.

An atoll is a fragile and precarious ecosystem. Fakarava's lagoon-centred ecosystem is much less hospitable to human habitation than higher islands, which have more land and mountains to catch moisture-laden clouds. The strength of the ocean imposes itself from the periphery of the island and from the lagoon, linked as they are through passes and channels, which provide the lagoon with its water and fauna. Human life is only possible on the *motu*[1] perched atop the reef surrounding the lagoon. As Bachimon notes, 'with atolls, we are at the limit of the concept of island, as differentiation from the ocean environment is slim. There cannot be insular *oceanicity* more powerful than on an atoll'.[2] Here, Bachimon's notion of insularity is virtually swept away to be replaced by an even stronger concept, *absolute oceanicity*. From the biological point of view one must stress, however, the great biodiversity of atolls, which makes them oases in the middle of the ocean. While atoll's terrestrial biodiversity is relatively poor, their marine biodiversity is generally extremely rich.

Fakarava's lagoon ecosystem is prolific and therefore provides islanders with plentiful resources. Whether using its coral and shells, for food consumption or handcraft use, crustaceans or many species of fish, the *Paumotu* knew the full use of marine resources — their whole culture is oriented towards their use.

Reappropriation of the *rahui* concept

This chapter analyses the practice of *rahui* throughout pre-colonial, colonial and modern times, in order to describe the various adjustments to which this practice was subject, particularly in the case of the atolls of the Tuamotu Archipelago in general and Fakarava in particular. What was meant by *rahui* in the Polynesian context? Generally, the aim of *rahui* is the conscious management of marine and

---

1   *Motu*: a group of islets forming a ring-shaped atoll.
2   Bachimon, P., 1990. *Tahiti: entre mythes et réalités*. Paris: Ed C.T.H.S, p. 29.

terrestrial resources. It is an institution marked by sacredness and *tapu* and imposed by community leaders. The *rahui*, therefore, possesses a religious and sacred dimension prohibiting the exploitation of some resources or a specific area. A *rahui* could have several functions, one of which was to impose a leader's authority: the more important a *rahui* was (in its duration or in the size of the area subjected to the *rahui*), the greater the power of the leader. Secondly, the *rahui* could act to preserve a certain amount of resources in anticipation of a ceremony, or could simply be imposed to prevent a possible famine. In all events, as the practice of *rahui* referred to the concepts of *tapu*, sacredness played an important role. Anyone who did not respect this sacredness could be punished by the gods, such as by misfortune befalling him or his family.

Pre-colonial times

The atoll dwellers of Fakarava utilised a wide variety of food resources to survive in their relatively poorly endowed habitats. The lean soils of atolls did not allow the growing of crops on a significant scale and the population relied on pits (trenches that were filled with organic waste) to grow fruit trees and root crops. These pits allowed the culture to survive the atoll's extreme weather and hydrogeological conditions. Hence, the main food resources, with the exception of some pig farms, originated from the sea and, more specifically, from the lagoon. In addition, the *Paumotu*'s nomadic lifestyles naturally lead to the rotation of exploited areas. Due to the broad space available, and the lagoon's high biodiversity, the *rahui* during pre-colonial times was more a way for community leaders to demonstrate their power, than the expression of an ecological consciousness: *rahui* were laid on areas or species to ensure the abundance of resources for ceremonies. As the small populations did not put pressure on the ecosystem, the *rahui* was more a means for the leader to enforce and remind the population of the prevailing social and religious rules. The planning and provision of a quantity of resources for ceremonial purposes was the leading reason behind the concept of *tapu*, which has an important religious dimension. This practice anchored the *Paumotu* cosmogony in daily life, and reinforced social cohesion around common beliefs. Daily life was governed by rules centred on *tapu* and other religious bans: the building of a boat, going fishing and other activities, had to be implemented carefully to ensure success and security to their participants. The *rahui* was a practice that fitted the system of local beliefs and logically applied cultural standards in reference to divinities and practices of daily life. Hence, the *rahui* had sacred and religious dimensions through the *tapu*, which constituted its essence and provided the *rahui* with a real legitimacy. *Rahui* and *tapu*, in this context, went far beyond the simple management of available resources.

Colonial period

The practice of *rahui* took a new dimension during the colonial period when, in the late nineteenth century, French settlers imposed their view of the world and prohibited many indigenous cultural practices. From 1870, Catholic missionaries organised the atolls into intensive coconut cultivation so as to produce copra, which particularly suited the environmental conditions of the region. Thus coconut trees rapidly covered most of the exploitable land surface of the atolls. With evangelisation, loss of cultural references and the decline of local beliefs, the religious connotations of *rahui* progressively lost their importance and were replaced by new meanings for *Paumotu* people. These new meanings were more related to the economy. The practice of *rahui* soon ran according to the economic imperatives for copra production. Indeed, the practice has been diverted from its original use to meet the new French colonial economic guidelines for Polynesians: economy and profits have become the main concerns. Despite a nomadic lifestyle in Fakarava, it became essential to have a main village located on the boat passage (for instance, the village of Rotoava in the north, which is located closer to the great pass) to be the base for harvesting copra bags. This new system did not correspond to traditional values but to the realities of distant markets. The spatial organisation evolved to suit the exploitation of copra and the atoll was divided into three main production zones, with a fourth located on the neighbouring atoll of Toau. These areas were designated based on the productivity of their coconut groves and the entire village population moved from one zone to the other every three months. The copra harvest was delivered to the schooners that regularly connected the atoll with Papeete. This system allowed time for the recovery of coconut plantations. At each new displacement, the population was relocated to so-called *fare rahui*,[3] which were temporary dwellings. It appears that, despite the division of the atoll's land between four extended families, the *rahui* were not, at least initially, performed in a competitive way, but rather everyone was involved throughout the year in a collective, communal exploitation of various areas that were considered to be community assets. Thereafter, the importance of profit overtook the sense of community cohesion and every family started to run their areas separately while continuing to synchronise the rotation between zones.

The lagoon's exploitation was performed in parallel with the exploitation of the coconut trees so that the anthropogenic pressure on the lagoon's ecosystem was never too strong. When regulations on compulsory school attendance came into effect, part of the population was forced to stay in the main village. The last official *rahui* involving mass mobility that took place in Fakarava occurred in July 1975. Thereafter, the women remained in the village making craft objects and caring for children attending school, while men and teenage boys went to harvest and tend to less remote coconut tree fields. The length of stays has become shorter over time, but the social dimension remained important. As the village lifestyle is increasingly Westernised, the return to the coconut fields is seen as a return to traditional *Paumotu* lifestyle. The links to the family group and to the ancestral land narrow in the sector, and a lifestyle that could be considered an indicator of poverty in the context of the village is claimed as traditional. Currently, periodic visits to the fields involving stays of generally less than two weeks are undertaken by some family members.

Institutional reappropriation

Recently, the *rahui* concept has taken a new, ecological direction. New priorities have emerged since the atoll was declared a biosphere reserve. Environmental management is now an important consideration in the development of the atoll, and local and international institutions have proposed and implemented management models to ensure the sustainability of the atoll ecosystem's biodiversity. Three major management models are in operation, each set up by a different entity,

---

3   *Fare rahui*: provisional house built in *rahui* area.

but which are nonetheless complementary. The first was proposed by the MAB (Man and Biosphere program, associated with UNESCO) on all Fakarava territory, which divides the atoll into three zones: a central area, a buffer zone and a transition area. This model is designed as a tool for sensitising the population and tourists to key ecological considerations. It identifies important areas of biodiversity and biological heritage. The second model, the General Territorial Plan (PGA) applies land management laws and edicts to the land. The third model, the PGEM is the one most concerned with the *rahui*, and was validated in 2007. This model is the regulatory and legislative tool for the entire marine section of the atoll, from the lagoon to the outside reef slopes. Under the last two plans, management models have been developed: the Urban Department for the PGA and the Fishery Department for the PGEM. The same area may be part of different management models simultaneously, although the PGA and PGEM are legislative tools and are therefore defined by the French Polynesian civil code.

The goal of PGEM is to ensure management of maritime space, both in terms of exploitation of natural resources and the regulation of related human activities. This includes rational utilisation of resources and space, management of user conflicts, control of degradation and pollution of the marine environment, and protection of marine ecosystems and endangered species. The PGEM is thus a document for space management that defines the terms of use, management, support and recovery of the lagoon. The delineation of zoning has been made by means of a strong participatory approach towards the atoll's population, which was actively included in the decision-making process. Each activity sector has been consulted to reflect the opinion of each party and the cultural aspect has been prominent in establishing the structure. The space is divided into several zones, which define the procedures and rules for any activity. There are four areas on the lagoon: an activity area, a protected tourist area, a protected natural area and, of particular interest here, a *rahui* area. This last area is a marine area subject to active management intervention to ensure the maintenance of habitats and to meet the requirements of specific species. The main objectives are to provide communities living near the area with the opportunity to maintain a sustainable lifestyle and to focus on research and monitoring environmental management alongside ancestral practices.

The *rahui* area is located in the north-western part of the atoll and encompasses about a quarter of the lagoon. It is split into two zones, and each zone is open alternately every two years. When a *rahui* is promulgated in one zone by the standing committee (composed mainly of inhabitants of the atoll), fishing (fish only) is prohibited in the whole zone. Simultaneously, fishing is allowed in the second zone. There is a second type of *rahui* that concerns particular species. All species of lobster and the coconut crabs (*kaveu*) are protected across the atoll, which is also divided into two parts by a north–south border and open alternately every two years. This latter, land-based *rahui* completes the marine *rahui*. The enforcement of these *rahui* follows a conservation and preservation focus on, on the one hand, the environment and, on the other hand, on cultural practices inherent in the operation of this ecosystem.

The development of the PGEM not only took the richness and diversity of lagoons into account, but also, most importantly, the needs of the population. It is possible to enumerate several dimensions of *rahui* practice as it is formulated by institutions. There is, firstly, an ecological dimension aimed at the conservation of biological heritage, which is directly linked to the new issues of tourist-based development, and therefore economic development of the atoll. Secondly, a strong ethical vision pervades the system as it reconciles economic and social development of the population while preserving the environment at the base for the perpetuation of local and cultural traditions.

There is another type of *rahui*, imposed by the Fisheries Department that applies across French Polynesia concerning only certain species. The system has two operating periods during the year: a period during which the *rahui* regulates fishing activities and imposes a minimum size for species in order that they can reproduce at least once during their lives; and a period of *tapu*, which prohibits exploitation, trade and consumption of targeted species. There is, in these systems, an important contradiction to the sense of the word *rahui*: the PGEM implies a total prohibition of the use of resources on demarcated areas; whereas the Fisheries Service uses the word *rahui* for a period of legal and regulated operation, in parallel with a complete ban on operations during the *tapu* phase. The vagueness in the terms used and the overlay of local and national models has often made it difficult for the local population to understand and conform to the restrictions.

THE RAHUI

The reappropriation of the term and concept of *rahui* by government institutions demonstrates their determination to integrate, respect and value traditions and local cultural practices. But it appears that, due to a lack of information and communication from government, the majority of the population prefers to dismiss the model rather than to try to understand and adhere to it. It is perhaps too simplistic to suggest that the term *rahui* loses some of its meaning when used by government institutions, but it is undeniable that the reappropriation of the concept must be adjusted for, and maybe simplified to fully convince, the local population, who currently refuse to acknowledge it. During my fieldwork, I realised that the population was very poorly informed on this topic and that the PGEM was primarily understood as a ban. Indeed, most fishermen saw the *rahui* only as a means by the government and institutions to control their activities and therefore to reduce their freedom of action. This is, however, clearly not the purpose of PGEM, which only aims to manage and organise the harmonious ecological development of the lagoon by enforcing these new rules.

Our discussions with the different parties have revealed that many inhabitants did not know of the existence of these management regimes or, if they knew, they were not aware of the location of regulated areas. Lagoon users, because of their lack of information on this topic, prefer then to ignore the rules and continue to fish as they have always done. The size of the lagoon makes it difficult to control these activities. Self-control is the chief means of compliance advocated by the authorities, but it is rarely practiced because, in such a small population, family and friendship networks cancel its efficiency. The *rahui* within PGEM raises issues, as it refers to a practice that makes little sense to people who are supposed to implement and respect it, because respecting something in which they don't believe is not possible. And that is certainly the main issue of PGEM and of its *rahui* areas: the *Paumotus* do not believe anymore in the sacredness of the practice and the lagoon.

9

European contact and systems of governance on Tongareva

Charlotte N. L. Chambers

Tongareva is the northernmost and largest atoll in the Cook Islands and is often referred to as Penrhyn after the first European sighting of the atoll in 1788 when the crew of the ship *Lady Penrhyn* 'saw a low flat island, bearing east to north east, seven or eight miles distant'.[1] The first sustained period of European contact with Tongareva occurred in January 1853 when an American brig, the *Chatham*, was wrecked off the south-west coast. E.H. Lamont spent a year on the island as a result of this wrecking, and later wrote an account of his time in *Wild Life Among the Pacific Islanders*.[2] Although much coloured by the lens of the Victorian period in which it was written, this book is considered by many to be a definitive account of Polynesian life on Tongareva prior to European contact.[3] The first London Missionary Society (LMS) missionaries arrived on Tongareva in 1854, shortly after the rescue of Lamont. Following the early successes of using Pacific Islanders as missionaries, in March 1854 the LMS sent three 'native teachers' to the atoll because 'the fear of being devoured is gone and

---

1 Watt, Lt., 1789. 'Lieutenant Watt's narrative of the return of the *Lady Penrhyn* transport', *The Voyage of the Governor Phillip to Botany Bay*, edited by Anon., 222–24, London: Stockdale, cited in P.B. Roscoe 1987. 'Of canoes and castaways: reassessing the population of Tongareva (Penrhyn Island) at contact'. *Pacific Studies* 11(1): 43–61, p. 244.
2 Lamont, E.H., 1867. *Wild Life Among the Pacific Islanders*. London: Hurst and Blackett.
3 Buck, P.H., 1932. *Ethnology of Tongareva*. Bulletin no. 92. Honolulu: Bernice P. Bishop Museum.

our young men are anxious to be the first bearers of the Gospel torch among them'.[4] In 1862, Tongareva was visited by Peruvian slave traders and, according to Maude's meticulous account of this period, suffered a 66.7 per cent population decrease as a result.[5] When the LMS missionary Wyatt Gill visited Tongareva in 1863 he found only 40 inhabitants living in Omoka and 48 spread between the other villages.[6] After the sudden population decline engendered by the slave trade, the patrilineal *ariki* (chief, king) structure was likely to have been highly fragmented.[7] Gill, for example, reports that the remaining Tongarevans were unable to decide which remaining *ariki* should have prominence, suggesting that 'there is no chief whatsoever … so that the [Christian] teacher is virtually king'.[8] The remaining Tongarevan population was eventually centralised into the two villages of Omoka and Te Tautua, which remain the contemporary settlements on Tongareva today.

By the late 1800s, Tongareva was involved in trading pearl shell, for which its lagoon was renowned, and the export of copra, with Omoka functioning as the main port. In 1889, after Tongareva was included in Britain's annexation of the Cook Islands,[9] a body called the Hau was instituted: 'an informally constituted council of elders which was recognised as the local government'.[10] The Hau was designated responsibility for allowing access to the lagoon for the collection of the pearl oysters and also the management of the different *motu* (islets) for copra harvest. Although membership of the Hau would have likely reflected pre-existing kinship structures, Campbell notes that the Hau often had difficulties enforcing its decisions as 'their positions had, in effect, been created by the British administration'.[11] Campbell suggests that, at least initially, this colonial 'taint' would have affected the ability of the Hau to enforce judgements.

---

4   Buzacott, 1866. *Mission life in the islands of the Pacific*, cited in A.R.T. Campbell, 1985. *Social Relations in Ancient Tongareva*. Pacific Anthropological Records no. 36. Honolulu: Bernice P. Bishop Museum, p. 10.
5   Maude, H.E., 1981. *Slavers in Paradise: The Peruvian Slave Trade in Polynesia, 1862–1864*. Canberra: Australian National University Press.
6   Maude, 1981, p. 10.
7   Campbell, 1985.
8   Gill, 1887, cited in Campbell, 1985, p. 80.
9   See Gilson, R., 1980. *The Cook Islands 1820–1963*. Wellington: Victoria University Press.
10 Campbell, 1985, p. 13.
11 Campbell, 1985, p. 14.

The Hau on Tongareva was replaced by the island council in 1901, which comprised of six elected members: three members taken from the settlements at Omoka and Te Tautua respectively, two *ariki*, and the colonial resident agent, who functioned as president.[12] The island councils were empowered by the colonial administration to take on the role of mediator and manager of the trade relations by making local ordinances or by-laws. Only four such by-laws were established, between 1901 and 1965, in order to deal with issues of wandering pigs and the use of obscene language.[13] The island council could also use its ordinance powers to impose *rahui* over the gathering of copra and pearl shell.

The ability of island councils to establish by-laws for the island continued unchanged by the *Cook Islands Act 1915*. In the *Cook Islands Amendment Act 1957*, however, by-laws made by island councils were subject to approval by the high commissioner; thus, Section 51.3 of the Act reads: 'no by-law made by an Island Council shall become law until it has been assented to by the High Commissioner'.[14] In the *Cook Islands Outer Islands Act 1987*, there remains a clear hierarchy of decision-making powers, although any by-law made by island councils must first be approved by a national executive council in Rarotonga before eventually attaining the approval of the relevant member of parliament for the island and, finally, ratification by parliament. The present functions of island councils, then, are slightly ambiguous in that they enjoy relative autonomy in the outer island context, yet still require centralised government approval for the establishment of any by-laws.

As a consequence Tongareva, as an outer island, has a system of governance that is at once 'local' but also clearly associated with legislative priorities of the central government based in Rarotonga. Indeed, while those distant from Tongareva may construct the island council as an effective structure reflecting 'local' interest and needs, this belies the varying social, political and cultural differences that the island council must negotiate in producing local decisions and

---

12   Campbell, 1985.
13   Crocombe, R.G., 1964. *Land Tenure in the Cook Islands*, Oxford University Press.
14   See www.paclii.org/cgi-bin/sinodisp/ck/legis/ck-nz_act/ciaa1957212/index.html?stem=&synonyms=&query=Cook%20Islands%20amendment%20act%201957.

courses of action.[15] The colonial origins of the Tongarevan Island Council and its current relationship to both local and national structures of authority are important for understanding the varying levels of authority and respect garnered by the island council in its contemporary manifestation. This is particularly so with regard to its ability to institute *rahui*.

The use of *rahui* on Tongareva

Rahui or the Rarotonga equivalent, *ra'ui*, is a technique used by those in power to control or deny access to land, crops or areas of the sea.[16] *Rahui* were generally declared in response to declining resources, or to protect scarce resources from over-harvest.[17] *Rahui* works by 'bounding' or 'closing' physical areas, for example, *motu* in the case of copra, or areas of the lagoon in the case of pearl shell. These areas are protected by the invocation of *tapu* so that those who disobey or break *rahui* are subject to either physical or spiritual sanctions.[18] Tiraa discusses how on the southern Cook Island of Atiu, in pre-European contact times, punishments for breaking *rahui* could be as severe as execution, banishment or having one's house and other property destroyed.[19] Throughout the Cook Islands, breaking *rahui* was generally expected to be dealt with by community pressure or, in post-contact times, by sanctions imposed by the relevant island council.[20]

The fact that the practice of *rahui* remains in use on Tongareva is not insignificant, particularly as its use was legislated against in the Cook Islands through the 1908 *Te Mana Ra'ui Act*, which declared that 'the ancient right of *ra'ui* no longer existed in respect of any land which has been investigated by the Native Land Court'.[21] Moreover, that *rahui* continues to be used in a marine context is interesting given that the

---

15   See Robbins, P., 1998. 'Authority and environment: institutional landscapes in Rajasthan, India'. *Annals of the Association of American Geographers* 88(3): 410–35.
16   Crocombe, 1964.
17   Ama, A., 2003, 'Maeva – rites of passage: the highlights of family life'. In R. Crocombe & M.T. Crocombe (eds), *Akono'anga Maori: Cook Islands Culture*. Suva: University of the South Pacific, pp. 119–26.
18   Gilson, 1980.
19   Tiraa, A., 2006. 'Ra'ui in the Cook Islands – today's context in Rarotonga'. *SPC Traditional Marine Resource Management and Knowledge Information Bulletin* 19: 11–15.
20   Gilson, 1980.
21   Crocombe, 1964, p. 325.

1915 Act stipulated that '[n]ative customary title shall not extend … to any land below the high-water mark'.[22] Indeed, it appears that the isolated nature of the outer islands, such as Tongareva, combined with decentralised governance through island councils, has meant that these islands enjoy relative independence in their decision-making processes, one aspect of which is the persistence of *rahui*.

The survival of *rahui* also suggests something of its flexibility as a technique in responding to the changing situations and circumstances of the island as well as the ability of the islanders to make the most out of the cracks of recognition that continued to exist in the superimposed colonial systems. In pre-European contact times, *rahui* was a largely decentralised tool used by individual families on a day-to-day basis to protect coconut crops.[23] Lamont also notes, however, that there were instances where large-scale bans (what he terms *masanga* — synonym for *rahui*) were imposed by *ariki* and *taura* (priests) with the agreement of the *huaanga* (a ramage comprising a group of patrilineal extended families) in order to prevent starvation. As Lamont's account states:

> To '*masanga*' or put a ban on certain trees … is a matter of every-day occurrence with the economic landowner, that the supply of nuts may not fail, but to have the ban put on every tree throughout the island, and to be reduced to a very moderate allowance of food, was soon the case of great suffering … After a great deal of talking on the part of the natives [sic] with their usual excitement, the restrictions of the *masanga* were finally agreed to among themselves, and all the men placed around their necks a piece of platted sinnet as a badge of their acceptance of it.[24]

This *masanga* was devised in order to allow the coconuts on food lands to recover from over-harvesting. Yet, such was the dependency of the people on coconut, a decision not to exploit the resource located on their *motu* meant pressure to raid the coconut plantations on *motu* belonging to other *huaanga* around the island. In this case, then, a decision to protect and regenerate local coconut supplies through a ban on use resulted in conflict with surrounding groups. Such a drastic step thus required the consent of the whole *huaanga*

---

22 Crocombe, 1964, part 12, sec. 419.
23 Lamont, 1867.
24 Lamont, 1867, pp. 273–74.

as the consequences were far-reaching.²⁵ So important was longer term preservation of resources that *huaanga* contemplating *rahui* were willing to risk conflict with neighbouring *huaanga* and drastic reduction of food supplies.

Post-contact, with a growing reliance on imported goods, the emphasis was placed on protecting the resources (pearl shell and copra) that fell at the centre of the newly established trade relations upon which island income depended.²⁶ According to people interviewed during my fieldwork, *rahui* was also used to declare certain parts of the lagoon closed in order to allow pearl shell to replenish, with the last instance of this type of *rahui* occurring in the mid-1990s.²⁷

The way in which the Tongarevan people adapted practices such as *rahui* to the economic and social changes brought about by European contact is noteworthy. On the one hand, despite the seemingly negative hegemonic influence of the LMS missionaries and the colonial presence on Tongareva, the people were not simply passive in their reception of these forces and responded actively instead, modifying them to suit their purposes. These observations relate to a specific pragmatism noted by other scholars in relation to the alacrity with which Christianity, as one particular consequence of European contact, was adopted throughout the Pacific Islands. For example, writing with respect to the rapid conversion to the LMS-inspired Christian faith that spread rapidly throughout the Cook Islands, Buck notes that 'material benefit was associated with the new religion and, if such benefits could be obtained more readily by adopting that religion, why not adopt it?'²⁸ Cowling goes on to cite the LMS missionary John Williams, who made clear the relationship between missionisation and the subsequent expansion of commercial interests: 'Thus, wherever the missionary goes, new channels are cut for the streams of commerce'.²⁹ This, however, is not to imply that the Tongarevan people had total agency, as the 1915 *Cook Islands Act*

---

25   Buck, 1932.
26   Buck, 1932.
27   Papa R., pers. comm. with the author, 24 May 2006.
28   Buck, 1939. Cited in W. Cowling, 2006. 'Once you saw them, now you don't – the disappearance of Cook Island traditional craft production'. *Proceedings from the 2nd International Small Island Cultures Conference*. Sydney: Maquarie University Press, p. 30.
29   Williams, 1837. Cited in Cowling, 2006, p. 30.

best demonstrates. Nevertheless, the continued use of *rahui* suggests flexibility in terms of what such a designation could be applied to, although the basic premise of the technique remained unchanged.

In this respect, Hviding notes that customary mechanisms such as *rahui* can be characterised on the basis of their flexibility and their ability to be applied to changing situations and circumstances.[30] Although Hviding's comments pertain to a Melanesian context, he suggests with regard to the use of customary marine tenure (CMT) systems, that the success of CMT structures to adapt to change lies precisely in their unwritten and non-codified nature. This characteristic, he asserts, enables such systems to retain the capacity to rapidly adapt to any sudden changes that might occur, be it in terms of changes to usage patterns or ecological conditions. CMT systems are, therefore, able to perform 'functions in the modern context for which they were not designed'.[31] With respect to imposing closures on resources, Hviding further states that closures may not necessarily reflect absolute states of abundance or scarcity of a resource, but rather can be influenced by the 'perception of market prices, available transport and other factors that affect the demand for and number of potential harvests of the resource in question'.[32]

It appears, then, that there are many similarities between Hviding's perception of CMT systems and the flexibility in the way that *rahui* as a technique was used and adapted in the changing Tongarevan context. Moreover, although the structures by which *rahui* could be imposed changed from dispersed kin groups to a centralised island council, the island council system continues to depend on input from the Tongarevan people. Indeed, the inclusive structure of the island council, and the way *rahui* requires the agreement of the people it is attempting to manage in order to work, function to ensure it is a management tool that cannot simply be coopted by whoever is in power.

---

30   Hviding, E., 1998. 'Contextual flexibility: present status and future of customary marine tenure in Solomon Islands'. *Ocean and Coastal Management* 40: 253–69.
31   Polunin, 1984. Cited in Hviding, 1998, p. 255.
32   Hviding, 1998, p. 263. See also Chambers, C.N.L., 2008a. 'Bounding the Lagoon: Spatialising Practices and the Politics of Rahui, Tongareva, Cook Islands'. PhD thesis, University of Edinburgh.

THE RAHUI

Authorising *rahui*

In an interview with Papa M, I was given an eloquent description of the use of *rahui* when Tongareva was still involved in the copra trade. The use of *rahui* to close down *motu* around Tongareva was functioning up until the early 1980s and was used in order to allow the coconuts to replenish before the next harvest. Papa M's comments are significant, for they show how people were literally 'called in' to observe the *rahui* placed on particular *motu*:

> I recall I was a young boy, the *rahui* was still enforced over here. I still remember the time when the papa would come, an old man, with a *paatee* [slit drum], making a noise, calling out 'the *rahui*, the *rahui*', and the name of the *motu* that would be closed. He tried to make everyone aware that there would be a *rahui*. Then there would be a public notice put up by the island council. Everybody knew there would be a *rahui*. And if the *rahui* is enforced, no one was allowed to go over to that island. As a kid here, I know, I still remember, the time when we go [to the island], everybody would say a prayer. A prayer for the *rahui* to close, and then, for the *rahui* to open.[33]

As this quote from Papa M illustrates, the ability to 'call' the *rahui* was contingent on the whole community first being aware of the planned closure and second, abiding by the spiritually enforced sanctions, physically enacted by the people going to the site of the *rahui* and participating in prayer. Implied in his account is a community-wide recognition of the *mana* (respect, authority) of the elders who would call in the *rahui* and, in turn, respect for the *tapu* nature of the closed *motu*. As Papa M testifies, the *rahui* would start by producing a closure not just on the coconuts, but on physical access to the *motu* in question. This bounding of both resource and surrounding area as *tapu* was achieved by the imposition of a normative rule that, while relying on community recognition and adherence, also depended on the tacit recognition of the authority of the island council as the appropriate body to make such declarations and as having the right to punish those who disobeyed. Once the period of *rahui* was over, a prayer was again used to unbound the *motu* and open up the resource, once again allowing people to enter the area of land and harvest coconuts for copra. In terms of how the *rahui* works, then, the island council

---

33   Interview with the author, 24 May 2006.

played a key role in terms of adjudicating the need for *rahui*, where this *rahui* was to be located, and how long it would last. This role, at least according to Papa M's account, was endorsed by Tongarevan society more generally.

Comments made by other interviewees suggest a considerable shift between how Papa M recalled *rahui* to have worked in the past and the implications of placing a *rahui* on *pasua* at the time of my fieldwork. Instead of the ritualised 'calling in' of the *rahui* of old, and the clear and unproblematic obedience to the bounded *motu* and resource in question, other people suggested that placing *rahui* on *pasua* now would be problematic and difficult to enforce. In a group interview, for example, Papa T and his friend Papa J debated this point:

> Papa J: Well for the *pasua*, and how they are thinking of closing it now? I remember the last time, about 10 or 15 years ago, we started closing the shell, the mother pearl shell. They [the island council] closed the lagoon for two years. You know what happened? They never put someone in charge or whatever. People to look after the *rahui*. And by the time it came to open the lagoon, there was no shell! What was the point of closing it! What was the point? If they want to close it again now for the *pasua*, they need to get everyone, or select a team, make them police the boundary of the *rahui* ...
>
> Charlie: And monitor it?
>
> Papa J: And monitor it, yeah.
>
> Papa T: But the main thing with the *pasua*, they cannot close the *pasua* without the people's say.
>
> Papa J: That's what I said before!
>
> Papa T: Yes, they cannot do it.
>
> Charlie: Because people won't listen?
>
> Papa T: It is the people who will say close the lagoon or keep it open. It's the people who say. Not the council.[34]

Papa T's comments hint at a considerable shift in the authority vested in the island council. He emphasises the need to have 'the people' involved in deciding whether or not to 'close the lagoon or keep it

---

34   Group interview with the author, 16 May 2006.

open'. Moreover, if a closure was instated by the council alone, without the people's say, Papa J suggests that it would fail if it didn't also have people involved to monitor and enforce compliance. Indeed, concurrent with Papa J and Papa T's comments, it was not uncommon for people to suggest that a *rahui* on *pasua* would fail if it wasn't supported by the island populace as a whole. In the following interview, for example, Mama T questions how the island council would be able to enforce the proposed closure on the lagoon:

> Charlie: Do you think people will respect *rahui* now?
>
> Mama T: If it's a by-law. Only if it's going to be a by-law. If it's going to be a verbal meeting in the island council chamber over here, no. If it's just a notice up on the notice board there, that the council is saying there is no more *pasua* for selling, people won't listen. People will just ignore that notice. But they will respect it if it's a by-law. Because a by-law will give the police the right to check people's boats and follow it up. Only if it's a by-law. If it's just a verbal thing, people won't give a damn. They won't listen.[35]

Mama T's comments, echoing again the frustrations expressed by Papa J and Papa T, suggest that it would only be through legal means, by the island council generating a by-law for the police to enforce, that people would adhere to a *rahui* on *pasua*. Neither the power of the designation of *tapu*, nor a 'verbal meeting', nor even a 'notice' appear enough to guarantee compliance with the restricted access planned for the lagoon. Mama T's comments suggest that *rahui* needs to be combined with alternatively authorised structures, that of the by-law, to be effective. While the Tongarevan Island Council has, since its inception, had the legislative power to make by-laws, it appears that *rahui* has never previously required formalisation in the form of a by-law in order for it to be effective on Tongareva. Making the *rahui* a by-law would, as Mama T suggests, make the enforcement of the *rahui* a matter for the police, and in turn anyone who broke the *rahui* would be punishable by law. The implication of Papa J, Papa T and Mama T's comments is that the council lacks the ability to monitor and enforce *rahui* in relation to *pasua*. This suggests a significant change in the ability of the island council to effectively govern the marine environment in the current Tongarevan context.

---

35 Group interview, 16 May 2006.

The relationship between authority and *rahui* in contemporary contexts is not unique to Tongareva. Writing with regard to the recently re-established *ra'ui* on Rarotonga, Tiraa echoes the concerns of Mama T that the Koutu Nui, a formalised group of *mataiapo* (lesser chief), which sit underneath the House of *Ariki*, have lost the ability to punish people who fail to observe the five *ra'ui* areas established around the island.[36] There is ongoing debate on Rarotonga as to whether the various *ra'ui* could be given legal recognition under the *Environment Act 2003*, which would make the *ra'ui* a matter for the Ministry of Marine Resources and give the police powers to punish those who break it. Many support this proposal so as to limit the number of infringements and thus to increase the effectiveness of the *ra'ui* in protecting the marine environment. While some members of the Koutu Nui are supportive of this plan, other members see the lack of respect for *ra'ui* as a lack of respect for the *mana* of the traditional leaders. They feel that giving *ra'ui* a legal basis would further erode this respect as it would foster an approach to conservation learnt by fear rather than by traditional conventions of *mana* and *tapu*.[37]

Conclusion

The debates concerning the *rahui* on *pasua* at the time of my fieldwork speak to the complex relationships that surround practices of *rahui* and the structures of authority upon which they depend. In the Tongarevan context, contrasts in views concerning how *rahui* worked in the past with people's concerns as to how it might fail in the present, suggest that there is an important relationship between changing levels of respect accorded the contemporary Tongareva Island Council and the debates for and against a *rahui* on *pasua*. Indeed, residents such as Mama T appear to be pushing for a 'hybrid' *rahui*, one that still works on traditional principals, but has the added strength of legal protection in order to garner the necessary compliance.

Changes associated with missionisation and colonisation then, although changing the socio-spatial structures of authority in relation to land and resources, did not simply 'obliterate' pre-European contact

---

36   Tiraa, 2006.
37   Tiraa, 2006, p. 13.

knowledges and practices. Indeed, there were specific legal provisions for recognising these relationships and interests. Particularly in the outer island context of Tongareva, the island council was able to function in a relatively independent, though not locally uncontested, manner. *Rahui*, as a key 'tool' of the island council, survives as an example of 'traditional' knowledge and management practice in relation to land, water and resources. *Rahui*, however, is also a 'modern' product in that it is a form of governing resources that sits within a radically socio-spatially restructured Tongareva. In this regard, tradition, contra to the way in which it is commonly deployed as the binary opposite to the modern, is not meant to imply a state of fixity, of that which is unchanging or 'rooted'. Rather, as this article has briefly explored, tradition as invoked by the people of Tongareva in the context of *rahui* is inherently dynamic, mutable and ongoing in its negotiation today.[38]

---

38 I would like to thank the people from Tongareva who participated in my research as well as assistance from Dr Andrea Nightingale and Professor Jane Jacobs at the University of Edinburgh.

10

Traditional marine resources and their use in contemporary Hawai'i[1]

Alan M. Friedlander, Janna M. Shackeroff and John N. Kittinger

Introduction

Marine resources were important to the ancient Hawai'ians for subsistence, culture and survival. But in recent times, intensive fishing pressure, particularly in more populated areas, has led to substantial declines in many highly prized and vulnerable species.[2] Factors contributing to this include a growing human population, destruction of habitat, introduction of new and overly efficient fishing techniques (e.g. inexpensive monofilament gill nets, SCUBA,

---

1   This chapter is adapted from Friedlander, A.M., Shackeroff, J.M. & Kittinger, J.N., 2013. 'Customary marine resource knowledge and use in contemporary Hawai'i'. *Pacific Science* 67(3): 441–60.
2   Friedlander, A.M. & De Martini, E.E., 2002. 'Contrasts in density, size, and biomass of reef fishes between the northwestern and the main Hawai'ian Islands: the effects of fishing down apex predators'. *Marine Ecology Progress Series* 230: 253–64; Williams, I.D., Walsh, W.J., Schroeder, R.E., Friedlander, A.M., Richards, B.L. & Stamoulis, K.A., 2008. 'Assessing the relative importance of fishing impacts on Hawai'ian coral reef fish assemblages along regional-scale human population gradients'. *Environmental Conservation* 35: 261–72.

Global Positioning System or GPS), and loss of traditional conservation practices.[3] Further, there is poor compliance with state fishing laws and regulations and insufficient enforcement.

Owing to the failures of conventional marine management, government and local communities are increasingly interested in conserving marine ecosystems for future generations. Efforts underway throughout Hawai'i to better understand, manage and conserve ocean resources include a shift towards ecosystem-based management by government agencies, development of school curricula and university programs in natural resource management, and the inclusion of stakeholders in the management process. Integrating Native Hawai'ian traditional ecological knowledge (TEK)[4] and traditional practices into contemporary marine management is an important element in these approaches, and a number of communities around the state are implementing these strategies (Figure 22). These efforts face challenges deriving from such things as power and politics,[5] postcolonial legacies,[6] and epistemological differences.[7] How TEK is integrated into contemporary Hawai'ian marine resource management and the impact this has on ocean condition may provide insights into better management practices elsewhere and is the focus of this chapter.

---

3   Friedlander, A.M., Brown, E.K., Jokiel, P.L., Smith, W.R. & Rodgers, K.S., 2003. 'Effects of habitat, wave exposure, and marine protected area status on coral reef fish assemblages in the Hawai'ian archipelago'. *Coral Reefs* 22: 291–305.
4   Berkes, F., Colding, J. & Folke, C., 2000. 'Rediscovery of traditional ecological knowledge as adaptive management'. *Ecological Applications* vol. 10:1251–62.
5   Shackeroff, J.M. & Campbell, L.M., 2007. 'Traditional ecological knowledge in conservation research: problems and prospects for their constructive engagement'. *Conservation & Society* 5: 343–60.
6   Tuhiwai-Smith, L., 1999. *Decolonizing Methodologies: Research and Indigenous Peoples.* New York: Zed Books Ltd.
7   Agrawal, A., 2002. 'Indigenous knowledge and the politics of classification'. *International Social Science Journal* 54: 287–97.

10. TRADITIONAL MARINE RESOURCES AND THEIR USE IN CONTEMPORARY HAWAI'I

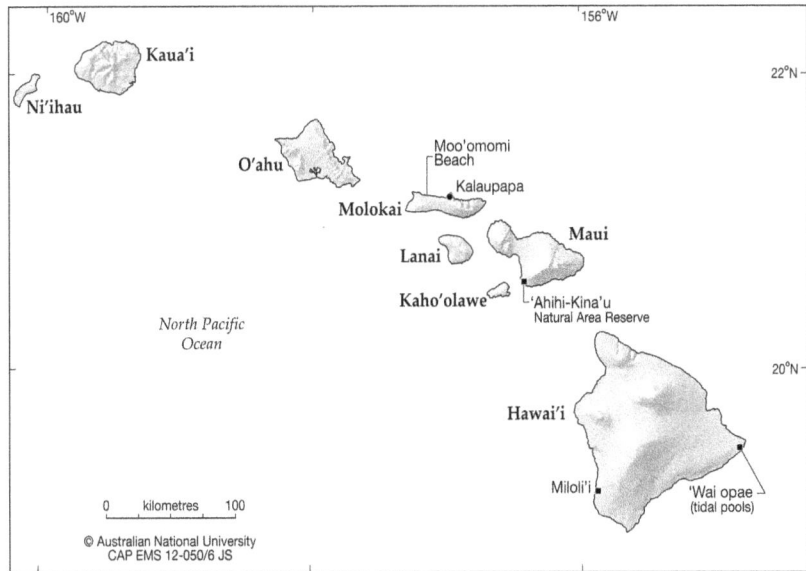

Figure 22: Map of Hawai'i
Source: © The Australian National University CAP EMS 12-050/6 JS

Marine resource use, knowledge and management in ancient Hawai'i

Hawai'ians of old (pre-1800) depended on fishing for survival, which motivated them to acquire a sophisticated understanding of the factors that caused limitations and fluctuations in their marine resources. Based on their familiarity with specific places and through much trial and error, Hawai'ian communities were able to develop social and cultural controls on fishing that fostered sustainable use of marine resources.[8] In traditional Hawai'ian society, the basic unit of land division and socioeconomic organisation was the *ahupua'a*, which radiated from interior uplands through valleys into the sea and was managed adaptively according to resource availability and fluctuations.[9] This type of land division allowed integrated

---

8 Titcomb, M., 1972. *Native Use of Fish in Hawai'i*. Honolulu: University of Hawai'i Press.
9 Kirch, P.V., 1989. *The Evolution of the Polynesian Chiefdom*. Cambridge University Press.

management of society and natural resources — forests, agricultural land, shoreline and ocean — by a single sociopolitical group at the local scale.

Within *ahupua'a*, fishing activities and catch distribution were strictly disciplined by *kapu* (rules). Harvest management was not based on a specific amount of fish but on identifying the specific times and places that fishing could occur so as to not disrupt basic processes and habitats of important food resources.[10] By allowing fish populations to replenish themselves, and by not interfering with important activities such as spawning, traditional Hawai'ian communities were able to maintain the productivity and fisheries yield near their villages.

Konohiki, land agents within *ahupua'a*, enforced *kapu* on behalf of *ali'i* (chiefs). Knowledgeable of the lunar and seasonal cycles that cause resources to fluctuate, *konohiki* were often advised by *kupuna* (elders) and *po'o lawai'a* (master fishermen). Master fishermen played a prominent role in the culture, were of a special lineage, and trained for years as apprentices. Their awareness of subtle changes in the environment made them sentinels of the ecosystem.[11]

Fishing activities and catch distribution were strictly disciplined by rules for which death was prescribed for severe transgressions.[12] Taking only so much so as not to diminish the supply, and not disrupting spawning cycles, represented some of the foundational rules. The first fish of the catch were reserved for *kupuna* and offerings to ancestors. *Ko'a*, or special aggregation sites, were tended and fished with care to prevent depletion. Certain species such as *moi* (Pacific threadfin) were reserved only for the chiefs. Other food such as *ulua* (jacks), *kumu* (an endemic goatfish) and *honu* (turtles) were the embodiment of the gods and were restricted for consumption by women. Many of these laws provided protection for important species and allowed Hawai'ians to derive sustenance from the ocean for millennia.

---

10   Friedlander, A., Poepoe, K., Poepoe, K., Helm, K., Bartram, P., Maragos, J. & Abbott, I., 2002. 'Application of Hawai'ian traditions to community-based fishery management'. *Proc. 9th Inter. Coral Reef Symp* vol. 2: 813–18; Poepoe, K., Bartram, P. & Friedlander, A., 2007. 'The use of traditional Hawai'ian knowledge in the contemporary management of marine resources'. In N. Haggan, B. Neis & I. Baird (eds), *Fishers' Knowledge in Fisheries Science and Management*. Paris: UNESCO, pp. 117–41.
11   Poepoe et al., 2007.
12   Titcomb, 1972.

Demise of the traditional system

Following Western contact, a variety of sociopolitical factors led to the demise of the traditional system of marine resource management in the late eighteenth to early nineteenth centuries. The Native Hawai'ian population declined precipitously due to introduced diseases, leading to widespread loss of knowledge and decline in the transmission of TEK. Western influences resulted in intensive resource extraction that was directed towards the acquisition of foreign goods and the beginnings of a cash economy. In 1848, the Mahele 'Aina (*Land Division Act*) established fee simple ownership of land, enabling foreigners to purchase land, which ushered in the plantation era and resulted in an influx of different ethnic groups.[13] While this led to the breakdown of the *ahupua'a* system, laws granting management of the near-shore fisheries resources by the *konohiki* remained. Annexation by the United States, however, and the *Organic Act* of 1900 that followed, repealed all *konohiki* rights and opened fishing to all citizens.[14]

The early 1900s saw the solidification of the cash economy and large increases in the commercial landing of marine resources. Japanese immigrants introduced new fishing technologies and replaced Native Hawai'ian people as the dominant commercial fishermen.[15] Just prior to the Second World War, commercial fishing in Hawai'i was a multimillion dollar industry that employed hundreds of people directly and thousands indirectly. But, after the war, many fishermen were unwilling or unable to return to commercial fishing. Recent decades have seen Hawai'i's rapid growth in tourism, an increasingly urban resident population, and the continued development of shoreline areas for tourism and recreation. The character of coastal fisheries is dominated by recreational anglers and a greater number of part-time commercial fishers who have curtailed their fishing to take advantage of more lucrative economic activities.

---

13 Chinen, J.J., 1958. *The Great Mahele: Hawai'i's Land Division of 1848*. Honolulu: University of Hawai'i Press.
14 Meller, N., 1985. *Indigenous Ocean Rights in Hawai'i*. Sea Grant Marine Policy and Law Report UNIHI-SEAGRANT-MP-86-01. Honolulu: UH Sea Grant College Program.
15 Schug, D., 2001. 'Hawai'i's commercial fishing industry: 1820–1945'. *Hawai'ian J. History* 35: 15–34.

Contemporary centralised management

Today, myriad state and federal authorities provide for the management of Hawai'i's coastal resources and do so based on Western science and implemented by government resource managers. As compared to traditional forms, contemporary fisheries management strategies are based on principles of maximum sustainable yield and conserving species at current levels. Knowledge is accrued through quantitative studies of single stocks with people considered separate from the natural world, and information transmitted in published literature. These, in addition to the scale, methods of assessment, fishing controls and planning horizons differ greatly from traditional Hawai'ian strategies of resource management.

Table 1. Comparisons of customary and conventional marine resource management in Hawai'i and application in integrated approaches.

Customary management	Description	Conventional management	Integrated approaches
Spatial	Areas closed to fishing (*kapu* zones), can be temporary or permanent (e.g. during Makahiki; rotating Aku/'Ōpelu *kapu*)	Marine protected areas, temporary fisheries closures	Community managed marine areas, with established *kapu* zones to replenish resources if needed
Temporal	Restricting fishing/harvesting activities during specific times. Often short duration, specific to certain species, and for specific events (e.g. religious ceremonies, protect spawning aggregations)	Closed seasons	Community-based moon calendars showing which species are spawning and should be *kapu*
Gear	Restrictions on certain harvesting methods or techniques; chiefly control of materials for fishing gear and boats, which limited access to some fisheries resources	Gear prohibitions	Restrictions on certain gear (e.g. for laynets, or no spearfishing with SCUBA)

Customary management	Description	Conventional management	Integrated approaches
Effort	Limits on access to certain areas (e.g. only residents of *ahupua'a* could access adjacent reef); limiting who can harvest certain species, use certain gear, or fish certain areas	Permitting territorial user rights systems for fisheries (TURFS) and limited entry fisheries	Community-based subsistence fishing areas with rules developed in an inclusive, place-based manner; permitted access for local families or residents in a district (*moku*)
Species	Prohibitions on consumption of certain species, often related to class, gender, or lineage	Protection of vulnerable or endangered species	Bans on certain species until populations regenerate; limits on harvest for culturally significant species or resources that contribute significantly to local food security
Catch	Restricting the quantity of harvest; social norms discourage wasting and other harmful practices	Total allowable catch; individually transferable quotas (ITQs)	Communal harvest events to sustain connections to local resources; educational and outreach programs to connect community members and build social capital
Aquaculture	Creation of fishponds, stocked with wild-caught juveniles, which sequestered nutrients from uplands and served as insurance against famine	Modern aquaculture	Rebuild and revitalise fishponds to provide fisheries resources to communities; explore creation of Community Supported Fisheries (CSF) models to connect communities to local fishponds
Enforcement	Violations of customary restrictions resulted in sanctions or punishments that could be severe	Fines; penalties; licence revocation	Develop and implement a penalty schedule of graduated sanctions that includes community service by violators in restoration activities

Source: Adapted from Cinner and Aswani (2007), McClenachan and Kittinger (2012), and Jokiel et al. (2011).

Hawai'i's contemporary coastal resource management reflects the historically sectoral-based governance of oceans in the United States, where at least 20 federal agencies implement over 140 ocean-related statutes.[16] It is well documented that contemporary marine

---

16 Crowder, L.B. et al. 2006. 'Resolving mismatches in U.S. ocean governance'. *Science* 313: 617–18.

management is riddled with gaps and overlaps.[17] Centralised, top down and sectoral twentieth-century marine management tends to address single species or single issues rather than the system holistically.[18] In Hawai'i's geography, centralisation means that most marine management is enacted in urban Honolulu, far removed from the local communities of the neighbouring islands.

Contemporary marine management in Hawai'i is complicated by additional problems. The heterogeneity of Hawai'i's marine resources, biogeography and the local communities is not well suited to centralised, top-down management. Issues surrounding political appointments, failed management strategies like rotational closures,[19] and some of the United States' lowest levels of resource management funding contribute to the failure of contemporary management.

Renaissance of traditional management in the Pacific

The renaissance of traditional management throughout the Pacific and rediscovery of traditional techniques has led to improved management of fisheries in the region.[20] Governments of many Pacific Islands are recognising customary marine tenure (CMT) rights by communities and are helping to facilitate more localised management of marine resources. In Fiji, a national network of non-governmental and government organisations supports over 200 locally managed marine areas that are leading to the revival of traditional resource practices to improve management and maximise benefits to local communities.[21]

---

17   Young, O. R. 2002. *Institutional Dimensions of Environmental Change: Fit, Interplay, and Scale*. Cambridge, Mass.: MIT Press.
18   Leslie, H. & McLeod, K., 2007. 'Confronting the challenges of implementing marine ecosystem-based management'. *Front Ecol Environ* 5: 540–48.
19   Williams, I.D., Walsh, W.J., Miyasaka, A. & Friedlander. A.M. 2006. 'Effects of rotational closure on coral reef fishes in the Waikiki–Diamond Head Fishery Management Area, Oahu, Hawai'i'. *Marine Ecology Progress Series* 310: 139–49.
20   Johannes, R.E., 2002. 'The renaissance of community-based marine resource management in Oceania'. *Annual Review of Ecology and Systematics* 33: 317–40.
21   Veitiyaki, J., Aalbersberg, B., Tawake, A., Rupeni, E. & Tabunakawai, K., 2003. 'Mainstreaming resource conservation: the Fiji Locally Managed Marine Area Network and its influence on national policy'. *Resource Management in Asia-Pacific*. Working Paper no. 42. Canberra: Resource Management in Asia-Pacific Program, Research School of Pacific and Asian Studies, The Australian National University.

Palau's traditional practice of *bul* involves the council of chiefs placing reef areas off limits to fishing during known spawning and feeding periods.[22] This traditional *bul* system has become the basis for Palau's network of protected areas and its protected area network law. These successes are not restricted to the Pacific Islands and, indeed, are found in many other regions around the world.[23]

Reviving traditional practices in Hawai'i

Reviving traditional practices and integrating them into contemporary activities is gaining momentum in Hawai'i. Despite the decline in traditional marine resource management since Western contact, there remain pockets of cultural continuity in Hawai'i where TEK and practice have persisted unbroken for millennia.[24] 'Cultural *kipuka*' represent areas of (usually rural) Hawai'i where cultural practice remains unbroken and authentic.[25] In these places, where TEK is intact and transmission of knowledge continues, *kupuna* and knowledgeable practitioners can be engaged as holders of expert knowledge. The continuance of subsistence fishing activities is one of the ways that knowledge, values and identity are transferred to succeeding generations. Cultural survival is thus entwined with resource conservation.

TEK is gaining attention in Hawai'i, as elsewhere, because ocean ecosystem structure and function continue to decline, despite conventional marine managements efforts. Persistent ecological decline, threats to the transmission of TEK, as well as the increase in power and political voice of Native Hawai'ian people represent potential reasons for the increasing attention to TEK. Hawai'ian scholars have recorded

---

22 Johannes, R.E., 1981. *Words of the Lagoon: Fishing and Marine Lore in the Palau District of Micronesia.* Berkeley: University of California Press.
23 Berkes et al., 2000; Cinner, J.E., Wamukota, A., Randriamahazo, H. & Rabearisoa, A., 2009. 'Toward institutions for community-based management of inshore marine resources in the western Indian ocean'. *Marine Policy* 33(3): 489–96.
24 McGregor, D., 2007. *Na Kua'aina: Living Hawai'ian Culture.* Honolulu: Bishop Museum Press.
25 McGregor, 2007.

TEK with attention to environmental change and practices,[26] and cross-cultural and interdisciplinary teams are beginning to elicit TEK to integrate traditional and Western scientific perspectives.[27]

Community involvement in marine resource management has increased markedly in the past few years. The following pages summarise the efforts across the state and case studies of local communities that are engaged in TEK.

Regulation and policy integrating TEK

Hawai'ian TEK is being enveloped into governance of marine resources, from the local community to the federal scale. For example, the Western Pacific Regional Fishery Management Council is now required by federal law to integrate Native Hawai'ian traditional knowledge into fisheries management plans, and the council is also incorporating the *ahupua'a* concept into management. In addition, the authorising regulations of Papahānaumokuākea Marine National Monument (PMNM), which manages the Northwestern Hawai'ian Islands, are based on *pono* (righteousness) practices, or a sense of Native Hawai'ian cultural integrity. PMNM's Monument Management Plan (2008) calls for the incorporation of TEK into day-to-day management.

At the state level, the Hawai'i Ocean Resources Management Plan has moved to a place-based approach, emphasising integration from mountain to sea. Traditional management is explicit in strategic actions, such as developing integrated natural and cultural resource planning and through demonstration *ahupua'a* projects. Additionally, it aims to establish island-wide support networks to increase community dialogue, develop a framework for education and build partnerships among various stakeholders.[28]

---

26 For example, Kamakau, S.M., 1976. *The Works of the People of Old (Na hana a ka po'e kahiko).* Translated from the newspaper *Ke Au 'Oko'a* by M.K. Pukui. Honolulu: Bishop Museum Press; Maly, K., & Pomroy-Maly, O., 2003. *Ka Hana Lawai'a a me na Ko'a o na Kai'Ewalu. A History of Fishing Practices and Marine Fisheries of the Hawai'ian Islands.* Honolulu: The Nature Conservancy.
27 For example, Poepoe et al., 2007.
28 Hawai'i Ocean Resources Management Plan (ORMP). 2008. *Final Report to the Twenty-Fourth Legislature, Regular Session of 2007 Coastal Zone Management Program.* Office of Planning, DBEDT.

Knowledge-sharing and capacity-building

A variety of community-based initiatives have emerged to ensure multigenerational knowledge-sharing and to build capacity across the state to protect and perpetuate traditional knowledge. Non-profit organisations, state and federal agencies, and communities are working in concert towards these ends. The Managing Better Together Learning Network, a project that brought together community marine practitioners to work toward improving their practice through sharing lessons and strategies exemplifies knowledge-sharing and capacity-building efforts that are bubbling up from Hawai'ian communities.[29] Since 2003, the network has grown from 12 to 22 participating communities and it is fostered by community-based organisations such as the Community Conservation Network and Hawai'i Community Stewardship Network.[30]

Enforcement

Much lore and intrigue surrounds the traditional Hawai'ian system of *kapu*, known for harsh enforcement of punishments for fishing infractions, sometimes with death. Traditionally, enforcement was enacted at the local level by *konohiki* acting upon real-time observations such as seasonality and population status. Contemporary communities in Hawai'i commonly complain about the lack of enforcement of marine regulations. As a result, community-based enforcement programs were initiated across Hawai'i, with Maui's 'Ahihi-Kina'u Natural Area Reserve in 1997 and, in 2003, with the Reef Stewardship Program at Wai 'Opae and Coast Watch at Miloli'i. These efforts gelled into 'Makai Watch', a formal partnership between the state and non-profit organisations that focuses on caring for near-shore marine resources with the active participation of local communities. Modelled after the Neighbourhood Watch program, Makai Watch volunteers in over 10 communities statewide serve as the 'eyes and ears' for conservation

---

29 Hawai'i Community Foundation, 2009. hawaiicommunityfoundation.org/index.php?id=257, Accessed 4 September 2009.
30 Hawai'i Community Foundation, 2009.

and resource enforcement officials. While not specifically a program integrating TEK, it represents a return to local enforcement and draws institutional parallels to traditional Hawai'i.

Examples of the contemporary use of traditional knowledge

Mo'omomi Bay, Moloka'i

The community in the Ho'olehu Hawai'ian Homesteads on the island of Moloka'i is actively engaged in managing their resources as well as educating users about traditional methods. Subsistence activities, including farming and fishing, supply about one-third of the food needed by the approximately 1,000 Hawai'ian residents of this community. The 1994 Hawai'i State Legislature created a process for designating community-based subsistence fishing areas. In response to this legislation, the local community created an organisation (Hui Malama o Mo'omomi), and prepared a fisheries management plan for the north-west coast of Moloka'i.[31]

Community resource monitors place an emphasis on high resolution monitoring using traditional observation methods that provide the basis for understanding local fisheries dynamics and adjusting fishing effort so that resources are not harvested at the wrong times and places.[32] By identifying peak spawning periods for important resource species, closures can be applied so as not to disturb the natural rhythms of these species. By observing spawning behaviour and gonad development, community monitors were able to develop a calendar identifying the spawning periods for the major resource species that can be used to validate the establishment of seasonal *kapu* to protect spawners.

An example of this strategy is the life cycle model developed for *moi*, an important resource both in ancient times and today. Ancient Hawai'ians had names for each life phase of the *moi*, and recognised

---

31 Hui Malama o Mo'omomi, 1995. Proposal to Designate Mo'omomi Community-Based Subsistence Fishing Area, Northwest Coast of Moloka'i. Prep. for Dept. of Land and Natural Resources, State of Hawai'i.
32 Friedlander et al., 2002.

that it changed sex. Traditional Hawai'ian conservation principles for *moi* included restrictions on the harvest of large females, depending on population structure, and restrictions on harvest during the spawning season. Minimising disturbance to spawning and nursery habitats was another important conservation practice.

Community-sanctioned norms for fishing conduct are reinforced through continual feedback based on site resource monitoring, education and peer pressure. The most effective means of eliciting proper conduct of fishing is through education of young people in the community to understand that they have responsibilities, as well as rights, for marine resource use. The continuation of traditional Hawai'ian practices in and around Mo'omomi Bay helps to maintain social and cultural identity and reinforces the values shared by the Ho'olehua community.

Kaho'olawe

For 50 years this island functioned as a de facto natural reserve since it served as a military bombing range until 1990. In 2003 access to Kaho'olawe was returned the state of Hawai'i and the Kaho'olawe Island Reserve Commission (KIRC) was established to manage the island and the surrounding waters in trust for the general public and the future Native Hawai'ian sovereign entity. This commission fosters access for Native Hawai'ians to practice cultural, spiritual and subsistence activities on the island and in the adjacent marine waters. The ocean management plan outlines fishing areas, cultural and subsistence activities, and enforcement policies that aim to integrate traditional practices with contemporary management.

Limited trolling is allowed in the reserve waters on two weekends each month. Vessel owners must register their vessel with the KIRC, apply for a permit and file catch reports. Applicants seeking to exercise traditional and customary rights and practices within the reserve must have their requests approved by the commission after review and consultation with cultural practitioners. Enforcement is conducted by state and federal agencies with additional surveillance provided by cultural practitioners. The KIRC mission also monitors the status of the ocean resources surrounding Kaho'olawe and improving the health of offshore areas.

Miloliʻi, Hawaiʻi

The predominantly Native Hawai'ian village of Miloli'i in 2005 secured *State Act 232*, establishing a community-based subsistence fishing area and thereby allowing the community to regulate its local coastal waters based on Native Hawai'ian principles. Act 232 directed the Hawai'i Department of Land and Natural Resources to develop proposed rules to ensure sustainable stocks of fish to preserve the traditional Hawai'ian lifestyle of the Miloli'i community. The Miloli'i community was once famous for the fishing of *'ōpelu* (mackerel scad). While *'ōpelu* is still fished by a few community members, traditional technology and practices have not been in regular use for over 50 years.

Numerous traditional practices associated with *'ōpelu* fishing helped to maintain healthy stocks. These included using only vegetable matter as chum, because fish-matter chum causes more rapid decomposition of dried fish and attracts predators that disrupted the spawning aggregations. Additional practices were returning a minimum of two reproductive fish to the water with each net haul, using nets that were not capable of removing entire aggregations, restricting fishing during spawning periods and strictly enforcing seasonal closures. Other aspects of traditional fishing for *'ōpelu* included an intimate knowledge of the aggregation sites (*ko'a*) and regular feeding of these *ko'a* prior to fishing. *Ko'a* would be tended at least three days per week by feeding vegetable matter to the aggregating fish. Certain *ko'a* were tended and subsequently fished by certain families. Tending would continue for approximately two months prior to fishing season. The fishing season would close during the seasonally rough winter months.

Today, some members of the Miloli'i community have started to fish *'ōpelu* again in the traditional way as part of an effort to teach youth about traditional practices and instill a sense of responsibility towards resource stewardship for many near-shore fisheries. One immediate manifestation of this effort is that, for the first time in over 60 years, a traditional *'ōpelu* canoe is now being used to fish in ways that once sustained both people and the fish stocks upon which they depended. Additional activities that accompany these efforts include teaching youth and other community members how to monitor biological resources in their areas, collecting historical knowledge from *kupuna* about changes in the area's marine resources and teaching youth how to collect, document and present marine resource knowledge through film, as well as being founding forces in the Makai Watch program. Key community members believe that the sharing of traditional knowledge and values with youth will help build a solid foundation for future wise choices in resource management.[33]

Kalaupapa, Moloka'i

The remote Kalaupapa Peninsula on the island of Moloka'i achieved notoriety in 1865 when the Kingdom of Hawai'i instituted a century-long policy of forced segregation of persons afflicted with Hansen's disease,[34] also known as leprosy. Former Hansen's disease patients, despite being free to leave, still live at Kalaupapa. Public access to this community is limited because of regulations safeguarding privacy.

Owing to its isolation and unique political structure, Kalaupapa has a semblance of local management and control of its resources. Residents abide by state regulations but visitors are restricted to pole fishing only. Violations of the Kalaupapa fishing policy or state regulations result in the visitor being declared unwelcome and banned from future visits to Kalaupapa. Boats can come within one mile of the shoreline but the community often expresses their displeasure with these actions.

Ni'ihau

Ni'ihau, the smallest inhabited island in Hawai'i, is privately owned with a resident population of about 130 Native Hawai'ians. The only Hawai'ian island where the Hawai'ian language is the primary spoken language, Ni'ihau has no stores and inhabitants fish and farm for subsistence. The Ni'ihauan's believe that the commodification of marine resources elsewhere in Hawai'i has led to serious declines in marine resources, and therefore they allow no commercial harvest by residents. Fishing is limited to castnets, spears and pole and line. Other conservation strategies include taking only what is needed, rotating fishing areas and fishing a variety of species so as not to deplete certain locations or stocks. Boats from Kauai often come to Ni'ihau but many residents have family on Kauai and intensive fishing by these outsiders is discouraged.

---

33 Walter Paulo, pers. comm. with the author.
34 www.nps.gov/kala/historyculture/hansens1.htm.

These case studies illustrate both the parallels in renewed traditional resource management, as well as their heterogeneity. In such cases, one of the more common tools used to help regulate fishing effort and timing is the moon calendar. Hawai'ians of old developed this tool for holistic understanding of marine and terrestrial environments,[35] and it is used today in select communities.[36] The moon calendar emphasises certain repetitive biological and ecological processes (e.g. fish spawning, aggregation and feeding habits) that function at different time scales (e.g. seasonal, monthly and daily). Fishermen can use moon calendars by validating it at specific locations and regulating effort accordingly.

Comparisons with other management strategies

Scientific surveys of various locations around Hawai'i show that locations under community-based management with customary stewardship harbour fish biomass that is equal to or greater than no-take marine protected areas. Both of these types of management have significantly greater biomass compared with partially protected areas and areas that are open to all fishing. From this analysis, it is clear that community-managed areas, where appropriate, are as effective as no-take areas. Additionally, partial protection is no more effective than areas with little to no regulation.

Ways forward

The return to the local scale of management represents a type of contemporary adaptation to traditional management practices. Each community will have to develop management strategies that are compatible with their unique situation. For a host of political, ethical and historical issues, it is not possible to directly implement traditional practices in the contemporary context.[37] Instead, reviving traditional practices most often represents a case of adaptation of traditional with contemporary practices rather than direct transference. Environment, history and resources dictate what type of management regime is most

---

35 Edith Kanaka'ole Foundation, 1995. Draft Ke Kalai Maoli Ola No Kanaloa, Kaho'olawe Cultural Use Plan. Kaho'olawe Island Reserve Commission.
36 Poepoe et al., 2007.
37 Shackeroff, J.M. & Campbell, L.M., 2007.

suited for each community. In areas where community ties are weak and multiple conflicting uses occur, more contemporary forms of management must be implemented.

In the United States, the landscape of federal ocean policy and management is undergoing dramatic change. A federal Ocean Policy Task Force is developing policies and standards for implementing ecosystem-based approaches and a marine spatial planning framework throughout US waters.[38] The integration of TEK into marine management is unquestionably necessary, given the increasing attention to TEK both locally and nationally. It will be particularly important to ensure that TEK and traditional knowledge-holders are engaged appropriately — ethically and politically.

Despite numerous anthropogenic stressors, many of Hawai'i's coral reefs, primarily in remote areas, are still in fair to good condition compared to elsewhere around the world.[39] It is therefore urgent to develop management strategies that can alter the current trajectory of resource declines and improve the quality of these resources for future generations before a tipping point is reached. Traditional knowledge and community are critical to achieving these goals.

---

38 Presidential memorandum, 12 June 2009. 'National policy for the oceans, our coasts, and the great lakes'. www.whitehouse.gov/sites/default/files/page/files/2009ocean_mem_rel.pdf. Accessed 17 August 2015.
39 Friedlander, A., Aeby, G., Brainard, R., Brown, E., Chaston, K., Clark, A., McGowan, P., Montgomery, T., Walsh, W., Williams, I. & Wiltse, W., 2008. 'The state of coral reef ecosystems of the main Hawai'ian islands'. In J.E. Waddell & A.M. Clarke (eds), *The State of Coral Reef Ecosystems of the United States and Pacific Freely Associated States: 2008*. NOAA Technical Memorandum NOS NCCOS 73. Silver Spring, MD: NOAA/NCCOS Center for Coastal Monitoring and Assessment's Biogeography Team, pp. 158–99.

11

Providing for *rāhui* in the law of Aotearoa New Zealand[1]

Jacinta Ruru and Nicola Wheen

In this chapter we examine the place and nature of *rāhui* in the law of Aotearoa New Zealand. The expression *rāhui* is used in legislation in New Zealand to describe certain conservation areas (*whenua rāhui*, *wahi rāhui*) and associated conservation agreements (*Nga Whenua Rāhui kawenata*), and to denote particular means or measures that can be utilised for conservation or sustainability purposes. By so adopting the idea or expression of *rāhui*, New Zealand law can be seen to be drawing on one of the three original uses of *rāhui*: to replenish resources. In this sense, *rāhui* can be defined as a 'mark to warn people against trespassing; used in the case of *tapu*, or for temporary protection of fruit, birds, or fish etc'.[2] This chapter focuses on *Nga Whenua Rāhui kawenata* and *rāhui* around and under the *Fisheries Act 1996* in particular, and discusses how the nature of and processes associated with *rāhui* have been defined by the legislation that applies in these two contexts.

---

1   This chapter is adapted from Wheen, Nicola and Ruru, Jacinta. Providing for 'Rahui' in the Law of Aotearoa New Zealand. *Journal of the Polynesian Society,* 20(2) 2011: 169–182.
2   Williams, H.W., 1971. *Dictionary of the Maori Language*. 7th edn. Wellington: GP Publications, p. 321.

Legislative incorporations of *rāhui* deserve analysis: *rāhui* was and is a key concept in Maori culture and, as a means of regulating human activities to sustain resources, it was and is widely utilised and understood. The extent to which resource management law in Aotearoa New Zealand accurately and sympathetically recognises, supports and affirms *rāhui* is a yardstick for how well environmental governance here complies with the New Zealand Crown's Treaty of Waitangi guarantee of *Maori rangatiratanga* (self-determination) over natural resources.

Ultimately, the analysis herein reveals some important differences between *rāhui* as originally understood and *rāhui* as a legislative construct. These differences may be rationalised or understood in more than one way. The differences may indicate a lack of understanding of *rāhui* on the part of legislators, or an unwillingness (again on the part of legislators) to create a legal form of *rāhui* that accurately replicates the practice and origins of the concept. On the other hand, the differences between *rāhui* as originally understood and described, and *rāhui* as it appears in legislation in Aotearoa New Zealand, may be seen, as indeed Maxwell and Penetito argue, to show that 'the custom of *rāhui* has changed and that *rāhui* are instated, enforced and lifted differently in modern times as compared to the original methods'.[3] In this case, the decisions that legislators have made about how to define *rāhui* and its associated processes and implications are part of the social fabric that, over the years, has remodelled and redefined what *rāhui* in Aotearoa New Zealand is and what it means.

Tikanga Maori and *rāhui*

The Maori phrase for law — *tikanga Maori* — involves an 'obligation to do things in the "right" way' or 'way(s) of doing and thinking held by Maori to be just and correct'.[4] The *tikanga* of *rāhui* is an integral

---

[3] Maxwell, K.H. & Penetito, W., 2007. 'How the use of rāhui for protecting taonga has evolved over time'. *MAI Review* 2: 2, www.review.mai.ac.nz.
[4] New Zealand Law Commission, 2001. *Maori Custom and Values in New Zealand Law*. Study Paper 9. Wellington: Law Commission, p. 16.

component of the Maori world. The effect of the *rāhui* is to 'prohibit a specific human activity from occurring or from continuing'.[5] According to Maxwell and Penetito:

> The definition of *rāhui* has not changed through time. Early accounts describe *rāhui* as a prohibition or to prohibit ... Modern definitions of *rāhuitai* include: banned, out of bounds, forbidden, prohibited, under sanctuary, reserved or preserved ... [I]nstalling a *rāhui* ... will 'prohibit the use of one or more resources in a given area'.[6]

However, as Maxwell and Penetito also go on to say:

> The literature suggests that the *custom* of *rāhui has* changed and that *rāhui* are instated, enforced and lifted differently in modern times as compared to the original methods ... The methods by which *rāhui* are instated have changed and it is likely that milder forms are introduced today.[7]

As Mead observes, the *rāhui* is a 'creative tool capable of being applied in a variety of situations for a wide variety of reasons'.[8] *Rāhui* have been used, and are regularly still used, to separate people from land and water (and their products) that have been contaminated by the *tapu* of death. *Rāhui* of a form Mead calls 'conservation *rāhui*':

> seem to have been associated ... with control of resources or the good of the whole community [and] also with the political use of resources. In the former, common-sense regulation of bird, fish and plant life seems to have been a consideration ... [It is also] evident that the conservation *rāhui* was sometimes used by the chiefs for political reasons which might have been related to the 'foreign policy' of the tribe or might have been for the personal aggrandisement of the rulers.[9]

Some more severe *rāhui* were originally instated by *tohunga*, calling on the 'dread powers of the gods to enforce them'.[10] Other 'milder' *rāhui* could be instated by a 'chief or *tohunga* [skilled spiritual person] ... simply stat[ing] that he is placing a *rāhui* over an area and it would

---

5   Mead, H.M., 2003. *Tikanga Maori. Living by Maori Values.* Wellington: Huia Publishers, p. 193.
6   Maxwell & Penetito, 2007, p. 1.
7   Maxwell & Penetito, 2007, p. 2, emphasis added.
8   Mead, 2003, p. 203.
9   Mead, 2003, p. 203.
10 Maxwell & Penetito, 2007, p. 2.

be so'.[11] A *pou rāhui*, or post, was almost always 'put up' to indicate that a *rāhui* was in place.[12] Prior to colonisation, the introduction of Christianity and the suppression of *tohunga*, transgression of *rāhui* was punishable by extreme measures including war, death and *muru* (ritual redistribution of wealth as compensation). As Mead states: 'Today, however, the *rāhui* is still honoured essentially because it is regarded as a sacred ritual of the traditional past [that is] still useful … '.[13]

As earlier stated, in this chapter we examine the place and nature of *rāhui* in the law — particularly the legislation — of Aotearoa New Zealand. Before beginning, it is necessary to provide some background on the law of Aotearoa New Zealand and *tikanga Maori*, the Treaty of Waitangi, and the status and ownership of land and resource management and conservation in Aotearoa New Zealand.

Necessary background

The Treaty of Waitangi, *Tikanga Maori* and the law

In 1840, Captain William Hobson, representing the British Crown, and over 500 Maori chiefs signed *te Tiriti o Waitangi* (the Treaty of Waitangi).[14] It is a short document, consisting of three articles. While the Maori version explicitly states that Maori ceded to the Crown governance only (article I), and retained *tino rangatiratanga* (sovereignty, article II) over their *taonga* (treasures), the British Crown assumed sovereignty over the country in accordance with the English version of the treaty and Aotearoa New Zealand became subject to colonial rule.[15] Henceforth, there were repeated and ongoing breaches of the Crown's guarantees in the treaty.

---

11 Maxwell & Penetito, 2007, p. 2.
12 Mead, 2003, p. 197, who notes that 'putting up' a post might have meant hanging a garment on a post, or smearing a post with red orchre, instead of actually erecting a post.
13 Mead, 2003, p. 202.
14 To view a copy of the Treaty, see First Schedule of the *Treaty of Waitangi Act 1975* or the NZ Government's official Treaty website: www.treatyofwaitangi.govt.nz.
15 Miller, R.J., & Ruru, J., 2009. 'An indigenous lens into comparative law: the doctrine of discovery in the United States and New Zealand'. *West Virginia Law Review* 111: 849–918.

11. PROVIDING FOR *RĀHUI* IN THE LAW OF AOTEAROA NEW ZEALAND

As colonial rule was applied to Aotearoa New Zealand so were English legal rules and constitutional assumptions. Formal law — made by parliament and interpreted and applied by courts — became the dominant regime, displacing *tikanga Maori*. Land was subject to private ownership and transfer. Central and local government was installed to provide infrastructure and manage and control natural resources. Significantly, parliament became the supreme lawmaker and the Treaty of Waitangi and its guarantees were — and still are — not part of domestic law unless included by parliament in legislation. Through until the 1980s, the colonial parliament and courts recognised few, limited instances of *tikanga Maori*.[16] During the 1980s and 1990s, however, references to the 'principles' of the Treaty of Waitangi and to *tikanga* concepts, such as *kaitiakitanga* (guardianship) and *wahi tapu* (sacred place), were persistently included in significant environmental legislation, including the *Environment Act 1986*, *Conservation Act 1987*, and *Resource Management Act 1991*. These legislative references to the treaty principles and to *tikanga* concepts reflected a wider policy shift on the part of government and parliament towards reconciling with, rather than assimilating, Maori.[17]

The shift towards reconciliation and away from assimilation was perhaps most obviously manifest in the establishment of the Waitangi Tribunal in the *Treaty of Waitangi Act 1975*. This permanent commission of inquiry is empowered to receive, report on and recommend redress for Maori-alleged Crown breaches of the principles of the Treaty of Waitangi.[18] Since it was established, the tribunal has reported on over 100 claims by Maori concerning matters ranging from the Crown's failure to protect *mahinga kai* (seafood gardens and other traditional sources of food) to the Crown's unlawful confiscation of land during the so-called land wars. Its recommendations have formed the basis of a number of settlements subsequently reached between the Crown and complainant Maori groups. More recently, the establishment within the Ministry of Justice of the Office of Treaty Settlements, with its mandate to resolve historical breaches of the Treaty of Waitangi,

---

16 Ruru, J., 2008. 'Finding solutions for the legislative gaps in determining rights to the family home on colonially defined indigenous lands'. *U.B.C. Law Review* 41(2): 315–48.
17 See Ruru, J., 2009. 'The Maori encounter with Aotearoa New Zealand's legal system'. In B. Richardson, S. Imai & K. McNeil (eds), *Indigenous Peoples and the Law: Comparative and Critical Perspectives*. Oxford: Hart Publishing, pp. 111–33.
18 See, generally, Hayward, J. & Wheen, N.R. (eds), 2004. *The Waitangi Tribunal. Te Roopu Whakamana i te Tiriti o Waitangi*. Wellington: Bridget Williams Books Ltd.

has played a pivotal role in reconciling with Maori. To date, more than 50 groups have successfully negotiated, or are in advanced stages of negotiating, tribal redress from the Crown.[19] More than 18 of these negotiated settlement agreements have been implemented in Acts of parliament. These Acts typically contain Crown apologies for wrongs done, various forms of financial or commercial redress, and redress recognising the claimant group's spiritual, cultural, historical or traditional associations with the natural environment.[20]

Land ownership and resource management

All land in Aotearoa New Zealand was once Maori customary land. Some of this land was unlawfully confiscated by the Crown, some land was legitimately sold or gifted to the Crown, but the majority of it became reclassified as Maori freehold land pursuant to the work of the then-named Native Land Court and was subsequently sold or confiscated. Today, about 6 per cent of the country is classified as Maori freehold land. A large chunk of the country is in Crown ownership, including 30 per cent of the landmass that is managed by the Department of Conservation. General, or private, land constitutes the other large component of land type.

The Department of Conservation was established in 1987 to manage natural resources held by it for conservation purposes (*Conservation Act*, s 6). The department, along with the New Zealand Conservation Authority and conservation boards, is responsible for devising and administering a policy and planning framework for conservation of lands and resources, and also for the day-to-day management and administration of those lands and resources. Much of the land administered by the department is Crown owned, but an increasing proportion is privately owned. Beyond the areas managed by the department, regional and local authorities and the Environment Court are responsible for land-use planning and for regulating access to and use of land, air and water (*Resource Management Act 1991*) and, importantly in the context of this chapter, the Ministry of Fisheries ultimately manages and controls customary, recreational and commercial fisheries (*Fisheries Act 1996*).

---

19   See Office of Treaty Settlements' website: www.ots.govt.nz.
20   For example, see: *Ngai Tahu Claims Settlement Act 1998* and *Te Roroa Claims Settlement Act 2008*.

Instances of *rāhui* in the law

The term *rāhui* appears only a handful of times in the legislation of Aotearoa New Zealand. In all cases, it is used to refer to a means or device 'to restore the productivity of land'[21] or to 'allow the *mauri* (life essence) of a resource or resources to replenish'.[22] In this section, we describe and comment on these references.

The first reference to *rāhui* appears in the *Ngati Awa Claims Settlement Act 2005*. This Act gives statutory effect to the settlement of Treaty of Waitangi claims between Ngati Awa *iwi* (tribe) and *hapū* (sub-tribe) and the New Zealand Crown. The Act refers to accounts of historic instances of the use of *rāhui* to support the association of Ngati Awa with two specific sites: Moutohora and Ohiwa Harbour.[23] Those accounts are manifest and recorded in the schedules to the Act. This is a simple acknowledgement both of the importance of *rāhui* as a form of social and environmental control, and of the fact that the authority to utilise *rāhui* attaches to individuals within the group holding *mana whenua* (authority) over the area.

Second, legislation has used the term *rāhui* to describe or refer to certain kinds of conservation land reserves: *Nga Whenua rāhui* and *whenua rāhui*. The inclusion of *rāhui* in the names given to these reserves indicates that these are places where activities may be restricted for restorative or conservation purposes.

Nga Whenua rāhui

Nga Whenua rāhui are areas of Maori land, or Crown land held under lease by Maori, that are being managed by the Department of Conservation pursuant to *Nga Whenua Rāhui kawenata* (*Conservation Act* 1987, s 27A or the *Reserves Act* 1977, s 77A(4)) or conservation covenants (*Conservation Act*, s 29 or *Reserves Act*, s 77). The minister of conservation has a statutory discretion to enter into a covenant or

---

21 Mead, 2003, p. 197.
22 Maxwell & Penetito, 2007, p. 6.
23 More precisely, the two 'statutory areas' in respect of which the assocation by Ngati Awa is affirmed are the 'statutory area' known as Moutohora (Whale Island) Management Reserve (*Ngati Awa Claims Settlement Act 2005* (No. 28), Schedule 7), and the 'statutory area' of part of the Ohiwa Harbour (Schedule 8).

THE RAHUI

Nga Whenua Rāhui kawenata with the owner or occupier of the land. Conservation covenants can be made with any such owner or occupier, but *Nga Whenua Rāhui kawenata* are specifically crafted for Maori landowners or occupiers. *Nga Whenua Rāhui kawenata* may be agreed to in order to 'provide for the management of the land in a manner that will achieve' the purposes of 'preserv[ing] and protect[ing]' the 'spiritual and cultural values which Maori associate with the land' or, either, the 'natural and historic values of the land' or 'the natural environment, landscape amenity, wildlife or freshwater-life or marine-life habitat, or historical value of the land' (Reserves Act, s 77A(1) and Conservation Act, s 27A(1)).

Nga Whenua Rāhui kawenata are administered by the *Nga Whenua Rāhui* fund, a contestible ministerial fund that was established in 1991. According to the Department of Conservation website, the 'criteria and mechanisms of *Nga Whenua Rāhui*, are geared towards the owners retaining *tino rangatiratanga* (ownership and control)'.[24] Each area is managed according to the terms of the applicable *kawenata* or covenant, and also according to the terms of the relevant legislation. Thus, for example, the offences prescribed in the Reserves and Conservation Acts for all reserves and conservation areas expressly apply to land administered under *Nga Whenua Rāhui kawenata* (Reserves Act, s 77A(1)(c) and Conservation Act, s 27(1)(c)).

Nga Whenua Rāhui kawenata may be agreed to for a specified term, or may be in perpetuity, either subject or not to a condition:

> that at agreed intervals of not less than 25 years the parties to the *Nga Whenua Rāhui kawenata* shall review the objectives, conditions, and continuance of the *Nga Whenua Rāhui kawenata*; and on such review the parties may mutually agree that the *Nga Whenua Rāhui kawenata* shall be terminated, or the owner or lessee may terminate the *Nga Whenua Rāhui kawenata* on giving such notice (being not less than 6 months) as may be agreed. The Crown shall have regard to the *manawhenua* of the owner or lessee in any such review.

McPhail observes that the option of a review within 25 years provides an important acknowledgement of some of the problems for landowners with conservation grants that are in perpetuity:

---

24 Department of Conservation website: www.doc.govt.nz/nga-whenua-rahui-fund.

11. PROVIDING FOR *RĀHUI* IN THE LAW OF AOTEAROA NEW ZEALAND

- Never having again the right to fully utilise their privately owned land.
- Changes in value over a period of years could make the amount paid for the purchase of the public good benefit look very small and inequitable.
- Aversion to parting with control over usage of land.
- No ability to review the terms of the deal after a reasonable period.[25]

Unfortunately, the option for review may be a reason for the Minister of Conservation having preferred, in some significant cases over the years, the option of a conservation covenant.[26]

Whenua rāhui

Whenua rāhui are sites identified as part of the Crown's Treaty of Waitangi claim settlement with Te Arawa Iwi and Hapū. This settlement is one of the negotiated treaty settlements earlier described. Several of these settlements have included some kind of statutory device that is designed to recognise Maori values in Crown land managed by the Department of Conservation. For example, one of the first settlement statutes, the *Ngai Tahu Claims Settlement Act 1998*, introduced the *topuni* device, which is derived 'from the traditional ... custom ... of persons of rangatira (chiefly) status extending their *mana* and protection over a person or area by placing their cloak over them or it'.[27] The 1998 Act's Schedules include Ngāi Tahu statements of value for 13 *topuni* sites, including *Aoraki*/Mount Cook. In both Acts, the values in each statement are acknowledged by the Crown, are to be notified and given particular regard by conservation authorities in managing the sites, and can provide the basis for the Crown and Ngāi Tahu or Affiliate Te Arawa (as the case may be) to agree on principles directed at the Minister of Conservation avoiding harm to values in the *topuni* or *whenua rāhui* site(s). If principles are agreed, the director-general

---

25 McPhail, D., 2002. *Constraints and Opportunities for South Island Landless Natives Act (SILNA) 1906 Indigenous Forest Utilisation*. Paper no. 3 from the research programme UoCX0004 Sustainability on Maori-Owned Indigenous Forest, School of Forestry. Christchurch: University of Canterbury, p. 52.
26 The two clear examples being the conservation covenants over the Waitutu and Lords River blocks (see the *Waitutu Block Settlement Act 1997*, *Tutae-Ka-Wetoweto Forest Act 2001*, McPhail (2002) and Wheen (2008)).
27 Te Rūnanga o Ngāi Tahu, 'Mana Recognition': www.ngaitahu.iwi.nz/ngai-tahu/the-settlement/settlement-offer/cultural-redress/ownership-and-control/mana-recognition/.

of conservation must take action in respect of them. Furthermore, the Governor-General is authorised to make regulations, and the Minister of Conservation may make by-laws, to regulate or prohibit public activities in or in respect of *topuni* or *whenua rāhui* and to prescribe offences and penalties for breaches of any such restrictions (*Ngai Tahu Claims Settlement Act 1998*, ss 239–244; *Affiliate Te Arawa Iwi and Hapū Claims Settlement Act 2008* ss 51–62).

The Act records the Crown's apology and provides cultural and commercial redress to the Affiliate Te Arawa Iwi. In s 11 of the Act, the Affiliate Iwi is defined as comprising 11 collective groups who, by *whakapapa* (genology) and choice, have agreed to this settlement with the Crown. An important component of settlement is the cultural redress package, which encompasses the use of the term *whenua rāhui*.

The *whenua rāhui* sites are legally described in s 4 of the Act. The schedule also recites a formal statement of affiliate values in each *whenua rāhui*. These statements describe the affiliate's traditional, cultural, spiritual and historical association with the *whenua rāhui* (s 49). These 'affiliate values' are expressly acknowledged by the Crown (s 51). The Act then authorises the Te Pumautanga o Te Arawa trustees and the Crown to agree on 'protection principles ... directed at' the Minister of Conservation 'avoiding harm to the Affiliate values in respect of the *whenua rāhui*' or 'avoiding the diminishing of Affiliate values in respect of the *whenua rāhui*' (s 53). The affiliate values and protection principles must be given 'particular regard' by the Crown, the New Zealand Conservation Authority (NZCA) or conservation boards when they consider and approve conservation documents or proposed changes to the conservation status of *whenua rāhui* (ss 54 and 55). The trustees are entitled to make submissions to the NZCA on any draft conservation strategy in respect of a *whenua rāhui* (s 56).

The formal declaration of a site as *whenua rāhui* must be publicly notified via conservation documents and the *New Zealand Gazette* (ss 57 and 58). The declaration obliges the director-general of conservation to 'take action' to implement the protection principles (s 59, although note that the director-general 'retains complete discretion to determine the method and extent of the action to be taken'). The Act also authorises the director-general to initiate changes to conservation documents to include objectives relating to the protection principles, and the Governor-General to make regulations — or the Minister of Conservation

11. PROVIDING FOR *RĀHUI* IN THE LAW OF AOTEAROA NEW ZEALAND

to make by-laws — to implement those objectives, or to regulate or prohibit activities in respect of *whenua rāhui* (ss 60–62). *Whenua rāhui* status does not, however, affect the existing classification of the site as a national park, conservation area or reserve (s 63). Nor do the terms of the Act create, grant or provide evidence of any estate, interest or rights in respect of *whenua rāhui* (s 67).

It is too early to comment on the success of the use of *whenua rāhui* as compared to other common cultural redress devices used in the conservation estate. It will be interesting to see if other *iwi* seek to utilise this concept in regard to their specific forthcoming settlements.

As well as these instances where *rāhui* is used by legislation to denote the conservation, or restricted, status of *Nga Whenua Rāhui* and *whenua rāhui* areas, the term is also *expressly* used in legislation to refer to a form of fisheries control and to a device for restricting access to a wetland. But, before discussing these two references to *rāhui*, it is important to note that there are other occasions where legislation refers to or implements devices that look like *rāhui*, even though it does not actually call them *rāhui*. Two particular examples of this are formally referred to as *rāhui* in the literature about the relevant legislation. These examples concern access to fisheries and *tītī* (muttonbird or sooty shearwater, *Puffinus griseus*).

Tītī

Traditionally, *tītī* was both an essential food source and a tradable commodity for Ngai Tahu (the predominant *iwi* in the South Island). The Titi Islands constitute approximately 36 islands clustered together in three main groups to the east, south and west of Rakiura Stewart Island at the bottom of the South Island. The harvesting of *tītī* chicks has been 'an integral part of the Ngai Tahi economy for centuries'.[28] Traditional rights to harvest chicks on the islands are founded on genealogy. Over the centuries, the harvest has been controlled by traditional ecological knowledge including the application of *rāhui*. According to Williams, the islands were, and are still, not visited between the end of May and the following March.[29] Significantly, this

---

28 Te Rūnanga o Ngāi Tahu 'Four Specific Sites': www.ngaitahu.iwi.nz/About-Ngai-Tahu/Settlement/Settlement-Offer/Cultural-Redress/Four-Specific-Sites.php.
29 Williams, J., 2004. *E Pakihi Hakinga a Kai: An Examination of Pre-contact Resource Management Practice in Southern Te Wai Pounamu*. PhD thesis, University of Otago, p. 140.

centuries old *rāhui* is now codified in the Titi (Muttonbird) Islands Regulations 1978. Eligible persons may only enter the islands during the birding season, which is defined as a period commencing on 1 April in any year and ending on 31 May in the same year.[30] While the regulations do not themselves use the word *rāhui*, they do effectively implement the substance of this *rāhui*.

The regulations were made by the Crown but, since the Ngai Tahu Treaty of Waitangi claims settlement (see the *Ngai Tahu Claims Settlement Act 1998*), they are administered and the islands are managed by Rakiura Maori, and the islands are owned by Te Runanga o Ngai Tahu.

Tutaepatu wetland/lagoon

Tutaepatu Lagoon is a coastal wetland situated north of Kaiapoi in the South Island. In 1995 the Waitangi Tribunal made its report on certain ancillary claims by Ngai Tahu, one of which concerned the loss of the Tutaepatu Lagoon.[31] This lagoon was and is of importance to Ngai Tahu as '*kainga nohoanga* [permanent settlements], *mahinga kai* and *urupa* [cemetery]'.[32] Following the tribunal's findings, parliament enacted the *Ngai Tahu (Tutaepatu Lagoon Vesting) Act 1998*. The Act vests ownership of the lagoon in Te Runanga o Ngai Tahu (see s 6). Te Runanga o Ngai Tahu must manage the lagoon in accordance with the objectives set out in Appendix 3 of the Act (see s 7). The five objectives include, for example, restoring and maintaining the lagoon for the benefit of present and future generations and actively encouraging scientific research and observation of the flora and fauna. Principle two is of particular interest to us. It reads: 'Appropriate public access to the Lagoon/wetlands will be allowed except for those times when, after notification in the local newspaper, a *rāhui* is applied'. This legislation thus envisages the use of *rāhui* and, although it does not confer or affirm the power to install the *rāhui*, it recognises the authority of Ngai Tahu to do so and thereby protect the resources of the lagoon.

---

30 See regs 2 and 3; Stevens, M.J., 2006. 'Kāi Tahu me to Hopu Tītī ki Rakiura: an exception to the "colonial rule"?' *Journal of Pacific History* 41(3): 273–91.
31 See the Ngai Tahu Ancillary Claims Report, 1995.
32 Bennion, T., 1997. 'Ngāi Tahu (Tutaepatu Lagoon Vesting) Bill' *Maori Law Review* at www.maorilawreview.co.nz/1997/11/november-1997-contents/#more-300.

Fisheries — *mātaitai* reserves and temporary closures

Maxwell and Penetito argue that today, 'voluntary *rāhui* are primarily used to protect aquatic resources'. They cite examples of the use of voluntary (informal, non-legal) *rāhui* from the Mahia Peninsula and Kaikoura, noting that in remote places 'with a small population that respects either the *tikanga* of *rāhui* and/or the resource', voluntary *rāhui* may have strength but 'in areas of New Zealand that are readily accessible to larger populations, voluntary *rāhui* are becoming increasingly ignored'.[33] In such cases, formal temporary closures of the relevant fisheries by the minister or the chief executive of fisheries have sometimes followed. The *Fisheries Act* 1996 (ss 186A and 186B) allows for such temporary closures of fishing areas to fishing to provide for the use and management practices of *tangata whenua* in the exercise of their customary, non-commercial fishing rights. According to the Ministry of Fisheries website:

> Temporary closures are designed to respond to localised depletion of fisheries resources. Note that in this context, *Tangata Whenua* means the *hapū* or *iwi* that hold *manawhenua* in the area. Anyone (not just Tangata Whenua) can request a s 186A (North Island/Chathams) and 186B (South Island) temporary closure, but the legislation is designed for customary purposes so must meet that purpose and have the support of *Tangata Whenua* if they are not the applicants.[34]

Although the *Fisheries Act* does not refer to such closures as *rāhui*, the ministry's official website frequently does so. As discussed below, this may prove to be a more significant point than it at first appears.

The one occasion when fisheries legislation in Aotearoa New Zealand *expressly* employs the term *rāhui* is in the context of *mātaitai* reserves. A *mātaitai* reserve is defined as an identified traditional fishing ground established pursuant to the Fisheries (South Island Customary Fishing) Regulations 1999, the Fisheries (Kaimoana Customary Fishing) Regulations 1998 and the *Fisheries Act 1996*. Along with temporary closures and *taiapure* fisheries (a local management tool established in an area that has customarily been of special significance to an *iwi* or *hapu* as a source of food or for spiritual or cultural reasons — see

---

33 Maxwell & Penetito, 2007, pp. 8, 9.
34 www.mfish.govt.nz.

s. 174 of the *Fisheries Act 1996*), *mātaitai* reserves comprise one of the legislation's key measures for recognising and providing for Maori customary fishing rights and interests. According to customary fishing regulations, the minister may establish a *mātaitai* reserve in traditional fishing grounds in order to recognise and provide for customary management practices and food gathering (Fisheries (South Island Customary Fishing) Regulations 1999, reg 20, and Fisheries (Kaimoana Customary Fishing) Regulations 1998, reg 23). The *tangata whenua* can nominate Tangata Tiaki or Kaitaki (nominations must be confirmed by the minister following a process of public consultation) who are authorised to make by-laws restricting or prohibiting commercial fishing in reserves if this is considered 'necessary for the sustainable management' of the fish, aquatic life, or seaweed therein (Fisheries (South Island Customary Fishing) Regulations 1999, reg 25 and Fisheries (Kaimoana Customary Fishing) Regulations 1998, reg 28). These by-laws are not called *rāhui*, although Tangata Tiaki/ Kaitiaki are further required to report annually to the *tangata whenua* on matters relating to the management of the reserve, including any *rāhui* in force in the relevant year (Fisheries (South Island Customary Fishing) Regulations 1999, reg 37 and Fisheries (Kaimoana Customary Fishing) Regulations 1998, reg 40). It is not clear if this reference is intended to link back to the power to make by-laws to restrict or ban commercial fishing in the reserve, but this may be implied. Thus the legislature may be seen to have envisaged the deployment of *rāhui* via by-laws within *mātaitai* reserves.

Comment

In summary, the legislation of Aotearoa New Zealand refers to or adopts the concept of *rāhui* somewhat inconsistently. In legislation, the term *rāhui* is always used to invoke the form of *rāhui* that involves allowing the *mauri* of a resource to replenish, or promoting resource sustainability or conservation. However, the legislation only sometimes recognises or affirms *rāhui* in its original or historic sense: as a device to be employed by those (Maori) with *mana whenua*, with enforcement and penalties for breaching the *rāhui* unclear, but potentially very severe. On other occasions, the *rāhui* of legislation is a device available simply to those with statutory or governmental authority, and which is enforced as a statutory offence. On these occasions, we may observe important differences between *rāhui* as originally understood and *rāhui* as a legislative construct. Thus, Maxwell and Penetito comment on temporary closures under the *Fisheries Act*:

> These temporary closures are also referred to as *rāhui*, possibly because they resemble voluntary *rāhui*. Temporary closures have been created from an anthropocentric worldview and not from a holistic worldview. Temporary closures are not designed to replenish *mauri* of the species in accordance with *kaitiakitanga*, but are designed to replenish the resource so the *tangata whenua* can continue to utilise the resource for the purpose of *manaakitanga* (providing food for their visitors). The current Minister of Fisheries is the only person who can install these temporary closures, based on anyone's recommendation, so long as the have the support of the majority of the community. Originally this was the right of only a person with *mana* ... So the role of the *tohunga* and chiefly members of a *hapū* (sub tribe) or *iwi* (tribe) effectively become the same as any other New Zealand citizen, as an advisor to the Minister of Fisheries and not an authority on the use of *rāhui*.
>
> ...
>
> On a positive note, temporary closures are legally enforceable which brings the 'teeth' back into this type of *rāhui*. A Fisheries Officer can apprehend anyone caught violating the terms of a temporary closure and if found guilty they can be financially penalised ... *Tangata whenua* do not have the right to arrest or penalise an offender of a temporary closure or a voluntary *rāhui* however they can [like any other person] assist the Fisheries Officer ... [35]

As we earlier observed, these differences between traditional conceptions and legislative constructions of *rāhui* may be rationalised or understood in more than one way. They may indicate on the part of legislators either a lack of understanding of *rāhui* or a simple unwillingness to create a legal form of *rāhui* that accurately replicates the traditional form (perhaps because this implies affirming the authority of Maori to make and enforce *rāhui* for the community as a whole). On the other hand, the differences may be seen to show how, ever flexibly, *rāhui* has adapted — or been adapted — to meet the needs and operate within the context of modern times.

---

35   Maxwell & Penetito, 2007, p. 9.

12
Uncanny rights and the ambiguity of state authority in the Gambier Islands

Alexander Mawyer

On Mangareva, in French Polynesia's Gambier Islands, the legitimacy and warrant of the state to regulate and oversee pearl cultivators in the exploitation of local marine resources is being contested. This chapter considers *ra'ui*, a traditional Mangarevan conception of governance in the regulation of common resources, to bring into focus a contemporary response to the modernising state and the actions of one branch of its executive, the Ministère de la Perle, which is tasked with administering the important business of cultured pearls. These contestations draw attention to contemporary ambiguities in the character and qualities of resource rights and labour, particularly those mediating the relationships of Mangarevans to the state of Polynésie Française that today claims them. Moreover, this chapter suggests that the discursive contestation of the state, and of its representation in the communicative actions of the agents of the pearl ministry, raises the possibility that contemporary Pacific political regimes are haunted by their predecessors, certainly including France but perhaps also prior governments that were absorbed and displaced by France after the nineteenth-century annexation of the Gambier. This chapter is thus in conversation with work elsewhere in the contemporary Pacific that has demonstrated the appropriateness of attention to problematic realisations of modernist state forms, and how historically embedded social orders and cultural institutions, including various legacies of earlier political regimes, interfere with and complicate the articulation of governance in a Pacific context. Attention to the murky and nebulous character of everyday economies of power in French Polynesia seems timely, given the complexity of state formations, erosions, revaluations and instaurations over the last two centuries and in the last decades as the various statutes chartering state formation begin to sediment over one another in an incommodious political topology.

Drawing on doctoral fieldwork conducted in the village of Rikitea in French Polynesia's Gambier Islands, this chapter considers the contemporary relevance of the traditional concept of *ra'ui* for making sense of attempts to control and restrict marine resources, domains and activities. Assessing the character of politics in French Polynesian everyday life continues to be challenging after years of intense inter- and intra-party conflicts and regular overhauls of the presidency and territorial assembly, as well as periodic statutory overhauls of the relationship with France — a period widely referred to as the *Taui* (Change). The first section proposes that attention to *ra'ui* as a local conception of authority can contribute to the visibility and intelligibility of contemporary Mangarevans' contestations of regional and national legislation and regulations bearing on pearl labours. The second section turns to a series of sign postings bearing on local debates about the regulation of pearl labour in which, in the political churn and froth of the region's last decade, the *fact of the state* can seem to be a primary site of political life. By fact of the state, I mean the way that the state itself seems to be the concrete and focal object of political contest. Visible in the discursive intervention of these signs, however, is a claim that the presence and potency of the state should not be taken at face value. The final section turns to the question of what the recent politically and socially fraught decade in French Polynesia reveals about the character of the state's claims on the labours and rights of persons in French Polynesia's outer islands. It considers how the contestation of the state, the practical negotiation of its reach and significance in everyday life, highlights the curious endurance of other cultural and social institutions, including traditional cultural values, understandings and the practical orientations to action that they make possible.

12. UNCANNY RIGHTS AND THE AMBIGUITY OF STATE AUTHORITY IN THE GAMBIER ISLANDS

Unrestricting *ra'ui*

Scepticism about the character and constitution of the state-form in French Polynesia seems particularly warranted in the context of the uncertain disestablishment of the rule of chiefs in French Polynesia's Gambier Islands after the 1857 death of Maputeoa, the last *'Akariki Nui* (King) of Mangareva to unambiguously hold the *ao* (the sacred rule of the Gambier). Following Osorio[1] and others[2] who have demonstrated the interpretive purchase offered by attention to traditional conceptions of community and polity, authority and agency, I want to join the other chapters collected here in suggesting that the right of chiefs to declare *ra'ui* and to apply restrictions over marine resources provides a historically sensitive micropolitical context for examining the problematic condition of state power and the ambivalent relation of its subjects to its impositions. In post-chiefly Polynesia the (in)effectual state sometimes becomes visible in the materiality of discourse over statutory and practical control of mundane powers. This, I believe, brings to light a critical question in the contemporary Pacific. What has happened and is happening to traditional cultures of governance? In places where they are not directly evident have they been utterly erased by history's tides or do they remain operating beneath or outside of statutory purview, just out of sight? Do they haunt the islands' administration as a spectral presence?

On Mangareva, the answers to these questions may be found in contemporary discursive engagement with the state in the areas of labour and marine resource use rights. In these areas, historical notions of *ra'ui* as the chiefly authority to restrict use rights are culturally highly salient and are curiously suggested by local political discourse. By way of teasing out a sense of the relevance of this concept, it is worth noting that the pre-contact practice of *ra'ui* in the Gambier was comparable to similar practices elsewhere in Polynesia. The earliest

---

1   Osorio, J.K.K., 2002. *Dismembering Lāhui: A History of the Hawai'ian Nation to 1887.* Honolulu: University of Hawai'i Press.
2   Kelly, J.D., 1997. 'Gaze and grasp: plantations, desires, indentured Indians, and the colonial law in Fiji'. In L. Manderson & M. Jolly (eds), *Sites of Desire, Economies of Pleasure: Sexualities in Asia and the Pacific.* University of Chicago Press, pp. 72–98; Kaplan, M., 2004. 'Neither traditional nor foreign: dialogues of protest and agency in Fijian history'. In H. Jebens, T. Otto & K. Heinz Kohl (eds), *Cargo Cult and Culture Critique.* Honolulu: University of Hawai'i Press, pp. 59–79; Kelly, J.D., 2005. 'Boycotts and coups, shanti and mana in Fiji'. *Ethnohistory*, 52(1): 13–27.

published dictionary of the Mangarevan language, Tregear's *Mangarevan Dictionary*, which is based on even earlier missionary works, offers this definition:

> *Ra'ui* To keep off, to defend; to prohibit, to forbid (said of lands, waters, of things which one declares *tapu*).
> *Ra'ui'ui* Plural of the action.
> *Rara'ui* Plural of the subject.
> *Ra'uiranga* The action of *ra'ui*.[3]

Thus, to early European observers on Mangareva, *ra'ui* appears to have been understood as something like a weakened and less significant version of *tapu*, a contingent feature of a more cosmic, divine authority to restrict and control everyday practices, as expressed in the mundane realm. Yet it seems worth noting that the invocation of *ra'ui* implies the possibility of its breach. Thus, Tregear:

> *Tara'ui* To steal a prohibited thing: said of the first who steals.
> *Tara'uiga* The action of *tara'ui*.[4]

On consideration, *ra'ui* does not appear to have been merely a cosmically efficacious power to be taken for granted, but a structural tension pointing to the contingencies of the everyday, to the play of power in a full matrix of social life, in effect one of the currencies of chiefly power.

Today *ra'ui* and *tara'ui* do not have currency in the spoken language of the Gambier. Indeed, informants claimed that they have not been invoked here since the time of the conversion of the islands to Catholicism in the 1830s, and certainly no later than the disestablishment of sacred chiefly rule in the decades after the death of Maputeoa. Yet, the contingencies of labour rights and marine resource use remain, and continue to be, a source of tension between prohibited labours and everyday use rights. Indeed, both the labour of Mangarevan individuals and families, their rights to the act(s) of their bodies and their use of marine spaces, and the material benefits thereof, appear to be in a sort of crisis that perhaps tells us something about the overall crisis of the state in French Polynesia's outer islands.

---

3   Tregear, E., 1899. *Mangareva Dictionary of the Gambier Islands*. Wellington: Government Printing Office.
4   Tregear, 1899.

Here it is not the legal imbroglio resulting from the region's statutory decolonisation and the political chaos that has characterised its government, but something at once everyday and practical and yet hinged to the ineffably historical — something latent in the way that rights to labour with respect to the (un)common goods and resources of the sea mediate understandings of the social.

The mad poster and perliculture's persistent crisis

During my doctoral field research in anthropology in French Polynesia's Gambier Islands in 2002 and early 2003, a series of publicly posted signs revealed the presence of enduring ambiguities in the character of state authority. Notably, the intensity of the French state's regional presence in its nuclear testing regime did not lead me to anticipate any ambiguity in the fact of the state on the ground. These signs suggested that, over a century after the gradual disestablishment of sacred chiefs in the Gambier Islands following the establishment of a French Protectorate in 1881, and the absorption of the Gambier into an administrative district with historically evolving regulatory regimes over subsequent historical periods, Mangarevans still ask *who* has inherited the *ao* (the rule of the land and the sea) including the rights to restrict their use.

In the Gambier, as in the Tuamotu, attempts to govern and administer the business of culturing pearls and daily labours on pearl farms seem to offer an excellent point of contact between Mangarevans' intimate experiences and the state from the age of the chiefs to the present.[5] In the current era, since the institution of the cultured pearl as the centre post of socioeconomic life in the Gambier in the 1970s and 1980s, economists, administrators and others have been charged with monitoring the market for so-called 'Tahitian' black pearls, bringing local labours into regional and global visibility. Even early on, such surveillance yielded disturbing indications regarding the stability

---

5   Rapaport, M., 1995. 'Pearl farming in the Tuamotus: atoll development and its consequences'. *Pacific Studies*, 18(3): 1–25.

of the pricing and volume of pearl sales.[6] For years, however, it was possible to ignore disquieting signs. This changed in February of 2001. A disastrous *vente aux enchères*, or scheduled auction of pearls on the international market, which was usually held once or twice annually, revealed a *crise persistante* and *tendance inquiétante* (persistent crisis and disquieting tendency) in the slowing growth, or actual decline, of the gem prices by lot.[7]

After years of loose oversight, the government's response was dramatic. Within months a Service de la Perliculture was implemented that was, shortly thereafter, restructured and promoted to a full Ministère de la Perle with sweeping powers to survey and regulate pearl culturing. What the agents of the new executive structure discovered as they began to take stock of the state of pearl culturing and labour over the following year was a discontinuity between the long-running official perspective and the facts of perliculture and labour in the Gambier. Apparently unrecognised by the government and ignored by the several syndicates that dominate the cultured black pearl market, the number of independent families and individual persons culturing pearls in the Gambier exploded in the 1990s. Administration agents expressed real shock in the discovery that the total number of *fermes*

---

6   As early as 1992, the Service de la Mer et de l'Aquaculture (SMA), which overlapped with and eventually replaced Etablissement pour la Valorisation de Activités Aquacoles et Maritimes (EVAAM) in the 1990s and preceded the Service de la Perliculture, reported a range of industry problems including the 'uncontrolled occupation of the lagoon', the absence of adequate legislation and a general 'lack of knowledge on the actual status of the industry'. To a large degree, the impossibility of monitoring the activities of producers was, at the time, seen to be cartographic — producing an inventory of pearl farming areas and subsequent monitoring was impossible, the service claimed, because of the 'non-availability of a homogeneous set of maps of the appropriate scale for the thirty-odd pearl farming areas: the existing topographic and hydrographic maps do not give comprehensive coverage and are not of much practical use (they do not, for instance, show the karena, or coral pinnacles, which pearl farmers use to attach their ropes)' (South Pacific Commission, 1992. *Pearl Oyster Information Bulletin* no. 4, February).

7   An administration report from the period offers further details. 'The 1998–2000 period saw an exceptional growth in the pearl industry, with a 75 per cent increase in the volume of exported pearl products, and a 38.7 per cent increase in the receipts generated by exports. This increase in exported volumes resulted in additional but less important (in terms of value) receipts. Indeed, the price of a gram of pearl has kept on falling for several years (XPF 2359/gram in 1998, XPF 1766/gram in 2000, XPF 1357/gram in 2001, and XPF 1326/gram in 2002). There was a reversal of situation in this sector in 2001, which resulted in a 28.4 per cent decrease in sales value abroad (–8 per cent in volume). Sales of pearl products reached, that year, XPF 15 billion with difficulty (the same amount of sales was reached in 1998). The pearl industry sector stabilised in 2002 at the same level of sales for rough pearls, finely-worked pearls, and for other pearl products' (www.presidence.pf/index.php?94).

(pearl farms) and, presumably, the quantity of gems entering the market far exceeded both official and unofficial estimates, to well over 100 pearl farms in 2002.

Most of these cultivators were out of compliance with the stringent statutes and regulations developed as the business of periculture matured after the 1970s. After pearl prices on the international market plummeted in 2001, one of the officers of the governmental inquiry claimed to me that fewer than 10 per cent of all Gambier *fermes perliers* were in compliance with the various regulations governing their labour. Perhaps this should not have been surprising since there is ample room for circumventing dozens of regulations, including the amount of sea space occupied, the number of oysters in cultivation, the periods of their harvest, and techniques bearing on the size of the implant used to seed the oyster.

The actions taken by the administration and the Ministère de la Perle in response to this perceived crisis eventually led to a series of widely attended public meetings on Mangareva in late 2002. It was in the midst of these meetings that a series of sign postings pointed to the ways in which local economies of power, individual and collective actions and the understandings of rights and duties that underlie them are experienced outside of, or perpendicular to, common sense conceptions of the presence and authority of the state. The first of these meetings, in October, ended in what could only be described as a disaster for administration representatives. Intended to be a simple presentation of the administration's new regulations, executive orders and practical actions in service of re-regulating periculture in the Gambier, the presentation was derailed by a series of deliberate moves to hold the discussion in Mangarevan, a language not shared by the administration's representatives. Moreover, the negotiation of the code shift into Mangarevan was followed by a topic shift to focus on what basis Mangarevans themselves would be entitled to address those assembled. These discursive moves drew attention to rifts in local understandings of 'us' and 'you'. Unable to speak, much less complete their presentations, the agents of the new pearl services left the island, cutting short their stay to report back to the administration under what I was told were emergency conditions.

In the weeks following this first abortive meeting, details of the unrealised presentation began to circulate. A flyer made available at the town hall listed a series of new regulations governing membership in a lawful pearl cooperative, and requirements for compliance by all those who had already begun culturing pearls. Most significantly, the new rules sought to regulate pearl labour, requiring potential farmers to sit various courses and pass exams in order to qualify as licensed producers. They also determined how many lines and oysters a person could cultivate, in how much space at sea, and how concessions of sea space would be allocated. Implicit in all of these proposed changes was the fact that any redistribution of space, rights to cultivate, or modification of the rules for participation in the industry would be equivalent to a redistribution of potential wealth, most likely favouring well-established senior men on the island as opposed to youths or latecomers to the business of culturing pearls.

In their effects, such impositions are, as Trouillot observes, the manner in which modernist states become visible.[8] Thus, in the new 'professional' requirements proposed in the meeting, we see what Trouillot identifies as the state's attempts to produce 'atomised individualised subjects molded and modelled for governance as part of an undifferentiated but specific "public"', along with their proposed 'realignment of the atomised subjectivities along collective lines within which individuals recognise themselves as the same' and 'production of both a language and a knowledge for governance and of theoretical and empirical tools that classify and regulate collectivities' as well as 'the production of boundaries and jurisdiction'.[9] Outer islands in a not-quite-postcolonial situation are thus unsurprisingly excellent candidates to witness the aggressive and assertive state in action. What is surprising, however, is the way that such acts of governance also summon into renewed relevance competing traditional authorities and powers such as those of chiefs to *ra'ui* the use of land and sea, thus refiguring noncompliant persons as *tara'ui* (usurpers).

As the date of a second meeting approached, inside the island's small goods shops one could hear people asking each other the rhetorical question, 'Ah, the meeting is next week, right?' Groups of men standing

---

8   Trouilliot, M-R., 2001. 'Anthropology of the state in an age of globalization'. *Current Anthropology* 42: 125–38.
9   Trouilliot, 2001, p. 126.

12. UNCANNY RIGHTS AND THE AMBIGUITY OF STATE AUTHORITY IN THE GAMBIER ISLANDS

outside began to joke about what they would do with the producers' badges and identity cards that the regulations posted at the town hall proposed they carry along with an official state-mandated compass and knife as they went about their work. The compass requirement in particular was the object of innumerable jokes — since the notion that Mangarevans need an aid to know where they are in their own lagoon is locally laughable, its vast size notwithstanding. Men and women spoke openly about their sense that the administration had an alien perspective on Mangarevan maritime domains as dangerous spaces and did not understand that they were already domesticated according to a variety of local understandings, traditions and contemporary conventions.

Finally, in the last week before the meeting, the semiotic equivalent of a string of firecrackers was set off in the village due to the activity of an obviously impassioned, non-administration aligned, politically subtle and clearly irate sign poster. Over the course of a week any number of signs were posted at key spots around the village. Evidently there were supporters of the administration's point of view as well. As soon as a sign went up and was discovered by the counter-party, down it would come. The removal of the posting led to countermeasures such as posting the signs in remote corners of the island where, although fewer villagers would initially see them, news of the signs would necessarily filter back into the collective discussion. This led to putatively invisible adversaries cruising around or lying in wait at obscure junctions on the island's thoroughfares to post or remove one or another sign. The poster battle lasted the course of the week leading up to the second meeting and became part of a discursive debate with control of the sea space and its resources as the stake.

I was not able to collect the text of most of the signs, and there were many. For example, the first two I saw were on the road *i mua* (the outward direction) from Rikitea where very few folks live. On the afternoon of 11 November, while out for a run, I spotted a series of flyers taped to the pillar of one of the meteorological service's weather stations, and recognised the oddity of their content. Since I did not have paper or pen on me I planned to return by bike but, by the time I did so only an hour later, they were missing, which was initially a complete mystery. Returning to the village I stopped in the first of the stores one comes to travelling in the *i roto* (inward) direction back into town, and asked if anyone had seen these curious things. I was told that someone was putting them up, that no one knew who and that someone else was taking them down. The several folks who were in the store noted that signs had been posted on the doors of several of the stores in the morning, on telephone poles in front of the post office and school, and in several other spots in town, but that they were never there for long. This semiotic contest lasted over the next several days. The text of two signs is representative. The first is from the morning of 13 November, the day of the second meeting:

> This lagoon is the heritage of the *Mangarevan People*. Recall the *regime* that has come to dispossess us of our lagoon, lands, culture. *President*, we are a vibrant and rich people, it is the Rikitea pearl that augments the market value of the *Pearl of* Quality.

Written in multicolour marker on the back of cardboard from a box, the fashioning of the sign seemed haphazard but aesthetically heartfelt. The morning after the meeting, a sign with the following text was posted on the pole that supports some meteorological equipment on the *i mua* stretch of the road, where I had first seen one of the signs quite out of town:

> The *King* conferred to the *Catholic Church* the protection and the development of these lands for the future of his *Mangarevan people* and to *France* the conservation of his lagoon and the protection of his resource 'la nacre' for her *children*.

Both signs present images of the conception of the historically inflected order of things, persons and their relation to forms of authority, of rights and the appropriate flow of rights from legitimate states. As is evident in these two signs, the local political order suffers from latent ambiguities. Is it the French Polynesian state or is it France that has the rule of the land and sea? Or did the Church, as a legacy of the mission period and the close attachments of the mission to the founding of the Mangarevan kingdom, acquire the authority of the previous political regime, a chiefly dynasty of 36 generations of *'Akariki*, and thus legitimate rule of the land, leaving the sea as the express ward of France with legitimacy from the same source?

In the first sign, the new state of affairs is construed as a regime that threatens Mangarevans' legitimate rights to inherit the goods and benefits of their own lagoon. The question is thus one of sovereign authority. As the implied addressee of the sign, the president of French Polynesia certifies this. He is the holder of the *ao* (the rule)

12. UNCANNY RIGHTS AND THE AMBIGUITY OF STATE AUTHORITY IN THE GAMBIER ISLANDS

of the land. And, accordingly, since the then long-serving President Gaston Flosse is Mangarevan, he might be expected to be particularly sentimental about and supportive of Mangarevan rights to choose when and how to use and restrict the resources of their lagoon. The second sign implies an entirely different descent of rights and an entirely distinct construction of Mangarevan persons. In this case, the implied addressee is the French state, the national mother, who has the obligation to protect her *children* from each other; i.e. to protect Mangarevans in the outer islands from the manipulation of the Tahitian majority operating from the territorial centre. In this case, Mangarevans appear as wards of the French nation-state, directly inherited from the last traditionally authorised ruler of the island, Maputeoa, before his death.

The discursive materiality of the French Polynesian state's engagements here in its so-called outer islands thus suggests that the crisis of the state finds expression in the relationship between efficacious historical actors, taken to be chief players, as it were, in the drama of the social, the structures of social order through which their authority and legitimacy is derived, and the events in which authority is expressed, negotiated, resisted and instituted *a la* Sahlins.[10] But, a century after the gradual disestablishment of sacred chiefs in the Gambier, it is unclear who has inherited the sacred power of the chiefs of yore. Who, or what, currently holds rights of sacred authority in this community is clearly a site of latent ambiguity, as is the relation of rights and obligations that pertains on the ground between Mangarevans and the state(s) that claims them as citizens. In the contemporary Gambier, such questions are of paramount importance, particularly as they bear on the potentially lucrative exploitation of marine resources and space, further contextualised in the Gambier because of the notorious intensity of the hierarchical social structure before regular contact with Western cultures,[11] and for the equal intensity of processes of Westernisation and the disestablishment of chiefly power.[12] When certain forms of state-sponsored agentive authority

---

10 Sahlins, M.D., 1985. *Historical Metaphors and Mythical Realities: Structure in the Early History of the Sandwich Islands Kingdom*. Association for the Study of Anthropology in Oceania, special publication 1. Ann Arbor: University of Michigan Press.
11 Sahlins, M.D., 1958. *Social Stratification in Polynesia*. Seattle: University of Washington Press.
12 Buck, P.H., 1938. *Ethnology of Mangareva*. Bulletin no. 157. Honolulu: Bernice P. Bishop Museum.

attempt to assert themselves and legitimate their authority over rights to spatial practices and everyday labours in the Gambier, they can be challenged by other sorts of historically embedded notions of legitimate authority. The result appears to be a sort of spectral conflict, as otherwise ineffable historically superseded political regimes, here made temporarily discursively visible, return to discursive relevance and challenge the current state's claims to legitimate authority here in the region's 'outer islands'.

Uncanny rights, prohibited labours

I think we are right to ask whether attention to states' micropolitical practices has been too often displaced in ethnographic assimilations of the Pacific and perhaps especially Eastern Polynesia, not because ethnographers were uninterested in power and politics but because state effects did not fit the representational models of certain durable and consistent understandings to which the diverse facts of regional cultures had been reduced. Consider ethnographers' long-enduring fondness for traditional conceptions of power in Polynesia. An abstract otherworldly force given concrete substance in the term *mana* on one hand[13] and reified in towering hierarchical structures on the other,[14] power has been taken to be a key hinge in the unfolding historical engagement of Western social science and Pacific cultures. This vast literature, however, is dominated by a relatively small set of persuasive if potent *mot essentiaux*[15] and *idées maîtresses*[16] (key words and determining ideas) which belie the complexity and variety in the everyday economies of power across diverse historical and sociopolitical contexts. Specifically, the closely associated ideas

---

13 Keesing, R.M., 1984. 'Rethinking mana'. *Journal of Anthropological Research* 40(1): 137–56; Shore, B., 1989. 'Mana and Tapu: a new synthesis'. In A. Howard & R. Borofsky (eds), *Developments in Polynesian Ethnology*. Honolulu: University of Hawai'i Press, pp. 137–74; Tomlinson, M., 2006. 'Retheorizing mana: Bible translation and discourse of loss in Fiji'. *Oceania*, 76(2): 173–85.
14 Sahlins, 1958; Douglas, B., 1979. 'Rank, power, authority: a reassessment of traditional leadership in South Pacific societies'. *Journal of Pacific History* 14: 2–27; Valeri, V., 1985. *Kingship and Sacrifice: Ritual and Society in Ancient Hawai'i*. Paula Wissing (trans). University of Chicago Press.
15 Baré, J-F., 1987. *Tahiti, Les Temps et Les Pouvoirs: Pour Une Anthropologie Historique du Tahiti Post-Européen*. Paris: Éditions de l'Orstom.
16 Mauss, M., 1973 (1923–24). *Essai sur le don: Forme et raison de l'échange dans les societies archaïques* In *Sociologie et Anthropologie*. PUF, Collection Quadrige, pp. 149–279.

of *mana, tapu* and chiefliness have been the standard currency of the discursive fashioning of Polynesian persons and their structures of practice and experience.

In the deliberation of the *longue durée*[17] played out between competing representations of agency and authority, structure and event, legitimacy and contestation,[18] as realised through these terms, one wonders whether the ethnographic literature on Polynesia has a disquieting tendency to interpret the operations of power too exclusively in terms of structurally amplified authority, the *mana* inhering in vertically assembled individual persons and traditional institutions, and the potent warrants thereby produced or enacted. Following work in Hawai'ian and Pacific studies, it seems clear that scholars have systematically overlooked the importance of other traditional conceptions of mundane powers, the everyday micropolitical clashes of successive legal frameworks and administrative regimes as historically emergent governing states grapple with the legacies of their predecessors and institute the constitutional developments that will bedevil their successors.[19]

Given the tendency of Pacific anthropologists to eschew the mundane in favour of the cosmic, the ambivalent comportments of individuals in favour of vertically structured institutions, we might well ask with Keesing[20] and Jolly[21] if ethnographers have too often gone native in a curious and at times fantastic archipelago of ideas, too removed from what are ultimately the intimate experiences of real people.[22] Attention to everyday discursive contestations between states and individuals engaged in daily labours within common spaces appears to be a timely and well warranted turn in contemporary Pacific and Polynesian studies. With reference to the contested character of the state made

---

17 Thomas, N., 1989. 'The force of ethnology: origins and significance of the Melanesia/Polynesia division'. *Current Anthropology* 30(1): 27–34; Thomas, N., 1997. *In Oceania*. Durham: Duke University Press.
18 Dening, G., 1980. *Islands and Beaches: Discourse on a Silent Land: Marquesas 1774–1880*. Chicago: The Dorsey Press; Sahlins, 1985.
19 Kame'eleihiwa, L., 1992. *Native Lands and Foreign Desires, Ko Hawai'i Aina a me Na Koi Pu'umake a ka Po'e Haole*. Honolulu: Bishop Museum Press.
20 Keesing, R.M., 1985. 'Conventional metaphors and anthropological metaphysics: the problematic of cultural translation'. *Journal of Anthropological Research* 41: 201–17.
21 Jolly, M., 2007. 'Imagining Oceania: indigenous and foreign representations of a sea of islands'. *The Contemporary Pacific*, 19(2): 508–45.
22 Shore, B., 2005. 'Reading Samoans through Tahitians'. *Ethos* 33(4): 487–92.

discursively material, as in signposting practices, among any number of analogous quotidian engagements between local persons and the otherwise all too translucent tentacles of the ghostly leviathan of the states that attempt to govern them, I am encouraged to think that Pacific scholars can identify terms and forms of everyday power that clarify Pacific lives in ways that reference to standard understandings of *mana*, for instance, may not. What attention to the concept of *ra'ui* as it contextualises political discourse bearing on marine resources may suggest is that the very action of the state, visible also in its effects, is producing uncanny feelings and sentiments,[23] disconcerting senses of familiar labours and common sense rights as *strange* here raising into visibility the spectre of the past and the previous rule of chiefs.

Like many manual labours, working on a pearl farm is a daily grind involving repetitive tasks centered on the health of the developing oysters, the security of lines and nets, and the maintenance of tools and vehicles. Periods of intense excitement are short-lived, few and far between. They punctuate days that consist of motoring out into the lagoon and free diving for a few dozen nets that must be taken back to the farmhouse. The farmhouse is typically a platform resting a few metres above sea level some distance from shore on concrete pillars poured in old gas barrels and put in place by producers who have essentially 'staked a claim' to a certain seaspace, either in conjunction with governmental authorisation (a concession to a domain), or according to purely local understandings of appropriateness of use reckoned through attachment of the incipient producers to lands recognised as their own *kaiga* (property), or *nuku* (maternal places).

The communicative assemblages that are latent in public meetings, sign postings and the equally potent discursive engagements latent in sign-removal, offer an example of concrete points of articulation between the contemporary French Polynesian state and its supposed subjects, as they make such everyday manual labours appear far from ordinary. The way that these signs summon ambiguously layered historical mentalities and competing understandings of the implications of the past for the present points to the incomplete

---

23   Artexaga, B., 2003. 'Maddening states'. *Annual Review of Anthropology* 32: 393–410; Throop, J., 2005. 'Hypocognition, a "sense of the uncanny", and the anthropology of ambiguity: reflections on Robert I. Levy's contribution to theories of experience in anthropology'. *Ethos* 33(4): 499–511.

12. UNCANNY RIGHTS AND THE AMBIGUITY OF STATE AUTHORITY IN THE GAMBIER ISLANDS

realisation of what is, after all, only the latest French Polynesian state, operating under a new statutory charter of autonomy as a Pays d'Outre Mer Territoire d'Outre Mer since 2004 with respect to continuing colonial France. They point to the uncanny presence of the shadows of states past, and the obligations and rights of its citizens in the Gambier. Here, such shadow states include the Territoire d'Outre Mer, the Etablissments Francaise d'Oceanie, the spectral protectorate, the short-lived statutory Kingdom of Mangareva, the also brief instauration of the Catholic Mission and, ultimately and originally, the enduring *ao* of traditional chiefs, the *'Akariki* and *Tongo'iti*, before their entanglement with Western governmental regimes. These signs are best seen as short, historically sensitive commentaries on state rights of restriction. In these postings over time it becomes clear that the traditionally legitimate authority to regulate and restrict everyday labours and common resources in French Polynesia, once understood through the lens of *ra'ui*, is now coexistent and yielding contemporary interference effects with successive projects of state(s) modernities.

These signs inherit or atavistically recapitulate past discursive contestation over legitimate marine rights and labours, *ra'ui* and their illegitimate counterparts, *tara'ui*. My ongoing investigation of the territorial archives in Papeete suggests that regulatory regimes bearing on pearl extraction and labour, and the discursive contest about them, were a central feature of the governance of these islands from the arrival of European ships bearing pearl divers in the early nineteenth century, often from elsewhere in Polynesia, into the protectorate period at the time of the demise of the Mangarevan kingdom in the late nineteenth century, and lasting until the Second World War. Hence, thinking about Osorio's work in Hawai'i,[24] I cannot help but speculate that the inability of the traditional chiefs, the Gambier's *'Akariki* and *Togo'iti*, to control labour in and the resources extracted from marine spaces, played a role in the instauration of the mission and its governance power,[25] the eventual formation of the Mangarevan kingdom and, on its collapse, the subsequent and evidently complicated implementation of the protectorate and acceptance of French colonial rule over several decades.[26] Official and unofficial letters, orders, reports, notes written in the margins of accounting documents of the town hall, minutes of

---

24   Osorio, 2002.
25   In the Gambier, the mission was regularly accused of having usurped the rule of the islands.
26   Vallaux, F., 1994. *Mangareva et les Gambier*. Tahiti: Etablissement Territorial D'Achats Groupes.

meetings and reports of the Mangarevan Grand Council between 1886 and 1937[27] show that requests for dispensations from a putatively 'central state' were virtually an annual affair, and that the independent action, *tara'ui*, of local and exterior persons in the absence of state authorisation was common in the exploitation of the Gambier's marine resources, particularly the lagoon's pearl oysters. Over the subsequent 150 years, marine resources remained a constant site of discursively constructed regimes of labour and restriction, and through them points of contact and friction between more or less efficacious state power and daily life.

Current state attempts to effectually govern pearl labour and marine resources, including new legislation and administrative discourse and action, may suggest to Mangarevans who are engaged in routine work on their pearl farms that they are engaged in *tara'uiga*, the usurpation of the legitimate restriction of a resource. As these signs suggest, this could literally be the case because the descent of the rights to *ra'ui* these resources is ambiguous. The result is that today, some Mangarevans are working to articulate an understanding of themselves as entitled and legitimate users and owners of these marine spaces and their product, what I identify as a set of *uncanny rights*. In the everyday fact of their labour, despite state attempts to prohibit it, the local rejection of the state's attempt to deny the rights to marine resource use, or labour activities, Mangarevans can be reminded that the authority to *ra'ui* various marine spaces has somehow not fallen into the hands of the current state that claims it. Again, this raises the question where has the right to *ra'ui* gone? Who holds it, the *ao*, of land and seascapes in the Gambier?[28]

---

27 Such requests are specifically notable in deliberation records from the years 1886, 1900, 1901, 1902, 1907, 1910 and 1937 (non-indexed manuscripts in the Territorial Archives, Papeete).
28 I want to thank Tamatoa Bambridge for urging me to work on this piece and for incisive suggestions. I also owe an *aloha* imbued thanks to Jeff Martin for his insights and generous guidance in reading in the anthropology of the state, and to Gary Mawyer and several anonymous reviewers for comments on an early draft. Thanks are also due to Bruno Schmidt, Yves Scanzi, Teri'i Seaman and many others in the *punui* of Rikitea and Papeete for gifts of friendship, time and insight into the politics of pearls. I want to particularly thank Monika Richeton, Rikitea's mayor, for her generous welcome and numerous supports, and for inviting me to be present at a number of formal events of governance during my time on Mangareva. The doctoral field research on which this chapter is based was conducted with the support of the US Department of Education Fulbright-Hays Program and the Wenner-Gren Foundation.

CONCLUSION
What are the lessons to be learned from the *rahui* and legal pluralism? The political and environmental efficacy of legal pluralism

Tamatoa Bambridge

Our analysis of the *rahui* owes much to the theoretical and methodological contribution to the study of legal pluralism in common law and in Germano-Roman contexts, the conditions that encourage the preservation of the *rahui* in various contemporary situations, and the authors' contributions to the research on the legal pluralism theory combined with anthropologically informed fieldwork.

This collection makes two major contributions to legal pluralism theory on both conceptual and methodological levels. First, all authors demonstrate that legal pluralism can and does occur without the presence of a modern centralised state, and that it fulfils a need and does so effectively. In Polynesia, Rigo; Torrente; Ottino-Garanger, Ottino-Garanger, Rigo and Tetahiotupa; and myself show, precisely, the profound pluralistic nature of Polynesian societies, in diverse fields related to the *rahui*. As such, the social order within activities (Rigo) and the coexistence of distinct legal orders depending on one's status and territorial category (Bambridge) account for traditional pluralism. Polynesian people recognise norms or even differentiated legal orders that rely on the communities' and their chiefs' autonomy (Torrente; Ottino-Garanger et al.). As a matter of fact, Ottino-Garanger et al.;

Rigo; and Torrente emphasise the pluralistic nature of pre-European societies in the Tuamotu and the Marquesas archipaelagos from the point of view of religion and social organisation. Even institutions are plural. *Tapu* and *rahui* cannot be treated as synonymous nor can they be analysed along a continuum between gods, man and nature. *Tapu* is a sacred prohibition by nature; *rahui* is a sacred prohibition through the medium of social organisation and status. The conclusions go beyond recognising the importance of this difference.

Torrente's and my own findings demonstrate that, notwithstanding their status, all people can implement a *rahui* on his territory or a specific resource. Pluralism crosses all social statuses. Indeed, Chapter 6 demonstrates that the status of *ari'i* (political leaders) is not the only status that justifies the establishment of a *rahui*; *manahune* (common people) can also control their territory, whether it be terrestrial or maritime in nature. This, with the fact that all societies studied in this book were not centralised societies, provides a pluralistic view of society pre-European contact. Even most of the anthropoly of law theories do not go so far when theorising about the pluralistic nature of societies, with the notable exception of Vanderlinden (2013), who considers that societies are plural because individuals create and generate norms at different levels according to the realm of their activities.

As far as state and customary institutions are concerned, Ghasarian, Thorax, Chambers, and Ruru and Wheen all note and describe local political hybridisation processes. State institutions are sometimes diverted from their primary goals, reorganised, or even reappropriated by local people, in order to create a new form of *rahui*. Thus, whatever the historical periods studied, one can find not only one but several types of legal pluralisms that vary between contexts.

Lastly, on a methodological level, Rigo, Ghasarian, Dixon and myself provide tools to analyse these legal pluralisms. From an anthropological viewpoint, one must study society in terms of ideology as well as social organisation (Conte). In the same perspective, Ghasarian, Torrente and Ottino-Garanger et al. stress the relevance of ethnographic principles when describing an institution. They do not, however, subscribe to the (somewhat static and institution-focused) principles used from the beginning of the twentieth century, which consisted in the recording of customs before their disappearance (see for example the Bishop Museum Expeditions, 1920–30) but to those that support a debated description and which take into account the aims of individuals to preserve or rehabilitate the *rahui*.[1] Conte suggests that legal pluralism can modify its nature, not because of a law or a belief, but because of a change in the fishing techniques used by the islanders. This represents a major contribution to legal pluralism theory which has largely neglected the relationships between the changes in techniques and the legal anthropological processes within Oceanic societies. Thorax and Mawyer's chapters help to place legal pluralism — associated with the tradition of the *rahui* — within new contexts, since they conduct their analysis on a micro-political scale and convincingly demonstrate how individual ambivalences are omnipresent in daily life. This is one of the main reasons why societies remain pluralistic: the state legal order has not managed to wholly impose itself and has produced some intrastate rights established by local people. Lastly, Ruru and Wheen assert that contradictions can be found not only in the state–custom connection but also within the internal dimensions of the state.

The resulting comparative analysis of *rahui* within French-speaking and English-speaking contexts influenced by different legal traditions are invaluable. The numerous case studies show that the underlying logic of the creation of a legal pluralism — after the emergence of a state — lead, in various ways, to the same outcome: an attempt by the states to control granted autonomies, that is to say a legal pluralism that is as minimal as possible.[5] This book's anthropological approach to the law enhances analysis that is based solely on legal traditions fixed in Eastern Polynesia since the colonial period. These different legal traditions matter less than power relationships for the state, and between indigenous communities and the state. Both relationships determine the leeway for legal pluralism. As noted, the legal pluralisms established after colonial settlements are ambivalent and problematic, for the modern state has revealed little capacity to concede sovereignty to local communities on some territories.

Moreover, we may wonder to what extent the claimed legitimacies appear to be different? On territorial control, the state seems to advocate environmental protection, whereas local communities insist on the preservation of their cultural heritage. Of course, the situation is never straightforward, with most authors in this book portraying this dichotomy as largely ambivalent.

---

1   Ghasarian, C., 2007. 'Art oratoire et citoyenneté participative à Rapa (Polynésie française)'. In Catherine Neveu (ed.), *Cultures et pratiques participatives. Perspective comparatives.* Coll. Logiques Politiques, Paris: L'Harmattan, pp. 135–53.

Another contribution that this book makes to the literature is in better outlining the conditions allowing a more cooperative and harmonious legal pluralism between state law and customary law. The lessons learned from the various works go beyond the instances located in Eastern Polynesia. Indeed, Ghasarian in Rapa, Friedlander, Shackeroff and Kittinger in Hawai'i and Dixon in Mangaia describe the conditions along which customary law leads to reluctance or willingness to acknowledge state law. Local social organisation has more impact on the establishment of a form of pluralism than the acknowledgement of the *rahui* by the state. The collective nature of property and sometimes the isolation of some communities from the state (Ghasarian, Chambers and Dixon), constitute discriminating factors in the preservation of a pluralistic society.

In these perspectives related to the *rahui* (Friedlander, Shackeroff and Kittinger, Ghasarian, Dixon, Bambridge), one can identify a certain degree of continuity between traditional pluralism and modern pluralism. The *rahui* operates when the relationships between the structure of collective property and family ties are identified and preserved, and when traditional values linked to the *rahui* have adapted to changing contexts. These observations are part of the political field rather than the environmental field. Thus, can we talk about some new forms of acknowledgement of a property right which is *sui generis*? Neither the states nor the local communities involved seem to have an answer, for now.

But the traditional pluralistic nature of society may also face profound breakages due to the monopolisation of power by modern states in Polynesia. Friedlander, Shackeroff and Kittinger describe situations where the *rahui* does not operate any longer. Mawyer emphasises the confusion of legitimacies, which develop in the minds of each individual. This collection of case studies has implications for legal pluralism in Eastern Polynesia. If many authors consider Eastern Polynesia as including the most colonised societies within Oceania, we also have to recognise that legal pluralism is the norm and is effective as a means of political empowerment and consensus-based environmental management in the context of multiple stakeholders. Traditional Eastern Polynesian ways have endured and continue to have efficacy.

POSTSCRIPT
What are the consequences of *rahui*?

Jean Guiart

The *rahui* maybe *the* institution belonging to island civilisation that has been least coloured with Western romanticism. Each author in this volume agrees more or less on the same features, the same rules and the same consequences. The same vegetable symbol is fastened to a coconut trunk, or built outside it, with the same coconut at different stages of maturity. More important, the story told about it is globally the same in Melanesia, Micronesia and Polynesia. This could mean that the *rahui* is in effect at the centre of all things, which conclusion may be regarded as slightly adventurous.

The frequent and relative consistency of any discourse about the *rahui* brings us to hunt around to make things clearer. The importance of the *rahui* is in its consequences and it is there that the professional stance falters so often. We have next to no analysis featuring numbers, the amount of food obtained and saved through the *rahui* for a given event, how it is brought in, where, in what quantities, by whom and how *exactly* it is shared and consumed.

The trouble so often is that any study aiming to generalise tends to cite all authors, all of whom are European. Some are good, some are bad, even very bad, some are in the middle, but all must be cited, even if they are only second-line cabinet anthropologists, who tend to repeat what everybody has said before. Anything told by a missionary should be under suspicion and checked in the field, given the set ideas that they brought to Polynesia from London, France or America about infanticide, cannibalism and human sacrifice, which they received from their superficial studies of the religious situation in the Roman Empire at the time of the beginning of the Christian religion, with the near Eastern messianic religions invading Rome and being *de facto* rivals of the nascent Christian faith. Only those who base their conclusions on solid field research should be cited. What is the value of a judgement about Polynesian culture and society by an author who has never been there? Or who has only passed through?

The classical rule, accepted through many centuries, is that a vernacular concept can only be analysed through taking all its known contexts in all vernacular texts available over the generations. Which is, or should be, amongst others, the job of authors of dictionaries. Analysing the interpretations by European authors only is a specific deviation from the rule by authors interested in Tahiti for the last 300 years. What Claude Lévi-Strauss calls normative anthropology is not the best way of analysing the cultures and societies of the islands. We have for so long disregarded facts and been satisfied with value judgements. Real facts were few and far between, in a sea of pure invention conceived by white self-imposed witnesses.

Texts uttered and taken down, or written down by vernacular authors themselves at leisure, at different dates in time, are what we need, and what we do not have (a very little in the Society Islands and none in the Marquesas). The Aotearoa New Zealand Maori written tradition is richer, so much so that we can ignore useless authors, such as Elsdon Best, who is useful only in precise instances. When he starts generalising, he is useless. This Maori universe represents, at least for a great part, the Society Islands as it existed 1,000 years before James Cook. This is a new field to be worked upon, abandoning for a time the imprecise conclusions of the *pakeha* (when they are not wholly wrong).

This brings us to the true consequences of *rahui*, that is the problem of *the circulation of goods and riches*, illustrated by Marcel Mauss's famed essay *The Gift*. There are some problems with this author, who was a cabinet sociologist (he never called himself an anthropologist) — this species survived long in France — and never went out of his study, except to see out his military service in Morocco, which means he did not always understand the details of the proceedings described by Malinowski or other authors. How can you apply a theoretical analysis to the exchange of yams when you have never seen a yam, much less eaten one, know how it is planted and looked after, and by whom? Mauss was so revered inside the French academic scene that nobody asked such an irreverent question, nor do they today.

The problem of method is thus to go back to reality. What are the *details* of the social and economic consequences of the *rahui*? One is evident: feeding a mass of people. The amount of food saved through the *rahui*, but *equally* through the physical labour allowing the yams and other tubers and *varia* to be grown is astounding. The two always go together. Tons of food are needed to satisfy the ceremonial appetite of approximately 3,000 people gathered together for five days, which was the usual length of any collective outburst of island privilege, prestige and power. They may stay another five days, but this was infrequent.

The rules of the game — as I know them from Southern Melanesia, which is so close, geographically and culturally, to Polynesia — are as interesting as they are unheralded. The principal one, which must not be infringed without dire consequences (it would be an insult) is that *the food one brings into the collective pot must never be found inside it*. The chief's first legitimate wife, known as *isola* inside the so-called chiefly language of the Loyalty Islands (used by commoners addressing chiefs, her individual name must never been used), has the difficult job, with a ceremonial man servant called *ahnyab*a (the man of the house), to check where the food brought from the outside is stored, so as never to give it back, as food or as a gift, to the exact people who brought it. This rule, which is equally valid in Vanuatu, has been little noted up to now. It underlines the essential function of the first-born lady having become the first legitimate wife of a chief, whom she always outranks.

The other, rarely described evidence relates to the circulation of goods. The reality is that there is very little circulation. Most of the food is eaten on the spot, it does not circulate in any way, except through the consequences of the biological function — the spot where one eats and the one where one defecates. This food has been brought directly from the gardens, far and wide, which also happens daily. There is no fundamental discrepancy with everyday life.

The only economic function of the tons of food put together is feeding the thousands of people for the duration of their stay. The economic consequence is that the same people, brought together on a single spot, will have only grown a percentage of the food brought together and put on exhibition before being consumed. They have come to eat, not to trade. But there is a physical limit to what they can eat.

Part of the prestige of a large feast is when there is more food left over than was needed, plus the gifts of food that are returned to the representatives — men, women and children — of the visiting descent lines, which will be shared at home, including with the old ladies who could not come to receive their rightful share. These specific gifts are theoretically *less* than what the recipients brought in, if they are linked to the paternal line of the husband of the married couple, or of the deceased man or woman; *more* if they are linked to the wife's line, or the maternal line of the deceased person. The fact is that *one never gets back the exact amount of what one has brought*, but either *more* or *less*, and this in varying amounts. This is one of the two great problems of the hosting group, to feed enough and well, and to give back what should be according to the available amounts, which must be calculated precisely before everybody arrives.

Various tricks are used to arrive at precise figures, which are checked at each stage of the preparations and of the five days, usually by using the fronds of the cycas palm tree. Creating heaps of 10 tubers fastened with a stone or shell to indicate the descent line that has brought the specific cycas frond in the first instance, and has chosen the added symbol.

The other reality is that, for the greater part, the same amount of food would have been grown, outside of any feast, so as to feed the same people. What has changed for the time is the method of allocation: centralisation of the same tons of food, for the same people, inside a single spot for five days. The validity of the process is symbolic, what is processed socially is not food but prestige, added to the demonstration of the legitimate forms of an island power of sorts. This is no form of tribute, part of the food coming from the chief's gardens and being the result of his own and his wife's physical exertions. The chief is the host, but he is equally one of the producers, and he too must not eat his own food. He would fall sick, hurt by the reverse operation of his own *mana*.

POSTSCRIPT

One may complete this kind of return to base by examining the concept of the circulation of riches. The first evident remark is that they are not consumed. They are never destroyed, ritually. They gain in prestige as they circulate, if they circulate. The problem is that they do not always circulate. The crown made from the hair of successive legitimate wives, over the generations of Te Ariki Kafika on Tikopia, worn by his wife does not circulate, it is added to at each generation. The necklaces made of green stone beads of the Loyalty Islands *isola*, and the New Caledonian first-born legitimate wives and first-born daughters are handed over, generation after generation, through the female line; they are never, as such, part of an exchange process. The riches that circulate are the shell money (*miö, adi*), and the circular shaped ritual axe (*gi o kono, sio*), built from a succession of male and female symbols.

The Latin motto '*Do ut des*', which has for so long governed anthropological interpretations, is completely wrong here. What is given is never wholly given back, if it is only something that can be divided in equal parts (so many dry coconuts, so many yams, so many taros, so many sugar canes — note that tubers are never cut into pieces except for cooking purposes). Some recipients do receive back an equal amount of anything, which is understood as a kind of insult intended by the island givers, but never understood by the European unconscious takers. It means only this, through a silent message: 'the present relation is hereby terminated, we do not want to build a long standing relation with you'. No white man, in the islands, has ever comprehended this disrespectful symbolic language. They may often have acted as if, in fact, they are only visitors, often invited for a short visit, and were effectively uninterested in a long-term relationship, as understood by the people, which, if started knowingly, could later become costly, costs growing along with the prestige claimed.

Another moot point is the one of the sanctions against those who did not respect the *rahui*. European authors dealing with the islands, be they missionaries, lay people, but also anthropologists, have from the beginning loved death (the one of island people, not their own) as a constant described sanction for any misdeed, violating *rahui* included. The fear of sanctions is given as an explanation for the start of a migration, somebody having for instance touched inadvertently the head of a chief's son. The whole social group goes overseas for fear of being wholesale murdered.

Having worked all over a wide area through searching for every single descent line, alive or dead, I have noted what happened to lines of which an ancestor had broken a *tapu*, for instance, by killing the paramount chief of the Wetr district in Lifou before the advent of the white man. The culprit's line was said to have been victims of a curse, mass murdered and died out through the lack of male members. The problem is that I found the descendants three miles away, they had been only obliged to change their name and as a consequence lost their former land tenure. They were on sufferance in their new environment, but apparently quite prosperous nevertheless. As of their preceding name, they had died out. As of those with the new name, they were shipshape. This is not the only instance of such a silent, peaceful change hidden behind a dramatic discourse for the benefit of expatriate curiosity.

Over the years, I have accumulated the knowledge of quite a few theoretically disappeared lineages, some close to Nouméa, who were meant to have died out here, but who are alive and kicking elsewhere. I do not believe anymore in sanctions by death for traditional reasons. The people have so often changed name and location at the same time, for all sorts of reasons — quarrels between siblings being quite a frequent explanation. Most culprits are just a little away — that is their descendants — and everybody knows it. Only a few are ever far away.

If the sanctions by death accumulated by the *pakeha, haole, pwopale* (north-east New Caledonia), *kamaadra* (men of the colour of blood, Lifou) authors had been genuine, plus human sacrifices, children killed by their *ari 'oi* mothers, victims of cannibals, how many islanders would there be left? That is the question none of these authors has ever answered over the last four centuries. The thousands of corpses have never been found, neither on land, nor inside the lagoons. The concrete consequence of their assertions, repeated over time, have never been considered by classical authors dealing with the Pacific islands. Going on saying that the violators of the *rahui* were punished by death is not believable today. Bring me a corpse with the necessary contextual data, and the physical traces of his execution. I have them in south central Vanuatu for quite different reasons. But they are there. They are absent in Polynesia, where massacres described by authors yield no material proof. Go down deep inside genealogies and get to the real sanctions, those that a healthy, living society could tolerate. I know of more chiefs killed or obliged to go into exile than of offenders of a *tapu*. Most offenders are found in the next island, or even the next Christian village today — that is their descendants — but who searched for them? Any stupid assertion by a missionary is regarded as being an unassailable truth. These clerics came from Europe and the Americas with those very ideas, so they interpreted everything according to their primitive views. White missionaries have been saying those things about everywhere: Madagascar, South Africa, India, China, and so on. Even from Ethiopia, where the people were Christians before us, and even from the Nestorian Christian Mongols of the famed Priest John along the Silk Road.

Another wrong idea is the use of poison as a hidden sanction for the breaking of a *tapu* or a *rahui*. This goes with the prevalent white idea of the presence of witchcraft, the theory of which was brought to the islands by missionaries. The islanders know well what plants are dangerous, but all use by them as poison is hearsay and again a nasty inventions by white authors. This idea by expatriates comes from a pidgin English linguistic transfer of signification, where the white man understood the use of vegetable poison, the islander was talking of having recourse to ritual tools for killing a man, making use of his hair or soil impregnated with his body liquids, or through curses asked from a local god (we have many such instances around the Shepherd Islands of Vanuatu).

This goes with what is the real authority of a chief? The general view of European authors is that chiefs represented a hierarchical system inside a stratified society. This is not at all how the islands' societies I know function, from New Caledonia to north Vanuatu. The stratified aspect is non-functional, except when one has recourse to the ceremonial lexicon. The respectful use of a so-called chiefly language between commoners and chiefly kin are equally used between *cipa*, younger brothers and their father and mother and their first-born sister or elder brother. The parallel respectful behaviour towards the paramount chief, who has been given a collective name, *angajoxue*, that is 'the chiefs', and the secondary chiefs of the lineages (*tixei i angete*) linked to the paramount chieftainship, are found to be the same, with somewhat less flourish, less complexity inside the devilish details, between children and their parents or elder brothers and sisters. The result is that it is unfeasible to bring about the concept of castes, as there is no fixed social status at birth. The name given to a child brings him at the same time his future social and land tenure status, but this name is the result of a discussion between a number of people, representatives of the lineage at birth and some outside people according to the demographic situation, and what lines need a new person to take over because there are no males left, or not enough. Thus, the situation of the new-born baby is not fixed, except by negotiations that might have started long before his birth.

In this context, one woman stands out — the *first-born sister* — whose social status is higher than that of her father and mother, higher than the elder brother (see Tonga, Samoa and Fiji, as well as New Caledonia, the Loyalty Islands and Vanuatu). If she is of high rank, she has been trained to exert a commanding position over men. I have never seen a man standing up to a first-born woman, not even her husband, who is also of lower rank than her. This was in Fiji the position of Lady Adi Lala, herself *Tui Rewa* or *Tui Dreketi*, Ratu Sir Kamisese Mara's wife, himself *Tui Nayau*.

In Lifou, this was the status of my mother-in-law, Charlotte Xutepec Wahnyamala, who chose a commoner as a husband but also talked as an equal to any of the three male paramount chiefs of the island. She never said to them *angajoxue*, as I would do, but called them by their personal names, which no one else would dare to do. She would be slightly more respectful with their legitimate wives, first-born women as she was. In fact, her husband was from another chiefly line, the Wanakamwe on Ouvéa, but this was never recognised openly.

The first-born sister has everywhere the choice of her husband. If she has a child out of wedlock, there maybe a special cadet ranking line available nearby where the child will be integrated, so as not to appear inside the official genealogy (on Tongariki, one of the Shepherd islands of Vanuatu, the blood samples taken from every single person, even new-born babies, have shown that 30 per cent of the members of this island community were not the sons or daughters of the parents they officially declared, which means that the biological descendants was not the working concept here). They did not deal in ideas of blood descendants, which are so loved by European authors. The status of a person is the result of a collective decision at birth, and genealogies are partly manipulated social tools, in which are looked for, and organised, the closest possible links with the persons having the greatest *mana*,

POSTSCRIPT

that is first-born ladies of yore. Another reason for such collective decisions at birth is to be the instrument of achieving access to land tenure rights that were previously not available.

The place is equally full of rejected elder brothers who have been found to be non-functional, that is brutal or stupid, unfitted to reign. A non-functional chief can be killed and there are numerous, well-documented cases of this. The lineage of the present Melanesian president of the local congress in Nouméa is one. The murder of Jean-Marie Tjibaou in Ouvéa is another, he being killed by the coherent collective will of the lineage chiefs, fathers of the young warriors who died in the cave. They could not accept that Tjibaou had not used his international stature at the time to save the life of their children, instead going to hide inside his tribe, claiming that he had had no previous knowledge of the project, when he was in effect the one to have given the marching orders. They were not concerned with the four members of the armed gendarmerie who were killed by their sons. My wife has close kin in Ouvéa, which helped greatly for a silent inquiry parallel and in complete contradiction to the official one.

The way local meetings are carried out on Ouvéa show a different picture than the one so often peddled around. The chief is present. When he talks, it is in a low voice. He is not the chairman, better playing subtly the role of a servant of his people. The men speaking in a strong tone are those who have inherited the right to do so. They speak as they wish, not specially referring to the chief's opinion, but saying what they have been trained to say. Contrary opinions can be voiced, which more often brings the discussion to a state of no decision, until the next time, a special dignitary being the one who will resume the discussion and state publicly if a decision has been or not been agreed to. During the meeting, children walk from the circle of women sitting on mats outside of the oval open meeting house, and go to speak in their father's ear. He then gets up and talks, telling what his wife has thus reminded him he should say.

The complexity of Melanesian chieftainships go from the outmost simplicity and in effect the lack of chieftainship (the Tchamba valley, north-east New Caledonia) to the affluent and celebrated chiefdoms in the Loyalty Islands, but also lesser known ones on Koumak, Gomen, Bondé and Pouébo in north New Caledonia, all the others being in between in all sorts of cunning ways. In the same way the Vanuatu situation moves from the absence of classical chiefs (Tanna) to the more elaborate situations in north Malekula (with patrilineal chiefs) and the area from Efate to Epi (matrilineal chiefs in the south, elected chiefs through a title system on the Shepherd Islands to the north).

This complexity is not an instrument of chiefs having the right of life and death on their subjects, as is expressed in so many white man's interpretations, but a way of creating, under all kinds of ritual or ceremonial pretences, real autonomies which protect such and such lines that can only be called upon for a specific task, the lineage chief sending a cadet to attend to the matter and never coming himself. Some lineages are only called upon to be present at ceremonial times, nothing being asked from them. Their chief is only meant to be what is called the 'shell' (*mo ni angajoxue*); that is, to be a kind of ornament at the chief's court. Catholic or Protestant missionaries tend to be considered as being of this kind, a prestigious piece of furniture. They rarely concur with this view, but they have rarely known about it.

The official explanations for all these autonomies are varied. There are no 'talking chiefs', such as on Samoa, Tonga and Fiji, but the list of privileges is still the one noted on Tonga by James Mariner, which is very little cited by anthropologists of all kinds, but is nevertheless one of the best things written about Polynesia. The original, primeval list is Melanesian, here on Ouvéa is:[1]

- the man who holds the right to speak for the chief, *hnyimen than, mutu de aliki*; he has been trained in all circumstances and knows what discourse he is to deliver in each instance; he is the introducer at all formal meetings;
- the man of the house, *ahnyaba*, he is the sole person allowed to sleep with the chief inside the *hnyeule*, round hut where are kept the yams brought at the first fruits ritual; he has the right to eat the bananas from the tree at the foot of which the chief, *than, aliki*, urinates and defecates at night; he is thus said to be another sort of wife for the chief, and said also, symbolically, to eat the chief's faeces, which some ill-disposed authors have taken as being the reality;

---

1   Quoted from Guiart, Jean, 1963. *Structure de la chefferie en Mélanésie du Sud*, Paris: Institut d'Ethnologie, Musée de l'Homme, Paris.

- *obotrkong*, the man whose duty is to conclude, positively or negatively, a meeting. He is the sole person allowed to say if a decision has been agreed to or deferred to another meeting;
- *hingat in than*, the man who is meant to be, or more than one man, an adviser to the chief; he holds also the right to remonstrate with the chief, or even beat him if what the latter is doing is not right by the traditional criteria (i.e. having sexual relations with a married woman); the *ta hingat* are also called upon to participate in, that is in the role of directing, construction work inside the chief's fence (*hag*);
- *tang tangen than*, the man who cares for and holds the chief's traditional riches (shell money, *sio*, etc.). Some in modern times have sold them to white men, or given them to Christian missionaries.

The island of Lifou adds to this list:

- the *angatresi* (*acania* on Maré island) are those who play the role of intermediate between the chief, *joxue* or *angajoxue*, and the *alalu* (because they are so often cited two by two) or *ten adro* (he who stands on the land), or *angete haze* (the men mastering the gods), according to context, in as much as they are meant to be the oldest inhabitants of the land, anywhere, are said to have chosen the chief on the area which is theirs and the only ones having the privilege of a direct relation to the gods (*haze*, *kaze* on Maré); for this reason their *men* (= *mana*) is great and their contact dangerous. Their contribution in yams for the first fruits ritual must go through each of their specific *atresi*, who keeps them and substitutes his own to go to the *angajoxue*, so as to protect him. This contribution, made in their name, is deposited outside, not inside, as with all the other contributions, the chiefly yard (*hag*);
- A specific line is called the 'chief's meat'. This has been interpreted by missionaries, and even by authors such as Maurice Leenhardt, as having the dubious privilege of giving one of its members when the paramount chief Bula wanted to taste human meat.

This interpretation is completely wrong. A man is said to have been 'eaten by the chief' when he has been chosen to be the one to take over the name (all the names linked to the dead lineage: place names, names of godly beings, names of places oozing with *men*) of a line without any male representative left, which gives him the benefit of that line's land tenure, which he holds in trust, redistributing the land as fast as he bears male children. If he has only daughters, it will be the job of his first-born daughter. He loses at the same time his birth names, and his previous land tenure. He is another man. All cannibal interpretations by white authors should go to the wastepaper basket.

Vanuatu systems have more or less the same list, to which they add the carpenter (*namataisau*) the one who has inherited the knowledge of the minute details of the building of large seagoing canoes (he exists also on Ouvéa). And also the *takoari* (the great warrior and executioner) found on the islands from Efate to Epi, but equally on north Malekula. The execution of the French settler Mazoyer, in 1939, on the orders of the chief of Tènamit (Big Nambas area), was done by the chief's *takoari*, who was sent home to fetch his gun and kill the white man while he was sleeping in his boat. The latter had abducted the three wives of a relative of the chief and would not give them back, even with the offer by the chief of a tusker pig. The *takoari* could not evade doing exactly what was his function. Such details are not from the devil, although he may be roaming around. They are functional, and they are at the basis of Polynesian ideology. Melanesian *rahui* predated the Polynesian ones by many thousands of years. Speaking of Polynesia only when dealing with concepts such a *tapu* and *mana* might be a fatal mistake for the profession.

A last remark is the unhappy effect of deeming so many things 'sacred', when 'sacredness' is a concept considered as being so natural as not being necessary to study. The parallel *vernacular* concepts of *tapu* and *mana*, could have nothing to do with 'sacrednessé', which is a *white man's* theological concept brought in by Protestant and Catholic missionaries. 'Sacred' may be the catchword of the anthropology of our time. It should be the theme of another book.

References

Adams, H., 1964. *Mémoires d'Ari'i Tamai*, Paris: Publication de la Société des Océanistes no. 12, Musée de l'Homme.

Adams, T., 1998. 'The Interface between traditional and modern methods of fishery management in the Pacific Islands'. *Ocean and Coastal Management* 40: 127–42.

Agrawal, A., 2002. 'Indigenous knowledge and the politics of classification'. *International Social Science Journal* 54: 287–97.

Allen, B.J., 1971. 'Shorter communication; wet-field taro terraces on Mangaia, Cook Islands'. *Journal of the Polynesian Society* 80: 371–78.

——, 1969. 'The development of commercial agriculture on Mangaia; social and economic change in a Polynesian community'. MA thesis. Massey University.

Ama, A., 2003, 'Maeva – rites of passage: the highlights of family life'. In R. Crocombe & M.T. Crocombe (eds), *Akono'anga Maori: Cook Islands Culture*. Suva: University of the South Pacific, pp. 119–26.

Anderson, B., 1989. *Imagined Communities. Reflections on the Origin and Spread of Nationalism*. London: Verso.

Appadurai, A., 1996. *Modernity at Large. Dimensions of Globalization*. Minneapolis: University of Minnesota Press.

Artexaga, B., 2003. 'Maddening states'. *Annual Review of Anthropology* 32: 393–410.

Aufray, M., 2002. 'Note sur les messages de végétaux: quelques exemples océaniens'. *Journal de la Société des Océanistes* 114–15.

Babadzan, A., 1993. *Les dépouilles des dieux*. Paris: Editions de la Maison des Sciences de L'Homme.

Bachimon, P., 1990. *Tahiti: entre mythes et réalités*. Paris: Ed C.T.H.S, p. 29.

Bakhtin, M., 1985. *The Dialogic Imagination: Four Essays*. Austin: University of Texas Press.

Bambridge, T., 2009. *La terre dans l'archipel des îles Australes. Étude du pluralisme juridique et culturel en matière foncière*. Institut de Recherche pour le Développement (IRD) et Aux Vents des îles.

———, 2007. 'Généalogie des droits autochtones en Nouvelle-Zélande (Aotearoa) et à Tahiti (1840–2005)', *Droits et Sociétés* 22(1).

———, 2005. 'Cosmogonies et juridicité en Océanie'. In *Anthropologies et Droits, état des savoirs*. Paris: Association française d'Anthropologie du Droit, PUF, pp. 392–95.

Bambridge, T. & Ghasarian, C., 2002. 'Droit coutumier et législation française à Rapa: les enjeux d'une traduction'. *Droit et cultures*, Traduction et droits 44: 153–81.

Bambridge, T. & Neuffer, P., 2002. 'Pluralisme culturel et juridique: la question foncière en Polynésie française'. *Hermès* 32/33: 307–16.

Bambridge, T. & Vernaudon, J., 2012. 'Espace, histoire et territoire en Polynésie: une appropriation foncière de l'espace terrestre et marin. In E. Le Roy (ed.), *La Terre et l'homme*. Paris: Editions Khartala, pp. 33–53.

Baré, J-F., 1987. *Tahiti, Les Temps et Les Pouvoirs: Pour Une Anthropologie Historique du Tahiti Post-Européen*. Paris: Éditions de l'Orstom.

Barth, F.,1969. *Ethnic Groups and Boundaries: The Social Organization of Culture Difference*. Bergen: Oslo; London: George Allen & Unwin.

Bataille-Benguigui, M-C., 1994. *Le côté de la mer. Quotidien et imaginaire aux îles Tonga, Polynésie occidentale*. Collection 'Iles et Archipels' no. 19. Bordeaux: Centre de Recherche des espaces tropicaux de l'Université Michel de Montaigne.

Beckwith, M., 1972. *The Kumulipo*. Honolulu: University of Hawai'i Press.

Beechey, F.W., 1834. (1831). *Narrative of a Voyage to the Pacific and Beering's Strait*. Vol. 1. New York: Da Capo Press.

Bellwood, P.S., 1978. *Archaeological Research in the Cook Islands*. Pacific Archaelogical Records no. 27. Honolulu: Bernice P. Bishop Museum.

Bender, A. & Beller, S., 2003, 'Polynesian tapu in the deontic square. A cognitive concept, its linguistic expression and cultural context'. In R. Alterman & D. Kirch (eds), *Proceedings of the Twenty Fifth Conference of the Cognitive Sciences Society*, pp. 131–38.

Bennion, T., (ed.), 2007. 'Māori Law Review' (see www.bennion.co.nz/mlr/1997/nov.html).

Bensa, A., 1982. *Les chemins de l'Alliance*. Paris: SELAF.

Benzaken, D., Miller-Taei, S. & Wood, L., 2008. 'Status of policy and target development and implementation for marine protected areas/marine managed areas in the Pacific Islands Region — a preliminary assessment and future directions'. Unpublished paper. Regional Forum for Oceania on MMAs convened by NOAA, UNESCO.

Berkes, F., Colding, J. & Folke, C., 2000. 'Rediscovery of traditional ecological knowledge as adaptive management'. *Ecological Applications* 10:1 251–62.

Bernardie, N. & Taglioni, F., 2005. *Les dynamiques contemporaines des petits espaces insulaires*. Paris: Karthala.

Best E., 1904. 'Notes on the custom of Rahui, its application and manipulation, as also its supposed powers, its rites, invocations and superstitions'. *Journal of the Polynesian Society* 13(2): 83–88.

Bhabha, H., 1994. *The Location of Culture*. New York; London: Routledge.

Buck, P.H., 1938. *Ethnology of Mangareva*. Bulletin no. 157. Honolulu: Bernice P. Bishop Museum.

———, 1934. *Mangaian Society*. Bulletin no. 122. Honolulu: Bernice P. Bishop Museum.

———, 1932. *Ethnology of Tongareva*. Bulletin no. 92. Honolulu: Bernice P. Bishop Museum.

———, Field Notes, Rarotonga MS Staff Collection, Box 3.03, Volume 1, Peter Buck Staff Archives, Bernice P. Bishop Museum, Honolulu.

———, MS Staff Collection, Box 4.15, Peter Buck Archives, Bernice P. Bishop Museum, Honolulu.

———, MS Staff Collection, Box 4, Peter Buck Archives, Bernice P. Bishop Museum, Honolulu.

———, MS Staff Collection, Box 3, Peter Buck Archives, Bernice P. Bishop Museum, Honolulu.

Bulletin de la Société d'Études Océaniennes (*BSEO*) March–June 1994, pp. 261–62.

Buse, J. & Taringa, R., 1995. *Cook Islands Maori Dictionary*. Rarotonga: Ministry of Education, Government of the Cook Islands.

Butaud, J.F., 2010. *Guide Floristique des Atolls Soulevés de l'archipel des Tuamotu*. Papeete: Direction de l'Environnement.

Caillet, F.X., 1930. 'Souvenirs de l'occupation des Marquises en 1843'. *Bulletin de la Sté des Études Océaniennes* (B.S.E.O.) 38(4).

Caillot, E., 1932. *Histoire des Religions de l'Archipel des Tuamotu*. Paris: Ernest Leroux.

———, 1914. *Mythes, Légendes et Traditions des Polynésiens*. Paris: Ernest Leroux.

Campbell, A.R.T., 1985. *Social Relations in Ancient Tongareva*. Pacific Anthropological Records no. 36. Honolulu: Bernice P. Bishop Museum.

Chambers, C.N.L., 2008a. 'Bounding the Lagoon: Spatialising Practices and the Politics of Rahui, Tongareva, Cook Islands'. PhD thesis. University of Edinburgh.

———, 2008b. 'Pasua and the politics of environmental management, Tongareva, Cook Islands'. *Scottish Geographical Journal* 124(2–3): 192–98.

Chaulet, G., 1899. *Supplément*. Nuku Hiva; Archives of the Congregation of the Sacred Hearts of Jesus and Mary, Rome.

———, 1879. Manuscript. Nuku Hiva; Archives of the Congregation of the Sacred Hearts of Jesus and Mary, Rome.

———, 1873–1900. *Notices géographiques, ethnographiques et religieuses sur les îles Marquises*. Manuscript, Catholic diocese, Nuku Hiva; Archives of the Congregation of the Sacred Hearts of Jesus and Mary, Rome.

Chazine, J.-M., 1985, 'Les Fosses de Culture dans les Tuamotu. Travaux en cours et Perspectives'. *Journal de la Société des Océanistes* 61: 25–62.

Chiba, M., 1998. 'Droit non-occidental'. In W. Capeller and T. Kitamura, *Une introduction aux cultures juridiques non occidentales. Autour de Masaji Chiba*. Académie Européenne de Théorie du Droit de Bruxelles. Editions Bruylant, pp. 37–44.

Chikamori, M., (n.d.). *Maraes in Mangaia*. Tokyo: Department of Archaeology and Ethnology, Keio Universty.

Chinen, J.J., 1958. *The Great Mahele: Hawai'i's Land Division of 1848*. Honolulu: University of Hawai'i Press.

Christian, F. W., 1910. *Eastern Pacific Lands; Tahiti and the Marquesas Islands*. London: Robert Scott.

———, 1895, 'Notes on the Marquesans', *Journal of the Polynesian Society* 4(3): 187–202.

Cinner, J. E., & Aswani, S., 2007. 'Integrating customary management into marine conservation', *Biol. Conserv.* 140: 201–16.

Cinner, J.E., Wamukota, A., Randriamahazo, H. & Rabearisoa, A., 2009. 'Toward institutions for community-based management of inshore marine resources in the western Indian ocean'. *Marine Policy* 33(3): 489–96.

Conte, E., 2000. *L'archéologie en Polynésie française*. Tahiti: Au vent des îles.

——, 1988. 'La pêche pré-européenne et ses survivances. L'exploitation traditionnelle des ressources marines à Napuka (Tuamotu-Polynésie française). PhD thesis. Université Paris.

——, 1987. 'Pêche ancienne au requin à Napuka (Tuamotu)'. *Bulletin de la Société des Études Océaniennes* 238: 13–29.

Conte, E. & Dennison, K.J., 2009. 'Te Tahata. Étude d'un marae de Tepoto (Nord). Archipel des Tuamotu, Polynésie Française'. *Cahiers du CIRAP* 1.

Cook Islands Administration, 1908. Correspondence with Resident Agents in the Outer Islands, Resident Commissioner's Office, Cook Islands Administration, Box 19/1, National Archives of the Cook Islands, Rarotonga.

Cowling, W., 2006. 'Once you saw them, now you don't – the disappearance of Cook Island traditional craft production'. *Proceedings from the 2nd International Small Island Cultures Conference*. Sydney: Maquarie University Press, pp. 26–35.

Crocombe, R., 1987. *Land Tenure in the Pacific*. 3rd edn. Suva: University of the South Pacific.

——, 1964. *Land Tenure in the Cook Islands*, Oxford: Oxford University Press.

Crook, W.P., 2007. *Récit aux îles Marquises, 1797–1799*. [An account of the Marquesas Islands 1797–1799] Mgr. H. Le Cleac'h, D. Koenig & G. Cordonnier (trans.). Tahiti: éditions Haere Po.

——, 1990. *Life in the Marquesas Islands, Missionaries' Narratives, 1797–1842*, Uvea-Wallis, published by Te Fenua Foou.

——, 1800. *An Account of the Marquesas Islands*. MS CIII, State Library of New South Wales.

Crowder, L.B., Osherenko, G., Young, D.R., Airumé, S., Norse, E.A., Baron, N., Day, J.C., Douvere, F., Ehler, C.N., Halpern, B.S., Langdon, S.J., Mcleod, K.L., Ogden, J.C., Peach, R.E., Rosenberg, A.A. & Wilson, J.A., 2006. 'Resolving mismatches in U.S. ocean governance'. *Science* 313: 617–18.

Danielsson, B., & Danielsson, M-T., 1964. 'Introduction'. *Mémoires d'Arii Taimai / Henry Adams*; trad. de l'anglais par Suzanne et André Lebois. Paris: Société des Océanistes.

Davies, J., 1851. *A Tahitian and English Dictionary with Introductory Remarks on the Polynesian Language and a Short Grammar of the Tahitian Dialect*. Tahiti, printed at the London Missionary Society's Press.

Davin A., 1886. *50 000 miles dans l'Océan Pacifique*. Paris: E. Plon, Nourrit & Cie.

de Bovis, E., 1978. *Etat de la société tahitienne à l'arrivée des européens*. Publication no. 4. Tahiti: Société des Études Océaniennes.

de Comeiras, J.R.A., 1846. *Topographie médicale de l'archipel de la Société et des Iles Marquises*. Montpellier, Printed by J. Martel ainé.

de Roquefeuil, C., 1823a. *Journal d'un voyage autour du monde pendant les années 1816, 1817, 1818 et 1819*. 2 vols. Paris: Ponthieu, Lesage, Gide fils.

———, 1823b. *Idem*: *A Voyage Round the World Between the Years 1816–1819*. London: Sir Richard Philips and Co.

———, 1818. t.1, p. 324, in Testard de Marans, A., 2004. *Souvenirs des îles Marquises. Groupe Sud-Est, 1887–1888*. Paris: Publication de la Société des Océanistes, no. 45, Musée de l'Homme, chap II.

Delmas, S. Manuscript. Archives of the Congregation of the Sacred Hearts of Jesus and Mary, Rome.

Dening, G., 1999. *Marquises 1774 – 1880, Réflexion sur une terre muette*. Papeete: Editions de l'association "Eo "Enata.

———, 1980. *Islands and Beaches: Discourse on a Silent Land: Marquesas 1774–1880*. Chicago: The Dorsey Press.

———, 1972. 'Tapu and haka'iki; an ethnohistory of the Marquesas Islands'. PhD. Harvard University.

Descola, P., 2005. *Par delà Nature et Culture*. Paris: Gallimard.

Devatine, F., 1992. *Tapu et Rahui*. Assises de la Recherche en Polynésie française, Document dactylographié, non publié. Papeete: Académie tahitienne.

Dieffenbach, E., 1843. *Dictionary, PART III: Grammar and Dictionary*, in *Travels in New Zealand with Contributions to the Geography, Geology, Botany, and Natural History of that Country*. Vol. II. London: John Murray, Albemarle Street.

Dordillon, R.I., 1931. *Grammaire et dictionnaire de la langue des piles Marquises*. Travaux et mémoires de l'Institut d'ethnlogie, Paris, Institut d'Ethnologie.

———, 1904. *Grammaire et dictionnaire de la langue des îles Marquises*. 2 vols. Paris: Imprimerie Belin Frères.

Douaire-Marsaudon, F., 1998. *Les premiers fruits*. Paris: CNRS Editions / Editions de la Maison des Sciences de L'Homme.

Douglas, B., 1979. 'Rank, power, authority: a reassessment of traditional leadership in South Pacific societies'. *Journal of Pacific History* 14: 2–27.

Doumenge, J-P., 2002. 'Diversité culturelle et constructions des identités collectives outre-mer'. In D. Wolton et al. (eds), *La France et les outre-mers: L'enjeu multiculturel*. Hermès 32–33, CNRS Editions.

Dumont D'Urville, J., 1842. *Voyage au pole Sud et dans l'Océanie sur les Corvettes. l'Astrolabe et la Zélée: 1837–1840*. Paris: Gide.

Edith Kanaka'ole Foundation. 1995. Draft Ke Kalai Maoli Ola No Kanaloa, Kaho'olawe Cultural Use Plan. Kaho'olawe Island Reserve Commission.

Elias, N., 1993. *Engagement et distanciation*. Paris: Fayard.

Ellis, William, 1972. *A la recherche de la Polynésie d'autrefois*. Paris: Publication de la Société des océanistes.

——, 1829. *Polynesian Researches, During a Residence of Nearly Six Years in the South Sea Islands*. Vols 1 & 2. Fisher, Son & Jackson.

——, 1831. *Polynesian Researches During a Residence of Nearly Eight Years in the Society and Sandwich Islands*. 4 vols. 2nd edn. London: Fisher, Son & Jackson.

Ehrlich, E., 2001 (1913). *Fundamental Principles of the Sociology of Law*. New Brunswick: Transaction Publishers.

Emory, K.P., 1975. *The Material Culture of the Tuamotu Archipelago*. Pacific Anthropological Records 22. Honolulu: Bernice P. Bishop Museum.

——, 1947. *Tuamotuan Religious Structures and Ceremonies*. Bulletin no. 191. Honolulu: Bernice P. Bishop Museum.

——, 1934. *Tuamotuan Stone Structures*. Bulletin no. 118. Honolulu: Bernice P. Bishop Museum.

Facon, T., 1990. 'Irrigation and drainage development, Mangaia, Cook Islands'. Draft technical report. FAO Project TCP/CKI/8852. Rome: FAO.

Firth, R., 1965. *Essays on Social Organization and Values*. Monograph on Social Anthropology no. 28. University of London, London School of Economics. The Athlone Press.

——, 1940. 'The analysis of mana: an empirical approach'. *Journal of the Polynesian Society* 49: 483–510.

Fraser, 1892. 'Notes and queries'. *Journal of the Polynesian Society* 1(4): 273–76.

Friedlander, A., Aeby, G., Brainard, R., Brown, E., Chaston, K., Clark, A., McGowan, P., Montgomery, T., Walsh, W., Williams, I. & Wiltse, W., 2008. 'The state of coral reef ecosystems of the main Hawai'ian islands'. In J.E. Waddell & A.M. Clarke (eds), *The State of Coral Reef Ecosystems of the United States and Pacific Freely Associated States: 2008*. NOAA Technical Memorandum NOS NCCOS 73. Silver Spring, MD: NOAA/NCCOS Center for Coastal Monitoring and Assessment's Biogeography Team, pp. 158–99.

Friedlander, A.M., Brown, E.K., Jokiel, P.L., Smith, W.R. & Rodgers, K.S., 2003. 'Effects of habitat, wave exposure, and marine protected area status on coral reef fish assemblages in the Hawai'ian archipelago'. *Coral Reefs* 22: 291–305.

Friedlander, A.M., Brown, E.K. & Monaco, M.E., 2007. 'Coupling ecology and GIS to evaluate efficacy of marine protected areas in Hawai'i'. *Ecological Applications* 17: 715–30.

Friedlander, A.M. & De Martini, E.E., 2002. 'Contrasts in density, size, and biomass of reef fishes between the northwestern and the main Hawai'ian Islands: the effects of fishing down apex predators'. *Marine Ecology Progress Series* 230: 253–64.

Friedlander, A., Poepoe, K., Poepoe, K., Helm, K., Bartram, P., Maragos, J. & Abbott, I., 2002. 'Application of Hawai'ian traditions to community-based fishery management'. *Proc. 9th Inter. Coral Reef Symp.* Vol. 2: 813–18.

Friedman, Jonathan, 1996. *Culture identity and global process.* London: Sage Publications.

Gell, A., 1998. *Art and Agency.* Oxford: Clarendon Press.

——, 1993. *Wrapping in Images: Tattooing in Polynesia.* Oxford Studies in Social and Cultural Anthropology — Cultural Forms. Oxford: Clarendon Press.

Ghasarian, C., 2014. *Rapa. Île du bout du monde, île dans le monde.* Paris: Demopolis.

——, 2007. 'Art oratoire et citoyenneté participative à Rapa (Polynésie française)'. In Catherine Neveu (ed.), *Cultures et pratiques participatives. Perspective comparatives.* Coll. Logiques Politiques. Paris: L'Harmattan, pp. 135–53.

——, 2002. *De l'ethnographie à l'anthropologie réflexive.* Paris: Armand Collin.

Ghasarian, C., Bambridge, T. & Geslin, P., 2004. 'Le développement en question en Polynésie française'. *Journal de la Société des Océanistes* 119(2): 211–22.

Giddens, A., 1984. *The Constitution of Society.* Cambridge: Polity Press.

Gill, W.W., 1979. *Cook Islands Custom*. Suva: Institute of Pacific Studies, University of the South Pacific

———, 1892. 'Mangaia (Hervey Islands), Proceedings of sections'. Section G. *Anthropology Australasian Association for the Advancement of Science*. Hobart: Government Printer.

———, 1885. *Jottings from the Pacific*. London: Religious Tract Society.

Gilson, R., 1980. *The Cook Islands 1820–1963*. Wellington: Victoria University Press.

Gilson, R.P., 1952. 'Introduction to the administration of the Cook Islands (Rarotonga)'. MSc, University of London.

Godin, P., 2000. 'Les ancêtres, essai de définition'. In F. Angleviel (ed.), *Religion et sacré en Océanie*. Paris: L'Harmattan, pp. 25–47.

Goldman, I., 1970. *Ancient Polynesian Society*. University of Chicago Press.

———, 1955. 'Status rivalry and cultural evolution in Polynesia'. *American Anthropologist*, 57(4): 680–97.

Graaner, J.A., 1983. 'Nukuhiva in 1819', in 'Journal of a Swedish traveller' (unpublished), B. Akerren in *Institut for Polynesian Studies*, vol. 7, no. 1, pp. 34–58.

Graaner, J.A., 2007. *Un Suédois aux Marquises en 1819*. BSEO no. 310.

Gracia, M., 1843. *Lettres sur les îles Marquises, ou mémoire pour servir à l'étude religieuse, morale, politique et statistique des îles Marquises*. Paris: Gaume frères.

Grand Conseil Gambier Islands, 1985. *Registre des Deliberations du Grand Conseil Mangarevien: 1881–1914*. Paris: Institut d'Ethnologie.

Grand, S., 1888. 'Lagon de Mangareva. Resume d'Observations Ostreicoles'. *Journal Officiel des Etablissements Francais de l'Oceanie* 36: 233–35.

Griffith, J., 1986. 'What is legal pluralism?' *Journal of Legal Pluralism* 24: 1–53.

Guiart, Jean, 2013a. *Malekula, l'explosion culturelle.* Nouméa & Pape'ete: Le Rocher-à-la-Voile.

———, 2013b. *Cultures on the Edge, Caught Between the White Man's Concept, Polynesia Opposed to Melanesia, from Efate to Epi, Central Vanuatu.* Pape'ete: Te Pito o te Fenua.

———, 2012. *Les Religions de l'Océanie.* 2nd edn. Pape'ete: Haere Po.

———, 1992. *Structure de la Chefferie en Mélanésie du Sud.* Paris: Institut d'Ethnologie.

———, 1963. *Structure de la chefferie en Mélanésie du Sud*, Paris: Institut d'Ethnologie, Musée de l'Homme, Paris.

Gunson, W.N., 1975. 'Review: Tahiti's Traditional History: Without Adams?' Reviewed work(s): *Mémoires de Marau Taaroa Dernière Reine de Tahiti traduits par sa fille la Princesse Ariimanihinihi Takau Pomare* by Marau Taaroa. *Journal of Pacific History* 10(2): 112–17.

Handy, E.S.C., 1971a. *Houses, Boats and Fishing in the Society Islands.* Bulletin no. 90, Honolulu: Bernice P. Bishop Museum.

———, 1971b (1923), *The Native Culture in the Marquesas.* Bulletin no. 9. Honolulu: Bernice P. Bishop Museum; New York: Kraus Reprint Co.

———, 1930. *History and Culture in the Society Islands.* Bulletin no. 79. Honolulu: Bernice P. Bishop Museum.

———, 1927. *Polynesian Religion.* Bulletin no. 34, Honolulu: Bernice P. Bishop Museum.

Hanson, A., 1989, 'The making of the Maori: culture invention and its logic'. *American Anthropologist* 91: 890–02.

———, 1973. *Rapa.* Paris: Publication de la Société des Océanistes no. 33.

———, 1970. *Rapan Lifeways. Society and History on a Polynesian Island.* Boston: Little, Brown.

Hanson, A. & Ghasarian, C., 2007. 'The land belongs to everyone. The unstable dynamic of unrestricted cognatic descent in Rapa, French Polynesia'. *Journal of Polynesian Society* 116(1): 59–72.

Hawai'i Ocean Resources Management Plan (ORMP), 2008. *Final Report to the Twenty-Fourth Legislature, Regular Session of 2007 Coastal Zone Management Program.* Office of Planning, DBEDT.

Hayward, J. & Wheen, N.R. (eds), 2004. *The Waitangi Tribunal. Te Roopu Whakamana i te Tiriti o Waitangi.* Wellington: Bridget Williams Books Ltd.

Henry, T., 2004. *Tahiti aux temps anciens*, Paris: Société des Océanistes.

——, 1988 (1968). *Tahiti aux temps anciens.* Paris: Publication de la société des océanistes.

——, 1928. *Ancient Tahiti*, Bulletin no. 48. Honolulu: Bernice P. Bishop Museum.

Hui Malama o Mo'omomi, 1995. Proposal to Designate Mo'omomi Community-Based Subsistence Fishing Area, Northwest Coast of Moloka'i. Prep. for Dept. of Land and Natural Resources, State of Hawai'i.

Hunn, E., 1993. 'What is Traditional Ecological Knowledge?'. In N. Williams & G. Baines (eds.), *Traditional Ecological Knowledge.* Canberra: The Australian National University, pp. 13–15.

Hviding, E., 1998. 'Contextual flexibility: present status and future of customary marine tenure in Solomon Islands'. *Ocean and Coastal Management* 40: 253–69.

——, 1996. *Guardians of Marovo Lagoon: Practice, Place, and Politics in Maritime Melanesia.* Honolulu: University of Hawai'i Press.

Hobsbawm, R. & Ranger, T., 1983. *The Invention of Tradition.* Cambridge University Press.

Hocart A.M., 1914. 'Mana'. *Man* 14: 97–101.

Hooper S.J.P., 1996. 'Who are the chiefs? Chiefship in Lau, Eastern Fiji'. In R. Feinberg & K. Watson-Gegeo (eds), *Leadership and Change in the Western Pacific: Essays presented to Sir Raymond Firth on the Occasion of his Ninetieth Birthday.* LES Monographs on Social Anthropology 66. Athlone Press, pp. 239–71.

Jardin, E., 1858. *Essai de l'Histoire Naturelle de l'archipel Mendana ou des Marquises*. Mémoires de la Société Impériale des Sciences Naturelles et Mathématiques de Cherbourg.

Johannes, R.E., 2002. 'The renaissance of community-based marine resource management in Oceania'. *Annual Review of Ecology and Systematics* 33: 317–40.

——, 1981. *Words of the Lagoon: Fishing and Marine Lore in the Palau District of Micronesia*. Berkeley: University of California Press.

Jokiel, P.L., Rodgers, K.S., Walsh, W.J., Polhemus, D.A. & Wilhelm, T.A., 2011. 'Marine resource management in the Hawai'ian archipelago: The traditional Hawai'ian system in relation to the western approach'. *J. Mar. Biol.* 2011: 1–16.

Jolly, M., 2007. 'Imagining Oceania: indigenous and foreign representations of a sea of islands'. *The Contemporary Pacific* 19(2): 508–45.

Journal of 'Messager de Tahiti'. Imprimerie du Gouvernement, Papeete, Aout 1878.

Kalaora, B., 1998. *Au-delà de la nature l'environnement. L'observation de l'environnement*. Paris: L'Harmattan.

Kamakau, S.M., 1976. *The Works of the People of Old (Na hana a ka po'e kahiko)*. Translated from the newspaper *Ke Au 'Oko'a* by M.K. Pukui. Honolulu: Bishop Museum Press.

Kame'eleihiwa, L., 1992. *Native Lands and Foreign Desires, Ko Hawai'i Aina a me Na Koi Pu'umake a ka Po'e Haole*. Honolulu: Bishop Museum Press.

Kaplan, M., 2005. 'Outside gods and foreign powers: Making local history with global means in the Pacific'. *Ethnohistory* 52: 1.

——, 2004. 'Neither traditional nor foreign: dialogues of protest and agency in Fijian history'. In H. Jebens, T. Otto & K. Heinz Kohl (eds), *Cargo Cult and Culture Critique*. Honolulu: University of Hawai'i Press, pp. 59–79.

——, 1995. *Neither Cargo nor Cult: Ritual Politics and the Colonial Imagination in Fiji*. Durham: Duke University Press.

Keesing, R.M., 1985. 'Conventional metaphors and anthropological metaphysics: the problematic of cultural translation'. *Journal of Anthropological Research* 41: 201–17.

———, 1984. 'Rethinking mana'. *Journal of Anthropological Research* 40(1): 137–56.

Kelly, J.D., 2006. 'Who counts? Imperial and corporate structures of governance, decolonization and limited liability'. In C. Calhoun et al. (eds), *Lessons of Empire*. New York: New Press, pp. 157–74.

———, 2005. 'Boycotts and coups, shanti and mana in Fiji'. *Ethnohistory*, 52(1): 13–27

———, 1997. 'Gaze and grasp: plantations, desires, indentured Indians, and the colonial law in Fiji'. In L. Manderson & M. Jolly (eds), *Sites of Desire, Economies of Pleasure: Sexualities in Asia and the Pacific*. University of Chicago Press, pp. 72–98.

Kirch, P.V., 2002. *On the road of the winds*. University of California Press.

———, 1997. 'Changing landscapes and sociopolitical evolution in Mangaia, Central Polynesia'. In P.V. Kirch & T.L. Hunt (eds), *Historical Ecology in the Pacific Islands*. New Haven: Yale University Press.

———, 1994. *The Wet and the Dry: Irrigation and Agricultural Intensification in Polynesia*. University of Chicago Press.

———, 1989. *The Evolution of the Polynesian Chiefdom*. Cambridge University Press.

———, 1977. 'Valley agricultural systems in prehistoric Hawai'i: an archaeological consideration'. *Asian Perspectives* 20: 246–80.

Kirch, P.V. & Green, R.C., 2001. *Hawaiki, Ancestral Polynesia, An Essay in Historical Anthropology*. Cambridge University Press.

Krämer, A., 1994. *The Samoa Islands*. Aotearoa: Polynesian Press.

Lal, Brij, 1998. *Another Way: The Politics of Constitutional Reform in Post-Coup Fiji*. Canberra: The Australian National University Press.

———, 1992. *Broken Waves: A History of the Fiji Islands in the Twentieth Century*. Honolulu: University of Hawai'i Press.

Lamont, E.H., 1867. *Wild Life Among the Pacific Islanders*. London: Hurst and Blackett.

Lavondès, H., 1975. 'Terre et mer; pour une lecture de quelques mythes polynésiens'. PhD thesis. Université Paris Descartes.

Lefils, F., 1843. *Description des îles Marquises*. Paris: Prevot.

Leslie, H. & McLeod, K., 2007. 'Confronting the challenges of implementing marine ecosystem-based management'. *Front Ecol Environ* 5: 540–48.

Lesson, P.A., *Pylade*, 4e voyage, t. 3 et *Documents divers, Marquises*. unpublished documents. The Corderie de Rochefort archives.

———, *Marquises, Documents divers*, unpublished MS, Corderie de Rochefort, no. 8147, pp. 647–48.

Levine, S. 2009. *Pacific Ways: Government and Politics in the Pacific*. Wellington: Victoria University Press.

Lévi-Strauss, C., 1964. *Le cru et le cuit*. Paris: Plon.

———, 1962. *La Pensée Sauvage*. Plon: Paris.

———, 1958. *Anthropologie structurale*. Paris: Plon.

Maly, K., & Pomroy-Maly, O., 2003. *Ka Hana Lawai'a a me na Ko'a o na Kai'Ewalu. A History of Fishing Practices and Marine Fisheries of the Hawai'ian Islands*. Honolulu: The Nature Conservancy.

Marchand, É., 2003. *Le voyage du capitaine Marchand, 1791: les Marquises et les îles de la Révolution, avec les Journaux de Marchand, Chanal et Roblet, by Odile Gannier & Cécile Picquoin*. Papeete: Au Vent des îles.

Maric, T. & Torrente, F., 2011, *Prospection archéologique de l'atoll de Anaa, Tuamotu*. Rapport préliminaire. Pape'ete: Service de la Culture et du Patrimoine.

Mark, M.V. 1976. 'The relationship between ecology and myth in Mangaia'. MA thesis. University of Otago.

Marshall, D.S., 1965. 'Descent, relationship and territorial groups, social categories relevant to the Mangaian Kopu discussion'. Unpublished paper. DS Marshall Archive, University of the South Pacific, Cook Islands.

———, 1958. Field Notes of Third Expedition 1957/58, Box 7.3, D.S. Marshall Archives, University of the South Pacific, Cook Islands Campus, Rarotonga.

———, 1955. Field Notes of Second Expedition 1954/55, Box 7.4, D.S. Marshall Archives, University of the South Pacific, Cook Islands Campus, Rarotonga.

———, 1953. Field Notes of the First Expedition 1951/53, Box 7.1, D.S. Marshall Archives, University of the South Pacific, Cook Islands Campus, Rarotonga.

Maude, H.E., 1981. *Slavers in Paradise: The Peruvian Slave Trade in Polynesia, 1862–1864*. Canberra: The Australian National University Press.

Mauss, M., 1973 (1923–24). Essai sur le don: Forme et raison de l'échange dans les societes archaïques In Sociologie et Anthropologie. PUF, Collection Quadrige, pp. 149–279.

Mawyer, A., 2006. '"TV Talk" and Processes of Media Receptivity in the Production of Identities in the Gambier Islands, French Polynesia'. PhD thesis. The University of Chicago.

Maxwell, K.H. & Penetito, W., 2007. 'How the use of rāhui for protecting taonga has evolved over time'. *MAI Review* 2: 1–15, www.review.mai.ac.nz.

McClenachan, L., & Kittinger, J.N. (2013). 'Multicentury trends and the sustainability of coral reef fisheries in Hawai'i and Florida', *Fish and Fisheries* 14(3): 239–55.

McCormack, F., 2010. 'Fish is my daily bread: owning and transacting in Maori fisheries'. *Anthropological Forum* 20(1).

McGregor, D., 2007. *Na Kua'aina: Living Hawai'ian Culture*. Honolulu: Bishop Museum Press.

McPhail, D., 2002. *Constraints and Opportunities for South Island Landless Natives Act (SILNA) 1906 Indigenous Forest Utilisation.* Paper no. 3 from the research programme UoCX0004 Sustainability on Māori-Owned Indigenous Forest, School of Forestry. Christchurch: University of Canterbury.

Mead, H.M., 2003. *Tikanga Māori. Living by Māori Values.* Wellington: Huia Publishers.

Meller, N., 1985. *Indigenous Ocean Rights in Hawai'i.* Sea Grant Marine Policy and Law Report UNIHI-SEAGRANT-MP-86-01. Honolulu: UH Sea Grant College Program.

Métraux, A., 1941. *L'île de Pâques.* Paris: Gallimard.

Miller, R.J. & Ruru, J., 2009. 'An indigenous lens into comparative law: the doctrine of discovery in the United States and New Zealand'. *West Virginia Law Review* 111: 849–918.

Moore, S.F., 1978. 'Law and social change: the semi-autonomous field as an appropriate subject of study'. In L. Nader (ed.) *Law as Process. An Anthropological Approach.* London: Routledge and Kegan Paul, pp. 54–81.

Moerenhout, J-A., 1835. *Voyages aux îles du Grand Océan.* Paris: Maisonneuve.

Morrison, J., 1981. 'Journal'. Paris: Société des Études Océaniennes.

——, 1966. *Le Journal de James Morrison, second maître à bord le la Bounty.* Traduit de l'anglais par B. JAUNEZ. Paris: Musée de l'Homme.

Morse, B.W., 1988. *Indigenous Law and the State.* Foris Publications.

Newbury, C., 1966, 'Aspects of cultural change in French Polynesia: the decline of the Ari'i'. *Journal of the Polynesian Society*, Wellington 67: 7–26.

New Zealand Law Commission, 2001. *Māori Custom and Values in New Zealand Law.* Study Paper 9. Wellington: Law Commission.

Ngata, H.M., 1993. *Māori-English Dictionary.* Wellington: Learning Media.

Nielsen, D., 1999. *Three Faces of God. Society, Religion, and the Category of Totality in the Philosophie of Emile Durkheim*. Albany: State University of New York.

Oliver, D., 1989. *Oceania: The Native Culture of Australia and the Pacific Islands*. University of Hawai'i Press.

——, 1974. *Ancient Tahitian Society*. 3 vols. Honolulu: University of Hawai'i Press.

Orbell, M., 1995. *Maori Myths and Legends*. Canterbury University Press.

Osorio, J.K.K., 2002. *Dismembering Lāhui: A History of the Hawai'ian Nation to 1887*. Honolulu: University of Hawai'i Press.

Ottino-Garanger, P., 2006. *Archéologie chez les Taïpi, Hatiheu, un projet partagé aux îles Marquises*. Papeete: Aux vent des îles/IRD éditions.

——, 1990. 'L'habitat des anciens Marquisiens: architecture des maisons, évolution et symbolisme des formes'. *Journal de la Société des Océanistes* 90(1): 3–15.

——, 1972. *Rangiroa. Parenté étendue, residence et terres dans un atoll polynésien*. Paris: Editions Cujas.

Papahānaumokuākea Marine National Monument, 2008. *Monument Management Plan Volume I. 2008*. Prepared by the United States Fish and Wildlife Service, National Oceanic and Atmospheric Administration, and State of Hawai'i.

Petersen G., 2007. 'Hambruch's colonial narrative.' *Journal of Pacific History* 42(3): 317–30.

——, 2005. 'Important to whom? On ethnographic usefulness, competence and relevance'. *Anthropological Forum*.

——, 1999. 'Sociopolitical rank and conical clanship in the Caroline Islands'. *Journal of the Polynesian Society* 108(4): 367–410.

Percy, S., 1901. 'Notes on the dialect of Niue Island', *Journal of the Polynesian Society* 10(4): 178–82.

Pidjot, J-M., 2002. *Le Mwa Tea Mwalebeng et le fils du soleil, Organisation de l'espace kanak en pays mwalebeng*. Nouméa: Le Rocher-à-la-Voile & les Editions du Cagou.

Poepoe, K., Bartram, P. & Friedlander, A., 2007. 'The use of traditional Hawai'ian knowledge in the contemporary management of marine resources'. In N. Haggan, B. Neis & I. Baird (eds), *Fishers' Knowledge in Fisheries Science and Management*. Paris: UNESCO, pp. 117–41.

Pomare, Takau, 1971. *Mémoires de Marau Taaroa, dernière reine de Tahiti, traduits par sa fille, la princesse Takau Pomare*. Publication de la Société des Océanistes no. 27. Paris: Musée de l'Homme.

Presidential Memorandum, 12 June 2009. National Policy for the Oceans, Our Coasts, and the Great Lakes. Accessed 4 September 2009. Available online at: www.whitehouse.gov/the_press_office/Presidential-Proclamation-National-Oceans-Month-and-Memorandum-regarding-national-policy-for-the-oceans/.

Radiguet, M., 1978 (1860). *Les Derniers Sauvages: Souvenirs de l'occupation française aux îles Marquises, 1842–59*. Tahiti: Les Éditions du Pacifique.

Rainbird, P., 2003. 'Taking the tapu. Defining Micronesia by absence'. *Journal of Pacific History* 38(2): 237–50.

Rapaport, M., 1995. 'Oysterlust: islanders, entrepreneurs, and colonial policy over Tuamotu lagoons'. *Journal of Pacific History* 30: 39.

——, 1995. 'Pearl farming in the Tuamotus: atoll development and its consequences'. *Pacific Studies*, 18(3): 1–25.

Raybaud, C., 2000. 'De la coutume à la loi dans les archipels de Polynésie orientale de 1767 à 1945'. PhD thesis. Université de Montesquieu Bordeaux IV.

Rigo, B., 2007. 'Le pouvoir politique et le sacré en Polynésie'. In M. Chatti, N. Clinchamps & S. Vigier (eds), *Pouvoir(s) et politique(s) en Océanie*. Paris: L'Harmattan, pp. 197–22.

——, 2005. 'L'espace et le temps, expression culturelle privilégiée'. In B. Rigo, *L'espace-temps*. Bulletin du LARSH no. 2. Papeete: Au vent des îles.

——, 2004. *Altérité polynésienne ou les métamorphoses de l'espace-temps*. Paris: CNRS Editions.

Robbins, P., 1998. 'Authority and environment: institutional landscapes in Rajasthan, India'. *Annals of the Association of American Geographers* 88(3): 410–35.

Robineau, C., 1984–85. *Tradition et modernité aux iles de la Société*. Paris: ORSTOM.

——, 1978. 'Réciprocité, redistribution et prestige, chez les Polynésiens des îles de la Société'. *Journal des Océanistes* 61.

Rodriguez, M., 1995. *Les Espagnols à Tahiti (1772–1776)*. Publication de la société des Océanistes no. 45. Paris: Musée de l'Homme.

Rollin, L., 1928. 'La maladie et la mort chez les anciens Maoris des îles Marquises'. *La Presse médicale*, 1er décembre 1928, no. 96.

——, 1974 (1929). *Moeurs et coutumes de anciens Maoris des îles Marquises* (*Les îles Marquises; Géographie, Ethnographie, Histoire, Colonisation et mise en valeur*). Papeete: Stepolde.

Royal, T.A.C. (ed.), 2003. *The Woven Universe – Selected Writings of Rev. Māori Marsden*. Masterton: The Estate of the Late Rev. Māori Marsden.

Ruddle, K., 1998. 'The context of policy design for existing community-based fisheries management systems in the Pacific Islands'. *Ocean and Coastal Management* 40(2/3): 105–26.

Ruru, J., 2009. 'The Māori encounter with Aotearoa New Zealand's legal system'. In B. Richardson, S. Imai & K. McNeil (eds), *Indigenous Peoples and the Law: Comparative and Critical Perspectives*. Oxford: Hart Publishing, pp. 111–33.

——, 2008. 'Finding solutions for the legislative gaps in determining rights to the family home on colonially defined indigenous lands'. *U.B.C. Law Review* 41(2): 315–48.

Sabetian, A., 2002. 'The importance of ethnographic knowledge to fishery research design and management in the South Pacific: a case study from Kolobangara Island, Solomon Islands'. *SPC Traditional Marine Resource Management and Knowledge Information Bulletin* 14: 22–34.

Sahlins, M., 1989. *Des îles dans l'histoire*. Paris: Gallimard/Le Seuil, p. 76 (1985. *Islands of History*. The University of Chicago).

———, 1985. *Historical Metaphors and Mythical Realities: Structure in the Early History of the Sandwich Islands Kingdom*. Association for the Study of Anthropology in Oceania, special publication 1. Ann Arbor: University of Michigan Press.

———, 1958. *Social Stratification in Polynesia*. Seattle: University of Washington Press.

Salmond, A., 1978. 'Te Ao Tawhito. A semantic approach to the traditional Maori cosmos'. *Journal of the Polynesian Society* 87(1): 5–28.

Salomon, A.K., Ruesink, J.L., Semmens, B.X. & Paine, R.T., 2001. 'Incorporating human and ecological communities in marine conservation: an alternative to Zacharias and Roff'. *Conservation Biology* 15(5): 1452–55.

Saura, B., 2005. *Entre nature et culture. La mise en terre du placenta en Polynésie française*. Tahiti: Edition haere Po.

———, 1996. 'Les codes missionnaires et la juridiction coutumière des TOOHITU au Iles de la Société et des Australes (1819–1945)'. *Revue de la recherche juridique de droit prospectif* 21.

———, 1995. 'Les règles coutumières en Polynésie Française'. In Paul De Deckker (ed.), *Coutume autochtone et évolution du droit dans le Pacifique Sud*. Paris: Editions l'Harmattan.

Schug, D., 2001. 'Hawai'i's commercial fishing industry: 1820–1945'. *Hawai'ian J. History* 35: 15–34.

Shackeroff, J.M. & Campbell, L.M., 2007. 'Traditional ecological knowledge in conservation research: problems and prospects for their constructive engagement'. *Conservation & Society* 5: 343–60.

Sharma, A. & Akhil. G. (eds) 2006. *The Anthropology of the State: A Reader*. United Kingdom: Wiley-Blackwell.

Shore, B., 2005. 'Reading Samoans through Tahitians'. *Ethos* 33(4): 487–92.

———, 1989. 'Mana and Tapu: a new synthesis'. In A. Howard & R. Borofsky (eds), *Developments in Polynesian Ethnology*. Honolulu: University of Hawai'i Press, pp. 137–74.

Sims, D., 1981. 'Erosion on Rarotonga, Mangaia and Atiu with recommendations and proposals'. Draft technical report. Rome: FAO.

Smith, J., 1974. *Tapu Removal in Maori Religion*. Memoir no. 40. Wellington: The Polynesian Society.

South Pacific Commission, 1992. *Pearl Oyster Information Bulletin* no. 4, February.

Stevens, M.J., 2006. 'Kāi Tahu me to Hopu Tītī ki Rakiura: an exception to the "colonial rule"?' *Journal of Pacific History* 41(3): 273–91.

Stevenson, R.L., 1995 (1880). *Dans les Mers du Sud*. Paris: Petite bibliothèque Payot/voyageurs [In the South Seas, being an account of experiences and observations in the Marquesas, Paumotous and Gilbert Islands in the course of two cruises on the yacht 'Casco' (1888) and the schooner 'Equator' (1889), London, ed. Neil Rennie (Penguin 1998)].

Stimson, J.F., 1937. *Tuamotuan Legends (Island of Anaa) Part I. The Demi Gods*. Honolulu: Bernice Pauahi Bishop Museum Bulletin.

———, 1933, *Tuamotuan Religion*. Bulletin no. 103. Honolulu: Bernice P. Bishop Museum.

Stimson, J.F. & Marshall, D.S., 1964. *A Dictionary of Some Tuamotuan Dialects of the Polynesian Languages*. Massachusetts: Peabody Museum of Salem; The Hague: The Royal Institute of Linguistics and Anthropology.

Stokes, J., 1930. *Ethnology of Rapa Island*. Honolulu: Bernice P. Bernice Museum.

Tautain, L., 1896. 'Notes sur l'ethnographie des îles Marquises'. *L'Anthropologie* 7: 543–52.

Te Rangi Hiroa (Sir Peter Buck), 1987. *The Coming of the Maori*. Wellington: Maori Purposes Fund Board; Whicoulls Limited.

Testard de Marans, A., 2004. *Souvenirs des îles Marquises, Groupe Sud-Est, 1887–1888*, Paris: Publication de la Société des Océanistes, no. 45, Musée de l'Homme.

Testart, A., 1986. *Essai sur les fondements de la division du travail chez les chasseurs-cueilleurs*. Paris: EHESS.

Thomas, N., 1997. *In Oceania*. Durham: Duke University Press.

——, 1989. 'The force of ethnology: origins and significance of the Melanesia/Polynesia division'. *Current Anthropology* 30(1): 27–34.

——, 1987. 'Unstable categories: *Tapu* and gender in the Marquesas'. *Journal of Pacific History*, 22(3–4): 123–38.

Throop, J., 2005. 'Hypocognition, a "sense of the uncanny", and the anthropology of ambiguity: reflections on Robert I. Levy's contribution to theories of experience in anthropology'. *Ethos* 33(4): 499–511.

Tiraa, A., 2006. 'Ra'ui in the Cook Islands – today's context in Rarotonga'. *SPC Traditional Marine Resource Management and Knowledge Information Bulletin* 19: 11–15.

Titcomb, M., 1972. *Native Use of Fish in Hawai'i*. Honolulu: University of Hawai'i Press.

Tomlinson, M., 2006. 'Retheorizing mana: Bible translation and discourse of loss in Fiji'. *Oceania* 76(2): 173–85.

Torrente, F., 2012. *Buveurs de mers, Mangeurs de terres, Histoire des guerriers de Anaa, archipel des Tuamotu*. Pape'ete: Te Pito o te Fenua.

——, 2010. *Ethnohistoire de Anaa, un atoll des Tuamotu*, Thèse de doctorat en Ethnologie, Anthropologie culturelle. Université de la Polynésie française.

Tregear, E., 1899. *Mangareva Dictionary of the Gambier Islands*. Wellington: Government Printing Office.

———, 1891. *The Maori-Polynesian Comparative Dictionary.* Christchurch, Wellington and Dunedin: Whitcomb and Tombs Ltd.

Troulliot, M-R., 2001. 'Anthropology of the state in an age of globalization'. *Current Anthropology* 42: 125–38.

Tuhiwai-Smith, L., 1999. *Decolonizing Methodologies: Research and Indigenous Peoples.* New York: Zed Books Ltd.

Tyerman, D. & Bennet, G., 1832. *Journal of Travel and Voyages by Rev. Bennet and Tyerman.* 3 vols. Boston.

Vallaux, F., 1994. *Mangareva et les Gambier.* Tahiti: Établissement Territorial d'achats groupés.

Valeri, V., 1985. *Kingship and Sacrifice: Ritual and Society in Ancient Hawai'i.* Paula Wissing (trans). University of Chicago Press.

Veitiyaki, J., Aalbersberg, B., Tawake, A., Rupeni, E. & Tabunakawai, K., 2003. 'Mainstreaming resource conservation: the Fiji Locally Managed Marine Area Network and its influence on national policy'. *Resource Management in Asia-Pacific.* Working Paper no. 42. Canberra: Resource Management in Asia-Pacific Program, Research School of Pacific and Asian Studies, The Australian National University.

von Benda-Beckmann, F., 2002. 'Who's afraid of legal pluralism?' *Journal of Legal Pluralism* 47: 37–83.

von Benda-Beckmann, K., 1991. 'Dispute sans fin sur la méthode de l'anthropologie juridique'. *Droit et Cultures* 21: 73–86.

von Benda-Beckmann, F. & K., 2006. 'The dynamics of change and continuity in plural legal orders'. *Journal of Legal Pluralism* 53–54: 1–44.

von den Steinen, K., 2005, 2008 (1925–28). *Die Marquesaner und ihre Kunst. Studien über die Entwicklung primitiver Südseeornamentik nach eigenen Reiseergebnissen und dem Material der Museen.* vol. 1, *Tatauierung*, 1925, vol. 2, *Plastik*, 1925, vol. 3, *Die Sammlungen*, 1928.

Ward, G., & Kingdom, E., 1995. *Land, Custom and Practice in the South Pacific.* Cambridge University Press.

Watt, Lt., 1789. 'Lieutenant Watt's narrative of the return of the *Lady Penrhyn* transport', *The Voyage of the Governor Phillip to Botany Bay*, edited by Anon., 222–24, London: Stockdale, cited in P.B. Roscoe 1987. 'Of canoes and castaways: reassessing the population of Tongareva (Penrhyn Island) at contact'. *Pacific Studies* 11(1): 43–61, p. 244.

Weber, M., 2010. *Économie et Société*. Paris: Édition Flammarion.

Wheen, N.R., 2008. 'Waitutu Block and Tutae-Ka-Wetoweto Indigenous Forests.' In K. Bosselmann, Ron Engel & Prue Taylor, *Governance for Sustainability – Issues, Challenges, Successes*. Switzerland: IUCN, Gland, pp. 227–36.

White, T., 1899. 'The ceremony of *Rahui*'. *Transactions & Proceedings of the Royal Society of New Zealand 1868–1869* 32: 352–57.

——, 1892. 'The *Rahui*'. Notes & Queries. *Journal of The Polynesian Society* 1(4): 275–76.

Wiber, M., Berkes, F., Charles, A. & Kearney, J., 2004. 'Participatory research supporting community-based fishery management'. *Marine Policy* 28: 459–68.

Williams, H.W., 1971. *Dictionary of the Māori Language*. 7th edn. Wellington: GP Publications.

——, 1852. *A Dictionary of the Maori Language*. London: D.C.L.

Williams, I.D., Walsh, W.J., Miyasaka, A. & Friedlander. A.M., 2006. 'Effects of rotational closure on coral reef fishes in the Waikiki–Diamond Head Fishery Management Area, Oahu, Hawai'i'. *Marine Ecology Progress Series* 310: 139–49.

Williams, I.D., Walsh, W.J., Schroeder, R.E., Friedlander, A.M., Richards, B.L. & Stamoulis, K.A., 2008. 'Assessing the relative importance of fishing impacts on Hawai'ian coral reef fish assemblages along regional-scale human population gradients'. *Environmental Conservation* 35: 261–72.

Williams, J., 2004. E Pakihi Hakinga a Kai: An Examination of Pre-contact Resource Management Practice in Southern Te Wai Pounamu. PhD thesis. University of Otago.

Williamson, R.R., 1937. *Religion and Social Organization in Central Polynesia*, Cambridge at the University Press.

Wilson, J., 1799. *A Missionary Visit to the Southern Pacific Ocean, Performed in the Years 1796, 1797, 1798, in the Ship Duff, Commanded by Captain James Wilson.* London.

Young, O.R., 2002. *Institutional Dimensions of Environmental Change: Fit, Interplay, and Scale.* Cambridge, Mass.: MIT Press.

www.ingramcontent.com/pod-product-compliance
Lightning Source LLC
Chambersburg PA
CBHW040320170426
43192CB00030B/2817